W9-DDH-773

FROM THE CAPITOL TO THE CLASSROOM:
Standards-based Reform in the States

FROM THE CAPITOL TO THE CLASSROOM:
Standards-based Reform in the States

One Hundredth Yearbook of the
National Society for the Study of Education

PART II

Edited by
SUSAN H. FUHRMAN

20 NSSE 01

Distributed by THE UNIVERSITY OF CHICAGO PRESS • CHICAGO, ILLINOIS

CABRINI COLLEGE LIBRARY
610 KING OF PRUSSIA ROAD
RADNOR, PA 19087

LB
5
.N25
100th
pt.2

#46815686

National Society for the Study of Education

The National Society for the Study of Education was founded in 1901 as successor to the National Herbart Society. It publishes a two-volume Yearbook, each volume dealing with a separate topic of concern to educators. The Society's series of Yearbooks, now in its one hundredth year, contains chapters written by scholars and practitioners noted for their significant work on the topics about which they write.

The Society welcomes as members all individuals who wish to receive its publications. Current membership includes educators in the United States, Canada, and elsewhere throughout the world—professors, researchers, administrators, and graduate students in colleges and universities and teachers, administrators, supervisors, and curriculum specialists in elementary and secondary schools.

Members of the Society elect a Board of Directors. Its responsibilities include reviewing proposals for Yearbooks, authorizing the preparation of Yearbooks based on accepted proposals, and appointing an editor or editors to oversee the preparation of manuscripts.

Current dues (for the year 2001) are a modest $35 ($30 for retired members and for students in their first year of membership). Members whose dues are paid for the current calendar year receive the Society's Yearbook, are eligible for election to the Board of Directors, and are entitled to a 33 percent discount when purchasing past Yearbooks from the Society's distributor, the University of Chicago Press.

Each year the Society arranges for meetings to be held in conjunction with the annual conferences of one or more of the national educational organizations. At these meetings, the current Yearbook is presented and critiqued. All members are urged to attend these meetings. Members are encouraged to submit proposals for future Yearbooks.

From the Capitol to the Classroom: Standards-based Reform in the States is Part II of the 100th Yearbook. Part I, published simultaneously, is entitled *Education Across a Century: The Centennial Volume*.

For further information, write to the Secretary, NSSE, College of Education, University of Illinois at Chicago, 1040 W. Harrison St., Chicago, Illinois 60607-7133.

ISSN: 0077-5762

Published 2001 by the
NATIONAL SOCIETY FOR THE STUDY OF EDUCATION
1040 W. Harrison St., Chicago, Illinois 60607-7133

© 2001 by the National Society for the Study of Education

No part of this Yearbook may be reproduced in any form without written permission from the Secretary of the Society.

First Printing
Printed in the United States of America

iv

Board of Directors of the
National Society for the Study of Education
(Term of office expires March 1 of the year indicated.)

LYN CORNO, Teachers College, Columbia University (2003)
NEL NODDINGS, Stanford University (2003)
THOMAS J. SERGIOVANNI, Trinity University (2002)
MARK A. SMYLIE, University of Illinois, Chicago (2001)
SAMUEL C. STRINGFIELD, Johns Hopkins University (2001)
KENNETH ZEICHNER, University of Wisconsin (2002)

MARK A. SMYLIE, University of Illinois at Chicago, Interim Secretary-Treasurer

Contributors to the Yearbook

SUSAN H. FUHRMAN, Editor, University of Pennsylvania

LOLA AAGAARD, Morehead State University
WILLIAM H. CLUNE, University of Wisconsin
PAMELIA COE, Education Consultant
ELIZABETH DEBRAY, Harvard University
JANET C. FAIRMAN, Rutgers University
WILLIAM A. FIRESTONE, Rutgers University
ROBERT E. FLODEN, Michigan State University
MARGARET E. GOERTZ, University of Pennsylvania
JANE HANNAWAY, The Urban Institute
PATRICIA J. KANNAPEL, Education Consultant
KRISTI KIMBALL, Princeton University
DIANE MASSELL, University of Michigan
GAIL PARSON, Harvard University
ANDREW C. PORTER, University of Wisconsin
CYNTHIA A. REEVES, Council of Chief State School Officers
JOHN L. SMITHSON, Wisconsin Center for Education Research
JAMES P. SPILLANE, Northwestern University
JONATHAN A. SUPOVITZ, University of Pennsylvania
SUZANNE M. WILSON, Michigan State University
KATRINA WOODWORTH, SRI International

Acknowledgments

I am grateful to the many individuals and organizations that enabled *From the Capitol to the Classroom: Standards-based Reform in the States* to become a reality. It has been a rewarding experience working with each of you. First, I'm indebted to Tom Payzant, Superintendent of the Boston Public Schools, for suggesting the idea for the book to the National Society for the Study of Education. I also wish to thank Kenneth Rehage and Lyn Corno for their support and assistance in preparing the book. The Society's Board of Directors provided many useful comments that helped to chart the course of this volume. I gratefully acknowledge the contributions of the twenty authors, who, for the last year, have toiled on their chapters, meeting deadlines and making revisions as necessary. I also wish to thank Fred Dolan of Pantagraph Printing and Debbie Miretzky of the University of Illinois for their support. Special thanks also go to Robb Sewell, communications manager for the Consortium for Policy Research in Education, for his work on this volume. Robb patiently worked with all authors, the Society, and the printer, and handled the logistics and copyediting for the volume.

Finally, the research reported in this book would not be possible if it were not for the financial support of the organizations that funded these studies. Specifically, the United States Department of Education's Office of Educational Research and Improvement, the Carnegie Corporation of New York, the Annie E. Casey Foundation, the National Science Foundation, the Pew Charitable Trusts, the Spencer Foundation, and the Education Policy and Practice Study (funded in part by Michigan State University). Opinions expressed in these chapters are those of the authors and do not necessarily reflect the position or policies of these organizations.

SUSAN H. FUHRMAN
Editor

Table of Contents

PAGE

THE NATIONAL SOCIETY FOR THE STUDY OF EDUCATION   iv

BOARD OF DIRECTORS OF THE SOCIETY, 2000-2001; CONTRIBUTORS TO THE

YEARBOOK   v

ACKNOWLEDGMENTS   vii

CHAPTER

   I. INTRODUCTION, *Susan H. Fuhrman*   1

Section One
The Standards-based Reform Approach

   II. TOWARD A THEORY OF STANDARDS-BASED REFORM:
       THE CASE OF NINE NSF STATEWIDE SYSTEMIC
       INITIATIVES, *William H. Clune*   13

   III. STANDARDS-BASED ACCOUNTABILITY:
       HORSE TRADE OR HORSE WHIP?, *Margaret E. Goertz*   39

Section Two
Assessing Reform Implementation and Effects

   IV. ARE CONTENT STANDARDS BEING IMPLEMENTED IN THE CLASSROOM?
       A METHODOLOGY AND SOME TENTATIVE ANSWERS,
       Andrew C. Porter and *John L. Smithson*   60

   V. TRANSLATING TEACHING PRACTICE INTO
       IMPROVED STUDENT ACHIEVEMENT, *Jonathan A. Supovitz*   81

Section Three
District Response to Reforms

   VI. BIG ISN'T ALWAYS BAD: SCHOOL DISTRICT
       SIZE, POVERTY, AND STANDARDS-BASED REFORM, *Jane Hannaway*
       and *Kristi Kimball*   99

   VII. THE DISTRICT ROLE IN STATE ASSESSMENT POLICY:
       AN EXPLORATORY STUDY, *Janet C. Fairman* and *William A. Firestone* . .   124

VIII. THE THEORY AND PRACTICE OF USING DATA TO BUILD CAPACITY: STATE AND LOCAL STRATEGIES AND THEIR EFFECTS, *Diane Massell* 148

Section Four
School Implementation and Instructional Effects

IX. PATTERNS OF RESPONSE IN FOUR HIGH SCHOOLS UNDER STATE ACCOUNTABILITY POLICIES IN VERMONT AND NEW YORK, *Elizabeth DeBray, Gail Parson,* and *Katrina Woodworth* ... 170

X. HEDGING BETS: STANDARDS-BASED REFORM IN CLASSROOMS, *Suzanne M. Wilson* and *Robert E. Floden* 193

XI. CHALLENGING INSTRUCTION FOR "ALL STUDENTS": POLICY, PRACTITIONERS, AND PRACTICE, *James P. Spillane* 217

Section Five
What Can Be Said About Reform Progress

XII. THE IMPACT OF STANDARDS AND ACCOUNTABILITY ON TEACHING AND LEARNING IN KENTUCKY, *Patricia J. Kannapel, Lola Aagaard, Pamelia Coe,* and *Cynthia A. Reeves* 242

XIII. CONCLUSION, *Susan H. Fuhrman* 263

NAME INDEX 279

SUBJECT INDEX 281

PUBLICATIONS OF THE SOCIETY 285

CHAPTER I

Introduction

SUSAN H. FUHRMAN

From the Capitol to the Classroom is about standards-based reform, which, in the 1990s, became the predominant policy approach of states and localities throughout the United States. After ten years or so of such reforms, it is time to look at results. While some evidence is emerging about student learning, since the reforms are still evolving and are in various stages of implementation, no overall verdict can be rendered. However, it is quite appropriate and not too early to ask whether classroom practice, which must change in order to produce increases in student learning, is improving in ways encouraged by reforms. This book focuses primarily on how schools and teachers are responding to standards policies.

In this introduction, I describe the development and progress of standards-based reform, and highlight the major questions that research on the reforms must answer. Then I preview the chapters in this volume and indicate how they address these questions.

The Development of Standards-based Reform

Standards-based reforms are reforms intended to anchor key aspects of policy—curriculum, assessment, teacher education, and professional development—around policy level statements of what students should know and be able to do. The idea was that states (although sometimes this happens at the district level, and some have argued for official, national standard setting) would develop content and performance expectations that would set direction for student achievement and for other policies aimed at increasing student performance.

When this reform notion emerged in the late 1980s, educators and policymakers were still experiencing the despair about lagging American achievement that drove the publication and response to *A Nation at*

Susan H. Fuhrman is Dean, and the George and Diane Weiss Professor of Education at the Graduate School of Education, University of Pennsylvania. She also is chair of the management committee of the Consortium for Policy Research in Education.

Risk. After the 1983 appearance of that Department of Education task force report, which charged that schools were characterized by "a rising tide of mediocrity,"[1] policymakers at the state and local level responded by raising standards for both students and teachers. They increased high school graduation requirements, greatly added to the amount of student testing, and, in many places, made high school graduation contingent on passage of a competency exam. Teacher certification requirements were tightened, as were regulations about teacher education. The "Excellence Movement," the term used to describe such belt-tightening efforts, was criticized by many educators as "top-down," too directive, and constraining to schools. By mid-decade a reaction occurred, taking the form of efforts to devolve more authority to schools and create school based decision making bodies. "Bottom-up" reformers also promoted school restructuring, rearrangements of school schedules to promote teacher collaboration, sustained teacher-student interaction, and in-depth subject matter blocks.

Both the excellence and restructuring reforms bore some fruit. High school course taking in academic subjects rose, without causing marked decreases in high school completion, and teachers seemed energized by efforts to give them more authority and control over their working lives. However, the nation's overall achievement continued to stagnate, and we still lagged in international comparisons. One reason for the emergence of standards-based reforms was the frustration policymakers were feeling—despite significant attention and resources (the 1983-88 period saw many significant state reform packages with funding increases), things were not much better. How standards-based reforms emerged as the proposed solution is an interesting story.

One reason for the appeal of standards-based reform was that our international competitors (those who scored higher than we did on the First and Second International Mathematics and Science Studies and other international assessments, those whose economies outperformed ours in the 1980s) used similar approaches. They had policy level (usually national) curricula, students and parents knew what was supposed to be learned, student assessment covered the stated curriculum, and teachers were prepared to teach that curriculum. This coherence of effort and consensus around school content appeared to be at least one factor giving other nations a leg up. The American Federation of Teachers—then under the leadership of Albert Shanker, a major standards proponent—put together a book of exams from other nations. The French baccalaureate essay prompt, "What does it mean to be free?" was widely discussed as an example of an intellectually challenging question that engaged the entire society in vigorous debate. It was presented as a stark contrast to the monotonous, hollow, typical multiple choice questions making up United States assessments.

A second reason for the attraction of standards reforms was the existence of seemingly successful American antecedents that could serve as models. The Advanced Placement (AP) program was a popular, well-known analog, which also carried a certain caché because of its college level course content. In that program, the curriculum, the examination, and teacher professional development were closely aligned. A similar model was presented by low level, remedial curricula in Title I. Although the content was very different from AP, remedial education frequently drilled students directly on standardized test material in a closely aligned fashion. Some commentators believed that the tightening of the achievement gap between less and more affluent students throughout the late 1970s and most of the 1980s could be attributed at least in part to this coherent educational approach.[2]

Third, research was showing that greater academic coursetaking, a result of the Excellence reforms, did not necessarily lead to greater learning because reliance on a single policy lever—course requirements—did nothing to assure that the content of the courses was improved or that teachers were well prepared to teach that specific content. Even more apparent was the fact that new graduation tests and the new course requirements sent contradictory signals about content. Requirements that students take more years of mathematics envisioned algebra and geometry, but graduation tests included mostly arithmetic. These were standardized tests designed for large groups of test takers, they were divorced from any specific curricula, and were typically used to assure that graduates had at least minimum skills. Given these sets of signals, schools often responded by providing more courses in mathematics to all students but kept the content focused on the graduation exam to assure student passage. Hence the existence of courses like "Informal Geometry," or geometry without proofs.[3] It seemed that more course requirements alone would not be sufficient, but that a much more comprehensive and coherent approach, using multiple policy levers of course requirements, curricula, teacher training, and assessment would be needed to improve student learning. This was a central part of the theory of standards-based reform: uniting previously diverse key instructional guidance mechanisms around common instructional goals.[4]

Fourth, standards-based reforms seemed to be one way to reconcile, or to unite, the Excellence and Restructuring movements. Standard-setting, specifying the content and skills students should know and be able to do, might be an appropriate central role for districts and states. They could set high goals and monitor achievement on those goals, in keeping with the spirit of the Excellence reforms. The monitoring or accountability function would address the prime worry of Excellence reformers: that relying on school based efforts would mean some schools would never improve and reforms would be too haphazard. However, figuring out how to reach the goals could be left to schools and teachers, thus preserving and enhancing the autonomy that marks professional judgment and that was the central focus of Restructuring reforms. The new "third wave" of reform, as standards reforms were sometimes called, seemed to offer the best of both earlier reform movements. The central role would be simplified and rationalized; because reforms would be more coherent and less confusing, there would be clearer incentives for achieving greater excellence. Central leadership would also have responsibility for assistance and resource provision. It was imagined that states and districts, having set clear directions, would also have to provide support for schools to achieve the directions. At the same time, the roles of professionals at the school would be enhanced by the presence of clear central direction and augmented support. They would not have to spend time and energy making sense of the muddle of policy surrounding them; instead they could focus all their energies on planning and executing improved instructional experiences to assure that students learned to new standards. This notion of distributed responsibilities, of making central guidance and school level initiative compatible, was another key element of standards-based reform theory.[5]

Finally, the standards reforms offered the hope of more equitable instructional opportunities for all children. It was envisioned that standards would embody content and performance expectations for all children, and that by tying assessment to the standards, states and districts could monitor whether all schools were striving to achieve them. No longer would groups of students be written off and offered less challenging curricula; instead, all students would be offered more ambitious curricula pegged to standards. No longer would student assessment tap only low level skills and therefore have salience only for lower-performing students; instead, assessments would be aligned to challenging standards and cause all students to strive to learn the same content. The concept that challenging standards for all students would lead to better instructional experiences for all students was another central component of the theory of action underlying standards reforms.

As initial standards-based efforts got underway, momentum increased. By the mid-1980s, California was incorporating high standards into curriculum frameworks and textbooks. By 1989, the National Council of Teachers of Mathematics (NCTM) had developed content standards for mathematics, proving that consensus was possible. National associations—including the Business Roundtable, the National Alliance for Business, the National Governors' Association, the Education Commission of the States, and the Council of Chief State School Officers—gave standards-based reform strong support. Professional associations in virtually every subject area embarked on content standard development. Prestigious national bodies—such as the National Academy of Sciences and the National Academy of Education—recommended standards-based reforms to enhance policy support for student learning. At the federal level, the Clinton administration used federal policies to support state standards reform efforts. The National Science Foundation's Systemic Initiatives program is based on the approach, as are state and local grants under Goals 2000 and Title I.

By the mid-1990s, every state but one was engaged in developing content and performance expectations for student learning; at least thirty-one states were trying to link assessment to such standards.[6] Standards-based reforms were also underway in most large cities, including New York, Chicago, and Philadelphia and in many medium-size, suburban, and rural districts as well. For example, with support from The Pew Charitable Trusts, the Pittsburgh, San Diego, Christina, Beaumont, Yonkers, New York City Community District #2, Lexington, and Portland districts were developing standards for student learning, adopting performance exams to measure attainment of the standards, and planning professional development related to the standards.

At the time this chapter was written, forty-nine states had standards in place,[7] forty-four of which have completed standards in English, mathematics, social studies, and science.[8] Thirty-eight states have revised or developed new standards over the last two years.[9] Twenty-one states have developed assessments intended to test whether students are meeting standards in all four academic subjects mentioned above;[10] many others have assessments in a subset of subjects. Currently, seventeen states base promotion and retention on a student's score on state and/or district assessments,[11] and twenty-six states have high school exit examinations in place.[12]

What Do We Know About Standards-based Reforms?

Several major questions must be raised about standards-based reforms. The first has to do with student learning and whether performance is improving. The other questions have to do with the theory of the reform. If standards-based reforms are working according to plan, the primary policy mechanisms are through policy alignment around standards—tying all the major instructional guidance mechanisms to challenging standards—and the creation of performance expectations through accountability systems. If the reforms are working according to plan, there must also be instructional improvement in the direction of the standards. In other words, is alignment—of curriculum, assessment, teacher preparation, and professional development—occurring? Are new performance expectations providing sufficient incentives? And, are schools and teachers responding in a way that leads to improved instruction?

The first question—are students learning more—is difficult to answer as many states are still implementing reforms. Some positive evidence exists. From research studies in specific sites, we have learned that students in more coherent instructional environments were achieving better. For example, students transition high school mathematics courses linked to ambitious NCTM-like standards (California's Math A and New York's "Stretch Regents" courses) were much more likely than general-track students to complete a minimal college preparatory sequence by the end of high school. On achievement tests, students in college preparatory mathematics courses gained slightly more than those in the transition mathematics courses, while students in transition mathematics gained more than those in general mathematics. Coherent approaches—such as linking professional development directly to the course content, curriculum, and pedagogy, such as the Math A training provided in California—helped teachers move toward an emphasis on problem solving, reasoning, and computing, and contributed to the achievement gains.[13]

Another study showed that professional development that was tied to the student curriculum influenced teacher practice and student achievement among California elementary teachers. Teachers taking workshops on one or more of the replacement units that mathematics educators had created to serve as curriculum for the reform changed their practice significantly and showed student achievement gains. This sort of professional development created a strong coherence between the curriculum of students' work and teachers' learning: teachers were studying how to teach specific mathematics topics to students, and learning both mathematics and mathematics teaching in the process. In contrast, professional development that is either generic ("classroom management"), or not focused on specific subject matter ("using mathematics manipulatives"), and did not show the payoff in student achievement.[14] Similarly, Knapp[15] found that district alignment of curriculum guidelines, textbook adoptions, and testing could be powerful supports for teaching for meaning or understanding. Effects were magnified when districts adopting such policies were in states with curriculum frameworks and testing approaches that encouraged "meaning-oriented" instruction.

Other evidence comes from assessment data in states and localities known for standards efforts. As examples,

- In Texas, student results on the Texas Assessment of Academic Skills have been very encouraging. Improvements have been seen in all grades, all subjects tested, and for all ethnic groups and categories of students. For example, in fourth grade, in 1994, 54.8 percent of all students passed all tests. The number for African Americans was 33.3 percent, and for economically disadvantaged it was 40.2 percent. In 1997, 72 percent of all students passed all fourth grade tests; the number for African Americans was 53.8 percent; and for economically disadvantaged, it was 59.8 percent.

- In Maryland, 30 percent of fifth graders scored "Satisfactory" on the reading portion of the Maryland School Performance Assessment Program in 1995 whereas the state goal is to have 70 percent at satisfactory (and the rest at excellent). By 1997, 36 percent had reached the satisfactory goal in that grade. Gains were spread across racial and ethnic groups.

- In Michigan and Connecticut, increases were seen in mathematics in the same years in both the state tests and in the National Assessment of Educational Progress (NAEP). These states had large-scale standards-based mathematics reforms underway as part of the National Science Foundation's State Systemic Initiatives Program.

- In Philadelphia, where standards have been in place since 1996, there were improvements in every grade and subject on the Stanford-9 test between 1996 and 1998. The number of students excluded from testing or absent from testing declined dramatically in the same period, which makes the test score improvement that much more impressive.

A third body of evidence comes from comparative studies of state achievement on the NAEP. Significant and sustained gains in North Carolina and Texas, two states that stood out from the rest in making progress between 1990 and 1997, have been attributed to the policy environment. Among policy factors deemed to influence progress were the creation of an aligned system of standards, curriculum, and assessment; accountability systems that held schools responsible for improvement by all students; and sustained business support.[16] In a newer study, Grissmer, Flanagan, Kawata, and Williamson[17] conclude that increases in NAEP mathematics scores from 1990 to 1996—controlling for demographics and participation in the test—probably reflect state reforms, although more research is needed. They find no major changes in resources that might have caused the gains. In addition, the gains, just like the structure and intensity of standards reforms, varied widely from state to state.[18]

While the evidence is promising, it's clearly not conclusive. More studies are underway, and we should learn much more in the next few years. The other questions about reform progress—is policy development occurring as reformers hoped and has classroom practice changed—are the focus of this book. The chapters that follow take up these questions specifically, shedding some light on the achievement question as well. One important caveat in terms of drawing conclusions about achievement has to do with a serious problem in policy development. If the alignment that underlies the theory does not really occur—if assessments are not aligned to curriculum and standards—one can't really measure the effects of reform. Not only do reforms in such circumstances fall short of the goal of a truly coherent instructional guidance system, but just as critically, we are hampered in reaching conclusions because assessments are not really measuring reform progress.

The first section of the book, *The Standards-based Reform Approach*, focuses on the overall theory of the reforms and the evolution of one particular, very salient aspect: the creation of performance based accountability systems. In Chapter 2, "Toward a Theory of Systemic Reform: The Case of Nine NSF Statewide Systemic Initiatives," William Clune unpacks the central thesis of standards reform, breaking it down into component elements linked in a causal sequence. Then he uses data from states supported by NSF to undertake standards reforms in mathematics and science, arrays the states on reform elements, and examines their assessment results. Finding the reforms "cost effective if not massively effective," Clune points out difficulties in assessing reform impact that other authors echo, the dearth of assessments pegged to standards, and the gap between standards and actual curriculum. Margaret Goertz's chapter, "Standards-based Accountability: Horse Trade or Horse Whip?" describes how state and local accountability systems are developing. As Goertz and other authors demonstrate, accountability systems that dole out rewards and punishments based on student performance are becoming the central drivers of standards-based reforms. It's one thing to set standards, and another to provide bonuses or deny promotion or graduation based on the achievement of standards. Attaching consequences to test scores provides bite to the standards movement. Goertz shows how accountability is strongly influenced by state and local context. However, across settings, policymakers face similar challenges: balancing student and adult accountability, closing the achievement gap, and improving alignment between standards and assessments.

The alignment issue is the central focus of the next section, *Assessing Reform Implementation and Effects*. Andrew Porter and John Smithson write about how to measure reform impact in "Are Content Standards Being Implemented in the Classroom? A Methodology and Some Tentative Answers." They examine alternative approaches to assessing the enacted curriculum and describe an eleven-state study that examines alignment between assessments and standards, and assessments and instruction. Finding alignment on these elements to be modest, the authors discuss the measurement issues that might contribute to the findings. In "Translating Teaching Practice into Improved Student Achievement," Jonathan Supovitz focuses on professional development. One can show that professional development aligned to standards influences practice much more easily than one can then link the alignment to student achievement. Why? The reasons are varied, including the assessment to standards alignment problem that every author so far has noted.

Before we get to the question of school and teacher response, we must ask how intermediate implementers, particularly local districts, are responding to state standards initiatives. In the third section, *District Response to Reforms*, there are three chapters. Jane Hannaway and Kristi Kimball report that large districts are better able to support standards-based reforms and offer assistance to schools. In "Big Isn't Always Bad: School District Size, Poverty, and Standards-Based Reform," they report the results of two companion national surveys. Janet Fairman and William Firestone also highlight the importance of districts in "The District Role in State Assessment Policy: An Exploratory Study." Large districts seem better able to buffer schools and teachers from political demands that sometimes detract from instructional improvement efforts. They also have more people—specialists and support staff—available to help teachers implement standards-based reforms. "The Theory and Practice of Using Data to Build Capacity: State and Local Strategies and their Effects" by Diane Massell indicates that increased local use of data is one important byproduct of reform. Since feedback about achievement on standards should serve as incentive for greater achievement and help pinpoint areas of curriculum or of the student body where educators need to exert concentrated effort, use of assessment data should be a key element of reform implementation. As reformers hoped, performance data are much more prevalent and influential, and data use is having some very noticeable effects on local educators.

Turning to schools and classrooms, the chapters in the fourth section of the book, *School Implementation and Instructional Effects*, share a common theme: some people are getting it and some people aren't. Variation in response to reforms is not a new story; it's the universal finding about reform implementation and effect. But for those who thought that standards reforms would mean standardization, to put a more negative spin on it, or common, high level instruction for all, to put a more positive spin on it, the findings presented in these chapters will provide contrary evidence. In "Patterns of Response in Four High Schools Under State Accountability Policies in Vermont and New York," Elizabeth DeBray, Gail Parson, and Katrina Woodworth show how accountability policies hit schools very differently. A critical aspect of their findings is that lower-performing schools, which were in fact the targets of state accountability policies, are frequently unable to respond except superficially. They might need to change the most, but they don't. Suzanne Wilson and Bob Floden, in "Hedging Bets: Standards-Based Reform in Classrooms," present pictures of teachers who vary in their interpretation of standards reforms and in how they change their practice. One reason, among many, for the piecemeal nature of change and improvement, is that teachers were sticking to some traditional practices they thought worked with their students. But what happens with respect to students who traditionally were exposed to weak curricula? What happens to students who had always been marginalized? Standards-based reform is explicitly aimed at encouraging teachers to improve instruction for those very students. If they protect low-performing students by giving them traditional dumbed down material, they defeat the very purpose of the reforms. James Spillane, in "Challenging Instruction for 'All Students': Policy, Practitioners, and Practice," finds that reforms were flatly rejected as inappropriate in four schools serving minority and poor children. Nothing about the way reforms were designed and implemented in these sites explicitly challenged underlying belief systems about what such children could achieve.

The final section of the book, *What Can Be Said About Reform Progress*, tries to put it all together and draw some conclusions about where reform is and where it is likely to go. "The Impact of Standards and Accountability on Teaching and Learning in Kentucky," by Patricia Kannapel, Lola Aagaard, Pamelia Coe, and Cynthia Reeves, takes a comprehensive look at reform in one state widely thought to be a standards leader. Evaluating the pluses and minuses, they see more positive than negative in Kentucky reforms. Substantial progress is balanced by concerns about more disadvantaged students, similar to the ones raised in other chapters. In the last chapter, the conclusion, I take up this theme and a number of the other issues that surface across the chapters to assess reform progress and prospects.

NOTES

1. National Commission on Excellence in Education, *A Nation at Risk: The Imperative for Educational Reform* (Washington, DC: Author, 1983).

2. Marshall Smith and Jennifer O'Day, "Systemic school reform," in Susan Fuhrman and Betty Malen, eds., *The Politics of Curriculum and Testing* (New York: Falmer Press, 1991), pp. 233-267.

3. William Clune and Paula White, "Education reform in the trenches: Increased academic course taking in high schools with lower achieving students in states with higher graduation requirements," *Educational Evaluation and Policy Analysis* 14 (1992): pp. 2-20.

4. Smith and O'Day, "Systemic school reform"; David Cohen and James Spillane, "Policy and practice: The relations between governance and instruction," in Susan Fuhrman, ed., *Designing Coherent Education Policy: Improving the System* (San Francisco: Jossey-Bass, 1993), pp. 35-95.

5. Smith and O'Day, "Systemic school reform."

6. American Federation of Teachers, *Making Standards Better: A Fifty State Progress Report on Efforts to Raise Academic Standards* (Washington, DC: Author, 1995).

7. Information available on the internet at www.achieve.org.

8. Education Commission of the States, *The Progress of Education Reform, 1999-2001: Standards* (Denver: Author, 2000), p. 3.

9. Ibid.

10. Education Commission of the States, *The Progress of Education Reform, 1999-2001: Standards*, p. 2.

11. Education Commission of the States, *The Progress of Education Reform, 1999-2001: Assessment* (Denver: Author, 2000), p. 3.

12. Ibid.

13. Paula White, Adam Gamoran, and John Smithson, *Math Innovations and Student Achievement in Seven High Schools in California and New York* (Madison, WI: Consortium for Policy Research in Education, University of Wisconsin-Madison, 1995).

14. David Cohen and Heather Hill, *State Policy and Classroom Performance: Mathematics Reform in California* (Philadelphia: Consortium for Policy Research in Education, University of Pennsylvania, 1998); David Cohen and Heather Hill, *Instructional Policy and Classroom Performance: The Mathematics Reform in California* (Philadelphia: Consortium for Policy Research in Education, University of Pennsylvania, 1998).

15. Michael Knapp, *Teaching for Meaning in High-Poverty Classrooms* (New York: Teachers College Press, 1995).

16. David Grissmer and Ann Flanagan, *Exploring Rapid Achievement Gains in North Carolina and Texas* (Washington, DC: National Education Goals Panel, 1998).

17. David Grissmer, Ann Flanagan, Jennifer Kawata, and Stephanie Williamson, *Improving Student Achievement: What State NAEP Test Scores Tell Us* (Santa Monica, CA: RAND, 2000).

18. Grissmer, Flanagan, Kawata, and Williamson, *Improving Student Achievement: What State NAEP Test Scores Tell Us*.

Section One
THE STANDARDS-BASED
REFORM APPROACH

CHAPTER II

Toward a Theory of Standards-based Reform: The Case of Nine NSF Statewide Systemic Initiatives[1]

WILLIAM H. CLUNE

This chapter has two main purposes: (1) testing the central thesis of standards-based reform, and (2) deriving lessons about the strengths and weaknesses of actual reform strategies that are used in policy and practice. Both purposes will be pursued through secondary analysis of a convenient source of data: case studies[2] of nine Statewide Systemic Initiatives (SSIs) funded by the National Science Foundation (NSF).[3] The case studies collect similar kinds of data in useful categories for all nine systemic reform efforts during the time period, 1992-96, thus permitting a methodologically controlled "snapshot" of parallel reforms. The case studies of SSIs also allow the sponsor of this chapter, the National Institute for Science Education,[4] to learn from the experience of the SSIs in its study of standards-based reform.

The Central Thesis of Standards-based Reform

As framed by Smith and O'Day,[5] the central thesis of standards-based reform is that creating greater coherence (or alignment) of instructional guidance policies (those affecting the content and quality of instruction in schools) is the only way to create large numbers of

William H. Clune is Voss-Bascom Professor of Law at the University of Wisconsin Law School, co-team leader of the National Institute for Science Education's Systemic Reform: Policy and Evaluation Team, and a senior researcher with the Consortium for Policy Research in Education.

effective schools (schools producing desirably high levels of student achievement). The specific kinds of policies mentioned in their model have persisted as the assumed components of standards-based reform: curriculum frameworks, instructional materials and curricula, inservice professional development, preservice professional development, student assessments and accountability, school site autonomy and restructuring, and supportive services from districts and the state. Although "policy" at the top was seen as the driving force for change, standards-based reform was not defined exclusively in top-down terms. Inservice professional development was seen as depending on active networks of teachers organized from the grass roots. School restructuring is another feature that might be stimulated by government action, but obviously could not occur at that level. Indeed, standards-based reform was proposed by Smith and O'Day partly as a way of generalizing (or going to scale with) successful models of school restructuring developed during a prior period of decentralized reform.

For Smith and O'Day, standards were the foundation of systemic reform: standards-based curricula utilized as the touchstone for policy alignment and modeled on the pioneering standards for mathematics developed by the National Council of Teachers of Mathematics (NCTM). Standards-based curricula aim for active learning by students and support teaching for understanding,[6] as opposed to the exclusive emphasis on basic skills that characterized some earlier (and probably somewhat successful) exercises of policy alignment, such as minimum competency achievement testing. Both the meaning of teaching for understanding and the proper emphasis to be placed on basic skills are hotly debated to this day.[7] But some kind of deepening (or upgrading) of the curriculum has remained a universally accepted goal of standards-based reform, especially for disadvantaged students. Thus the terms *systemic reform* and *standards-based reform* have become virtually synonymous.[8] While this chapter does examine standards-based reform at the state level, Smith and O'Day's exclusive focus on the state as the locus of policy has been broadened. Many large districts are creating their own systems, and NSF now has a program funding Urban Systemic Initiatives.

Building on this background, we can state the *central thesis of standards-based reform* as follows:

Systemic reformers can bring about a greater degree of alignment of policies of instructional guidance around new standards of learning, thereby producing widespread and substantial gains in the quality of teaching and learning for all students throughout the area affected by the policies.

Testing the Central Thesis:
A Theory of Standards-based Policy and Reform

In order to test the central thesis, we needed to develop a testable theory. The theory presented in this chapter follows the central thesis but also reflects the practice of the NSF-funded SSIs. Three researchers—William Clune, Eric Osthoff, and Paula White—gathered data about all of the SSIs from workshops, forums, interviews with systemic reformers and researchers, and documents, such as proposals and evaluations. A book manuscript applying the theory is planned based on the broader set of data. While this chapter applies the theory to the data set made available by the nine case studies, all three researchers found no major inconsistencies between the two studies except that, in the larger study, the ratings of SSIs (including the nine SSIs common to both) may be lower, and the findings about successful models more varied both across states and across reform components within states. Comparing our theory and findings with SRI International's provides an additional checkpoint on validity and usefulness, and we welcome feedback that might further shape the proposed book.

A good theory of standards-based reform should model the indispensable elements of the central thesis of standards-based reform: a *policy system* (including an unspecified mix of policies and intermediate organizations and activities) with a strong influence on *a rigorous curriculum as actually taught to all* students (though possibly a differentiated curriculum), and corresponding measured *high student performance* and *standards-based reform itself* (some set of activities that bring systemic policy into existence). These basic elements, shown schematically in causal relationship, appear as follows:

Standards-based reform (SR), through its purposeful activities, leads to
Standards-based policy (SP), which leads to
A rigorous, implemented standards-based curriculum (SC) for all students, leading to
Measured *high student achievement* (SA) in the curriculum as taught

This kind of system is dynamic even in its fully mature state (requiring constant communication and adaptation), and even successful reform will likely proceed incrementally (with more reform leading to gradually stronger policies, leading to gradually stronger curriculum for more students and greater gains in student achievement), so that standards-based reform obviously should be represented as a *continuous causal sequence*:

$$SR \rightarrow SP \rightarrow SC \rightarrow SA$$

where SR = standards-based reform, SP = standards-based policy, SC = standards-based curriculum, and SA = student achievement corresponding to the curriculum.

OPERATIONALIZING THE VARIABLES

To test the above model against real reform efforts requires three things beyond the schematic: first, the variables must be made specific and measurable (operationalized); second, they must be operationalized in a way that corresponds to the causal theory; and third, the measurement must show to what extent the goal of changing the entire system—rather than a few teachers, schools, or students—has been achieved.

We decided to meet all three requirements by conceptualizing the variables according to characteristics or elements that make them influential, and then rating overall variables (taking all elements into account) on five-point scales of breadth and depth. Breadth in our method refers to the scope of the variable across the elements, and a score of five would be given if all the elements were present. Depth refers to the strength of the influence, combined with its quality, or adherence to the model of standards-based reform, with a score of five being awarded for maximum quality and strength. An earlier version of this chapter included a detailed matrix that displays our rating system by variable, component of each variable, and criteria for rating the breadth and depth of each component.[9] A narrative summary of that matrix is provided below.

Standards-based reform. After studying data on all the SSIs, we decided to conceptualize standards-based reform as "reform leadership and management." The influence of this variable in any state involves the following elements: vision, strategic planning, networking with policymakers, networking with professionals, institutionalization of the reform structure, leveraging of resources, and public outreach and visibility. The reform would be considered broad to the extent it had all of these elements and the elements touched all the levers of policy, and deep to the extent that each element was strong and of high quality, defined as conforming to a standards-based vision of reform.

Standards-based policy. The components of the policy system that are rated for breadth and depth are curriculum standards; curriculum frameworks; student assessments; instructional materials; equity targeting policies; preparation and initial licensing of teachers; teacher recertification; professional development for teachers and administrators;

accountability for students, teachers, schools, and administrators; and district and school capacity building and improvement. The policy system would be considered broad to the extent that it covered the full range of influential policies in the area and that the policies themselves covered the full range of subjects, grades, and schools. The system would be considered deep to the extent that it has strong predicted influence on schools, teachers, and students, and pushed in the direction of high quality standards-based teaching and learning. We decided to conceptualize the strength of the policy components according to a set of attributes developed by Porter and colleagues for this very purpose.[10]

Standards-based policy's influence is defined by the strength of four attributes: authority, power, consistency, and prescriptiveness or detailed guidance, each of which can be reflected in a variety of specific policies and organizational forms depending on the context. *Authority* is provided through the backing of powerful institutions and individuals, such as the governor, legislature, or an intermediate network of teachers or professional organizations. Sometimes a particular policy instrument, such as student assessment, achieves a kind of authoritative recognition. Some states, particularly in the South, seem to have governmental authority structures that are especially well accepted in districts and schools. *Power* is attained through resources, such as professional development opportunities or financial rewards, or through other incentives, such as the stakes attached to a student assessment or an accountability system. *Consistency* is achieved when all of the elements of influence push in the same direction and are aligned around a common vision and content. *Prescriptiveness*, or detailed guidance, represents the extent to which the policy system gives a clear idea of exactly what schools and teachers are supposed to do through, for example, the availability of textbooks, replacement curriculum units, student assessments, and demonstration teaching tapes.

Standards-based curriculum. Content and pedagogy, the material actually conveyed to students in classrooms and the instructional methods by which it is taught, make up standards-based curriculum. Content refers to the knowledge or skill that students are supposed to learn in subject areas like algebra and geometry, as well as skill areas like computation, problem solving, and conceptual understanding. Pedagogy refers to the kind of teaching that is employed, particularly whether the demands on students match the content and skills that are being taught (for example, whether students actually solve and discuss problems if the goals are problem solving and communication). Breadth depends on the number of schools, teachers, grades, and subjects (mathematics, science, etc.) that demonstrate change. Depth depends on the extent and quality of the change. Deep change would refer to substantial upgrading of the content and a correspondingly strong change in pedagogy. Shallow change refers to smatterings or layerings of new content and pedagogy, a common finding for the extent of curriculum reform and perhaps its greatest challenge.[11] Also, pluses for curriculum breadth and depth are equity targeting in the curriculum, and school improvement aimed at curriculum change. We also considered the availability of good data on curriculum as part of its depth because good data help guide reform. But the availability of data would inevitably be reflected in the depth rating in any case because good data are helpful in showing deep curriculum change. As explained below, systematic observational data on the implemented curriculum were rarely available for the SRI case studies, but were considered a definite plus where they occurred (teacher surveys and observations at selected sites were common; other indicators are more indirect, such as whole school curriculum reform).

Standards-based student achievement. The primary measure of standards-based student achievement is gain on a student assessment that is in some way aligned with the reform (for example, gain after stronger policies were enacted, or gain in schools receiving more emphasis under the policies). Assessments commonly available in the states with SSIs included state assessments and the National Assessment of Educational Progress (NAEP). Some state assessments are better aligned with the goals of policy than others (a fact that would be reflected in the consistency rating of the policies). Gains in equity (gap closing) were counted as a plus, as were gains in course enrollment and attainment in later grades. Breadth of gain in student achievement depended, once again, on how many students, schools, grades, and subjects showed gains. Depth refers to the size of the gains, as well as the quality of the data on achievement. A gain over five years of one or two percentage points of the total number of students in the state reaching proficiency on a student assessment seems relatively small in terms of policy goals, and was at the small end of our sample (one on a scale of five), while a gain of eight or more points seems large, and was at the high end of the sample (five on a scale of five).

Methodology

The methodology for this chapter consisted of, first, reading and taking detailed notes on all nine of the SRI case studies of SSIs, focusing on what appeared to be strong evidence related to our theoretical categories; and, second, rating all the variables in every state on both depth and breadth according to our theoretical model and the rating system previously discussed.

For the 1998 case studies from which this chapter was drawn, SRI International used a model that depicted "SSI Activities" as affecting a foundation of policy, which in turn affected teachers, schools, and student achievement. The graphic form of the model is presented in Figure 1. Following this model, the case study researchers gathered data in each of the nine states according to implementation of the reform, effects on policy, effects on teachers (meaning effects on how teachers were trained and taught), and effects on students. These categories nicely fit the four main variables in our model of standards-based reform and management, standards-based policy, standards-based curriculum, and standards-based student achievement.

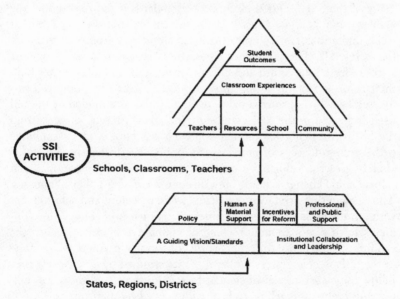

Source: Andrew Zucker, Patrick Shields, Nancy Adelman, Thomas Corcoran, and Margaret Goertz, *A Report on the Evaluation of the National Science Foundation's Statewide Systemic Initiatives (SSI) Program* (Menlo Park, CA: SRI International, 1998).

FIGURE 1
Model of Systemic Reform Used to Guide SRI Case Studies

The information in the SRI reports was translated into the theoretical framework used in this chapter in two steps. The appendix gives our narrative synopsis of each SSI by each of the four main variables (reform, policy, curriculum, and achievement) and, in addition, includes a general comment on the overall strength of the reform. The appendix is long and detailed, but readers unfamiliar with the data and looking for the human (or at least organizational) face of reform, should find it very helpful as a way of grounding the analysis. We used the narrative synopsis to develop a numerical rating of every element of every reform in both breadth and depth. The results of that rating are provided in the section on Results.

LIMITS FROM STUDYING THE NSF INITIATIVES, INCLUDING MEASURING PARTIAL CAUSATION

A number of readers of earlier drafts of this chapter asked whether our theory is of standards-based reform generally, or only of the NSF-funded Statewide Systemic Initiatives. The short answer is that we see many of the SSIs as good examples of standards-based reform and the whole group as a good test-bed for the theory, but we concede that some limitations and complexities of analysis flow from our focus on the NSF SSIs. The guidelines issued by NSF for proposals from the states reflected the Smith and O'Day formulation, and most states built their reforms roughly along those lines. It is true that some reforms focused heavily on professional development that was funded by the SSI itself (reflected in the SRI graphic by the arrow running directly from the SSI to the schools); another approach was pilot schools combined with varying degrees of emphasis on policy. Regardless of the actual approach of the reform, we tested the prediction in our model that reform could change schools only through increasing policy alignment. Thus a state that produced big changes in curriculum and achievement without affecting policy (solely through its own professional development activities, for example) would be counted as evidence against the validity of our theory. In other words, our model predicts that success of the SSIs in changing schools will be determined by how closely they follow the classic model of standards-based reform, and the states taking a different approach provide us with needed comparisons.

A second and related complexity is the relationship of the SSIs to other standards-based reforms, both in the same state and in other states not studied or funded. For related reforms in the same state, we had to judge (as did the SRI researchers) whether the SSI made a substantial contribution to the increased degree of alignment, if any. A similar sense of partial causality is seen in a statement on the Weather Channel, "The above average number of storm-related deaths in California this summer was undoubtedly due in part to El Niño." If we wanted to carry this analogy out, El Niño would correspond to the NSF-funded systemic reforms, the storms would correspond to policy alignment, the swollen rivers would correspond to an upgraded curriculum, and the storm-related deaths would correspond with student achievement. Given this model of partial causation, other reforms occurring in the state at the same time might also get credit for pushing toward standards-based policy, and, indeed, we found that the prior enactment of a standards-based student assessment was an important stimulus to reform. Another limiting effect of the focus on the SSIs is that we have no data on states that did not receive any NSF funding. From our database, we do not know whether other states achieved equal levels of standards-based reform without such funding.

The issue of partial causation and how to recognize it deserves further discussion because it operates at every stage of our model. Standards-based reforms join other forces in leading to stronger policies. Stronger state policies may not be the only cause of curriculum improvements (more advanced course requirements from an earlier time being another); and curriculum improvements may not be the sole cause of increases in student achievement (demographic changes being another candidate; for example, unmeasured, gradual increases in higher education among parents). We (and it is fair to say the SRI researchers) took two approaches to the recognition and measurement of partial causation: qualitative and quantitative. Qualitatively, we looked for anecdotal evidence that the activity at one stage of the model was being felt at the next stage—for example, that a curriculum designed by the reformers actually was adopted in policy, adopted by schools, and reflected in student achievement. Gains in student achievement that did not seem associated with the presence of reform in schools, or that occurred in a time period too early to reflect the impact of reform, would be assumed to be the result of some other factor. Quantitatively, once we had some confidence in the basic correspondence between activities in each stage of the model, we would then measure the breadth and depth of those changes and see whether high ratings at one stage corresponded to high ratings in the next. This methodology for measuring partial causation is fuzzy and inexact, but seems reasonably robust in practice. Reforms have a logic of action that can be plumbed by careful evaluation, as in the SRI case studies.

A third complexity is how much the limited time period analyzed in the case studies can tell us about the progress of reform over a longer period of time (especially since one of our findings is that the more successful reforms built on past reforms and typically were incomplete at the end of five years). The answer is that the case studies must be considered a "snapshot" of reform in progress over the five years. If a reform had reached the stage of greater alignments in policy, but had not reached many schools, it would get high ratings on policy but lower ratings on curriculum and achievement. As will be seen, Louisiana turned out to be a state where student achievement had not yet responded strongly to reform. A different case is where the reform strategy adopted in the first five years was judged ineffective and dropped in favor of a more promising strategy. A reform that was "just getting its act together" at the end of the first five-year period (as actually occurred in some cases) would get a low rating then, based on the National Institute for Science Education system, and would deserve that rating, but might get a high rating using the same criteria at a later point in time.

Results

RATING THE STATES

The results of the rating exercise are presented in Table 1, with the states listed from highest to lowest in the average of all ratings.

TABLE 1
BREADTH, DEPTH, AND AVERAGE RATINGS OF THE NINE SRI STATES

| STATE | REFORM | | POLICY | | CURRICULUM | | ACHIEVEMENT | | STATE |
	BR.	DP.	BR.	DP.	BR.	DP.	BR.	DP.	AVERAGE
Connecticut	4	4	4	4	3	2	4	4	3.6
Maine	4	4	4	4	3	2	4	4	3.6
Montana	3	4	2	4	2	3	2	4	3.0
Louisiana	4	4	3	2	3	2	2	2	2.8
Michigan	2	3	2	2	2	2	3	2	2.3
California	2	3	2	3	3	2	2	1	2.3
Arkansas	3	3	2	2	2	1	2	2	2.1
Delaware	2	1	1	1	1	1	1	1	1.1
New York	1	1	1	1	1	1	1	1	1.0
Average Over States	2.8	3.0	2.3	2.6	2.2	1.8	2.3	2.3	

Let's begin discussion with what can be concluded from this quantitative analysis. The question of whether strong Reforms led to stronger Policy, which led to a stronger Curriculum, which led to stronger Achievement, can be assessed by reading backward from Achievement. Higher ratings on Achievement are associated with higher ratings for the other variables, particularly Reform and Policy. Additional support for these relationships comes from the correspondence of our ratings with the funding renewal decisions of NSF (those decisions themselves emerging from careful performance reviews and ratings by panels of expert reviewers). Two of the top three states in Table 1 had their funding renewed by NSF (Connecticut and Maine). The third state getting renewed funding, Louisiana, ranked fourth in our analysis and had an average rating of 2.8, slightly behind Montana. Almost surely (but not entirely without controversy), Montana was downgraded because of its exclusive emphasis on high school mathematics, reflected in lower breadth ratings for our variables. As for Louisiana, some commentators have suggested that equity (percent of minority students) may have played a role in the refunding of this state. Equity is an announced goal of the SSI program (success for all students) and would be a legitimate basis for decision in a close case. Another compatible explanation is that Louisiana has the same high ratings for Reform as Maine and Connecticut. The strength of the reform base makes likely a strong future impact on Curriculum and Achievement.

A second set of observations can be made about the variables by looking at the average ratings of variables over states in the bottom row. Reform and Policy are stronger than Curriculum and Achievement, and, within Reform and Policy, depth (or strength of influence) is stronger than breadth (coverage of the whole state). Greater strength in Reform and Policy can be expected because of both the sequence of reform (with those areas receiving attention first) and the sheer difficulty of making an impact on teachers and students. Greater depth than breadth of reform might be expected because reformers will discover strong reform and policy tools before extending them to the whole system. The generally lower ratings for Curriculum and Achievement reflect some problems of policy design, plus major problems of data and measurement. Both of these issues are discussed further below. Examples of design problems are the lack of emphasis on curriculum content and whole school restructuring. The lowest average rating across states is for depth of influence in the curriculum, and exactly this—shallow influence on the curriculum—was identified as the chief failing of standards-based reform in an earlier research synthesis sponsored by NISE.[12] The main data problems with Curriculum were scant data and indirect measurement of what was going on in classrooms. The main data problem with Achievement was the lack of alignment of student assessments with the goals of reform, but the absence of good control groups for evaluation was a close second as a problem.

What can the ratings of the states tell us about the success of the NSF's SSI program? The highest possible standard of evaluation would be deep and broad change in every aspect of the system in every state. That standard, which would translate into an average of five for every state, was not met. Looking at the last column in Table 1, the states averaged from just below four to one on a five-point scale. Even the higher rated states reached at most fifty percent of this "whole system" target and did so with inconsistent depth and quality. But the standard of perfection is surely too high, given the limited time and resources available to the reformers, the complexity of the systems, and the highly experimental nature of the reforms themselves. A more reasonable standard is whether substantial change occurred in most states, and that standard was met. Only New York and Delaware made no progress; however, both of these states were retooling in promising directions at the end of the five-year period. Thus the reforms seem cost effective if not massively effective. A good argument for this point of view was that of Zucker and Marder in the Montana case study, which noted that the strategy of "concentration" producing deep change in one sector at a time in some strategic order may be as good an investment of resources as the "holistic" strategies of many states that produced broader but shallower change.[13]

THE IMPRECISE TASK OF TESTING CAUSATION

The primary indicator of causation, a correlation of all the standards-based variables, was satisfied as well as could be expected in a sample of nine states. Higher ratings go with higher ratings across all four variables. This rough correspondence should not be understood as anything like a rigorous statistical test. There were only nine cases, with the bulk of the measurements falling closely together in the middle ratings. Differences were small, given the sample size and the imprecision of the measurements, as in data on Curriculum and Achievement. And some qualitative judgments were made to derive the numerical ratings. For example, Michigan and Arkansas showed higher gains on statewide tests of student achievement than are reflected in their ratings. The reason for lower ratings of student achievement in both cases is that the gains shown were judged probably related to an earlier period of basic skills reform, a judgment supported by the intensity of the earlier period of reform, the timing of the gains in achievement, and the lack of any evidence that instruction changed, such as comparisons among units affected to a greater or lesser degree by the policy changes brought about by the SSI.

Generalizations and Cross-Cutting Themes

Discovering common patterns of organization and strategy across SSIs requires qualitative analysis, and for this the case study is indispensable. As background for the generalizations about reform that are discussed here, readers are again urged to read through all of the appendix, which consists of qualitative syntheses of each case study organized by the four variables in our model.

THE TYPICAL PROFILE OF SUCCESSFUL SSIs

The typical profile in the higher rated states, described according to the four variables of the theory presented in this chapter, looks like this: (1) *Reform.* A reform agency with independence but strong connections with the scientific disciplines in higher education; strong networking of reformers with supportive professional leadership organizations in the state; a mission including both mathematics and science; long–term support of key policymakers, especially the governor.[14] (2) *Policy.* A state assessment as a key building block of policy; intensive (consisting of at least four weeks per year) professional development aligned with standards reaching a substantial number of the state's teachers; development of teacher networking built around curriculum and instruction (usually involving both face-to-face and electronic contacts); a workable approach to school improvement; strong connections with preservice teacher education departments in the state universities. (3) *Curriculum.* A substantial but not transformative influence on curriculum and teaching in the direction of the new standards. (4) *Student Achievement.* A substantial positive impact on student achievement, something like ten points on a 100-point scale over five years (an average of two points per year).

This description of success also fits the lower rated states, where one or more important pieces of the composite picture are missing. In fact, some lower rated states are decisively stronger on selected components of variables. California's teacher networks, for example, probably were the model of design and impact, but political and policy support in that state disintegrated near the end of the initiative. Montana's strategy of curriculum replacement had the greatest impact on the classroom, but the scope of the initiative was limited to high school mathematics.

THE IMPORTANCE OF EARLIER PERIODS OF REFORM
AND THE TIME REQUIRED FOR SUCCESSFUL REFORM

A pattern that emerges in this group of case studies is that successful states built on pre-existing reforms of the 1980s, with continuity rather than discontinuity between the earlier period and the new period of standards-based reform. Usually the first piece was the state assessment itself, which acquired a base of statewide authority and acceptance strong enough to support subsequent modifications in a more standards-based direction. In Montana, the foundation was prior development of a standards-based curriculum and teacher enhancement projects, which then acquired the support of state policy. In any case, the lesson is that reform takes more time than the five years allowed in one cycle of NSF funding.

STUDENT ASSESSMENTS AND TEACHER NETWORKS
AS THE UNIVERSAL MIDDLE LINK

The combination of a state assessment as the lead policy instrument, and professional networking as a delivery structure operates as a kind of universal link between the top and bottom, regardless of whether state policy is built on central or local control. States with strong centralized policies need a way to bridge the gap between the top and the bottom, while local control states find that the assessment/network format is a politically acceptable way to provide strong instructional guidance. In both kinds of states, assessments and networking bridge the gap between the large "grain size" of the standards and the more specific tasks demanded by teaching and learning.[15]

LIMITS OF THE SEQUENTIAL CAUSAL THEORY:
"SYSTEMIC CAUSATION" IN MATURE CULTURES OF REFORM

The notion of reform becoming embedded in a student assessment, which in turn becomes embedded in the discourse of a network of teachers, points to a limitation of the sequential causal theory presented in this chapter. Once teachers are in the "net," they become part of all the "boxes" or variables of reform, namely reformers, policymakers, curriculum implementers, and facilitators of student achievement. They

are reformers and policymakers because they help construct each modification of standards and assessments, and they implement the curriculum and shape student achievement in their own classrooms. Sub-
groups of teachers take the lead in developing the examinations and
working with teachers from higher education, while others focus more
exclusively on their own classrooms. To some extent the entire system
becomes a "learning organization," in which the causal processes of
reform are distributed across roles.[16] This kind of causation in mature
systems might be called "systemic causation." Some dispersed causation can be captured within the confines of the NISE model used in this
chapter, which is labeled a "continuous causal sequence" and whose
notion of "depth" does include deeper understanding by all system
actors and even cultural change. Further, the multiple roles of teachers
can be thought of as adding authority to the policy system. But at some
point a system of simultaneous, multidirectional communication
requires a more elaborate model.[17]

Some Missing Pieces in the Reform Landscape

The previous section dealt with commonalities observed across successful reforms, but the interstate overview provided by the case studies also reveals a number of glaring deficits, or missing pieces, in the
reform landscape.

THE ABSENCE OR INDIRECTION OF INFLUENCE
OVER CURRICULUM CONTENT

Although it is true that student assessments and teacher networks
served as the link between top and bottom in the reforms, that link
would have been stronger with a more powerful means of influencing
curriculum. The common problem is the focus on pedagogy rather
than content. Reforms typically were aimed at classroom processes
such as the use of manipulatives, collaborative learning, and inquiry
learning. Especially early in the reforms, direct means of influencing
curriculum such as model curricula, new materials, and model teaching units were relatively rare.

Criticism of the pedagogical orientation could easily be overdrawn.
Not only is active learning supported as effective by research from cognitive psychology, but the distinction between content and pedagogy is
not entirely clear. Well-conceived active learning techniques raise the
level of cognitive demand or complexity in any given domain of content. Graphing, for example, is not simply a technique of representing

a function but a different kind of content and a means of seeing more deeply into the material. Furthermore, many teacher training programs incorporated content as part of the training when, for example, inquiry-based science in elementary school required restructuring the curriculum, or curriculum units were used as part of teacher training. Nevertheless, it is surprising how few reforms focused on *what* the students were being taught as opposed to only *how*. The gap between pedagogy and content narrowed as the reforms progressed, partly as a result of productive prodding by NSF. By the mid-1990s, many of the stronger reforms were using new materials, model teaching units, or curriculum replacement units.[18]

THE DEARTH OF FULLY ALIGNED STATE ASSESSMENTS

Despite the importance of student assessments in reform, the absence of assessments that are aligned, or fully aligned, with the reform objectives is a constant source of frustration. Reform objectives are neither advanced nor well measured by mismatched assessments. It is true that progress was made during the 1990s as new assessments were developed, piloted, and implemented. And, even in the absence of a fully aligned assessment, a major contribution to testing causal influence could be made by a more detailed understanding of which items on various state assessments are more and less matched to the objectives of reform.

THE ABSENCE OF GOOD DATA AND EVALUATION OF THE IMPACTS OF REFORM ON CLASSROOMS AND STUDENT ACHIEVEMENT

The impact of standards-based reform can be recognized without the strongest data on changes in classroom practice and student achievement, but good data and design around these variables would lend considerably more confidence to such judgments. Any theory or evaluation of standards-based reform requires testing causal links in complex systems on the basis of relatively few cases (observations). The task would be much easier, and the case much more convincing, if there were more direct and precise data on teaching and learning that could be associated with varying degrees and phases of reform. States were certainly moving in that direction with, for example, evaluations that compared gains in student achievement with the number of SSI-trained teachers in schools; but the effort is truly in its infancy. In one sense, no excuse exists for not gathering better data on teaching and learning, because adding the measurements is relatively easy and inexpensive compared to the daunting task of changing systems. True, the difficulty of measurement can be underestimated. Measurement of instruction, for example, must include not only pedagogical techniques like active learning but also the rigor and importance of the mathematics or science concepts being taught, appropriate sequencing and connections, and articulation without unnecessary repetition between grades and levels of schooling.[19] The greatest challenge is not in the difficulty but in the timing. The hard part is building good measurement and evaluation design into a program that is being invented and implemented on the fly and always has more urgent priorities. Fortunately, a funding agency is well equipped to insist on a solution to this problem of timing and priority, and improvement of evaluation should be and has become a major priority in the standards-based reform program of NSF.

THE SLOW GROWTH OF INCENTIVES AND MECHANISMS FOR WHOLE SCHOOL RESTRUCTURING

Another "late bloomer" on the reform landscape was building incentives for whole school restructuring. Many reforms were better at going to scale with the training of teachers within schools than changing the schools (and districts) in which the teachers would operate, and school restructuring proved a serious challenge. Gradually, components aimed at school restructuring, such as administrative outreach and workshops, became more common. At least one SSI not reviewed in this chapter has a powerful model of school restructuring.[20] But this component appears sufficiently underdeveloped that it deserves further cross-site study as the basis for better technical assistance during the reforms.

THE UNEXPLORED TERRITORY OF ADEQUACY AND CULTURAL CONTEXT IN URBAN SCHOOLS

One problem that appeared in such a fragmentary way that it is barely on the radar is the adequacy, or instructional capacity, of urban schools and districts. This problem requires further study to understand its basic dimensions. In the urban areas in some states, the obstacle is shortages of key resources, such as textbooks, materials, and computers. In others, materials are plentiful, but special problems of training exist, due to, for example, rapid turnover. In still others, the obstacle identified is a complex and resistant urban school bureaucracy. Another challenge is making the new curricula accessible in the ethnically pluralistic urban context.[21] Finally, student mobility may raise special problems for an articulated multi-year course of instruction and associated data systems on instruction and achievement. The special obstacles to reform in urban districts, as well as, perhaps, the special advantages, deserve further study. Some research already exists,[22] and the rapid expansion of the Urban Systemic Initiatives offers an opportunity to look more deeply.

Conclusion: Making a Difference Using Theory to Build New Reform

This chapter examined how a particular theory of standards-based reform can be used to conceptually simplify, describe, evaluate, and draw conclusions from case studies of reforms in different states. But the theory also has prospective and practical applications. Every component that is important to success in other reforms can become part of the design of new ones—for example, the independence of the reform agency and its connections with policymakers, teachers, and schools. The historically most powerful tools of policy, such as student assessments and teacher networks, can be raised in priority. Deficits found in earlier reforms can be addressed at the beginning of new reforms, such as influence over curriculum content, assessments or items on assessments aligned with reform objectives, whole school restructuring, and good evaluation design. Indeed, it is quite clear from reading the case studies that there has been a learning curve in the standards-based reform movement nationally that is a by-product of lessons learned in individual states. Hopefully, the theory offered here can help strengthen that learning process in the future.

APPENDIX

Nine Statewide Systemic Initiatives Studied in SRI Case Studies Synopsized and Ranked According to the NISE Theory[23]

CONNECTICUT

Reform. Independent science, mathematics, and technology "Academy" has influence in the department of education, the legislature, most school districts, major professional organizations, and the department of higher education. Academy has affected the curriculum in nineteen needy districts, forty professional development providers, the state assessment, and state teacher certification. The Academy also has a public relations campaign.

Policy. This state has a "top-down, bottom-up, through-the-middle" strategy of an authoritative, challenging state assessment (no high stakes), plus voluntary aligned program development in schools, districts, and professional organizations; and aligned changes in state assessment and teacher certification. The state assessment had been through several cycles of design and modification prior to the SSI, thereby contributing to its quality and authority.

Curriculum. Survey of curriculum in nineteen needy districts shows active learning pedagogy, increased enrollment in advanced courses, and changes in some district curriculum guidance.

Student achievement. From 1993-97, six to nine percent more students score "proficient" on state mathematics assessment in fourth, sixth, and eighth grade. From 1992-96, seven to eight percent more students score "basic/proficient" on NAEP mathematics in fourth and eighth grades. From 1995-96, two to three percent more students score "proficient" on the tenth grade state science test.

General comment. Policy infrastructure created by Academy appears to have reinforced strong state assessment.

MAINE

Reform. The reform agency is an independent "alliance" with links to the governor, legislature, department of education, higher education, and business groups. It had an impact on curriculum frameworks and assessments, trained a large group of teachers, and developed a technical assistance network. The agency probably is sustainable on the basis of its reputation and influence.

Policy. In response to *A Nation at Risk*, Maine established a state assessment with content tests in fourth, eighth, and eleventh grades in 1984. In the 1990s, the SSI worked on alignment of a new set of frameworks, "learning results," and a new version of the state assessment. A group of seven districts received technical assistance from the SSI and in turn provided technical assistance on a regional basis. Summer academies in mathematics and science provided intensive professional development. A "leadership consortium" of teachers and others meets to develop common goals and works with the subject matter professional organizations. The combination of these institutions changed SMET educational culture in the state.

Curriculum. About twenty percent of the state's teachers have received intensive training, while another forty percent have received some information and assistance. The training has been evaluated to be of high quality and effectiveness. A survey of the classrooms in the technical assistance districts showed high levels of active learning techniques (e.g., ninety-three to one hundred percent of elementary teachers emphasizing levels of learning beyond recall; high school classrooms had lower levels, in the fifty to seventy-five percent range). There do not seem to have been any comparisons of reform and non-reform groups, nor of reform groups over time.

Student outcomes. Maine students showed substantial gains on the state tests of mathematics and science at all tested grade levels in the 1990s (twenty to sixty-five points on a 300-point scale). Students in assisted schools started and ended this time period about twenty points ahead of students in the rest of the state.

General comment. Maine's SSI established strong links with all levels of the system (policymakers, delivery infrastructure, schools, and districts), and there were corresponding changes in policy, educational culture, and practice. Students appear to have made strong gains on a state assessment, although the students in assisted schools did not appear to gain more than others.

MONTANA

Reform. The high school mathematics curriculum reform was led by people active in the National Council of Teachers of Mathematics standards movement, and the Montana Council of Teachers of Mathematics was a leader from the beginning. Awareness of the SSI was high in high schools, as "practically every mathematics teacher" knew it. Two successive governors supported the reform, and the legislature provided $3 million for a related technology initiative. Seventy mathematics teachers developed the curriculum itself. The SSI had a public relations arm and published over 600 articles in the media. At its end, the SSI formed an integrated mathematics and science society (partly because of pressure from NSF) and developed an integrated mathematics and science curriculum framework. Still, the absence in the reform mission of science, and of the lower grades in mathematics, lowers the rating.

Policy. The SSI developed and tested an integrated four-year high school curriculum (SIMMS) with the first two years intended as a core curriculum for all students. The curriculum was similar to the NCTM model in terms of its vision, topics, technology requirement, applications, and collaborative learning. Adoption of the curriculum was voluntary. There was no state assessment, but a new accreditation law required the districts to have a district-mandated curriculum and appropriate assessment, creating a demand for the new curriculum. Within this policy framework, the SSI used consensus building and technical assistance to disseminate the reform. Intensive professional development was expected of every mathematics teacher using SIMMS, and workshops were held for thousands of school administrators. State universities contributed overhead on grants to buy computers for teacher preparation. There was a new teacher accreditation requirement, the universities designed new teacher education courses, and state colleges and universities agreed to recognize three years of integrated mathematics as meeting the admissions requirement. Again, almost the only weakness was the limitation of the high school mathematics effort, though a different NSF grant supported middle school mathematics. There has also been a decline in state spending and cuts in the Department of Education, which the SSI avoided because of its location in a university (rather than in the Department of Education).

Curriculum. The SIMMS curriculum, instituted in a majority of the high schools, was used by forty percent of mathematics teachers and taken by twenty-five percent of the state's high school students, or one-third of those enrolled in mathematics courses, and a quarter of the Native American students. Some professional development was provided for seventy-five percent of high school mathematics teachers. Use of the SIMMS curriculum was even higher outside the academic track where teachers often preferred more traditional courses, especially in the later grades.

Student outcomes. Students in the first two years of the course sequence scored between fourteen and twenty-three points higher on a SIMMS open-ended test; students in the third year scored less, but these were most likely students who previously would not have taken advanced mathematics. Students in the first two years of SIMMS showed no advantage on the PSAT relative to the control group (interpreted to mean that the basic skills levels of SIMMS and non-SIMMS students were equal).

General comment. Montana is a study in contrast between the depth and breadth of its reforms. Looking just at high school mathematics, the strategy was among the most systemic and powerful of all (at least allowing for future scale-up beyond the number of schools already reached). The strategy of developing a new curriculum to meet demand created by a new school certification requirement, plus intensive training of teachers, resulted in rapid adoption of the new courses, especially among those previously not in the academic track. The reform had high visibility in secondary schools, partly because of well-organized professional associations.

LOUISIANA

Reform. A quasi-independent agency (with politically and organizationally skillful leaders from higher education) obtained funding from the state boards of higher and of K-12 education, and had success in obtaining and coordinating other federal grants. Its governance council includes top policymakers, and its staff includes a full-time public relations coordinator. A new governor and reform task force support SSI innovations in frameworks and assessments.

Policy. In the first five years, seventy to seventy-five percent of resources were spent on high quality, intensive professional development in mathematics and science for 4,100 primarily K-8 teachers (out of about 45,000 teachers in the state), teacher preparation projects in most colleges and universities, and new teacher certification requirements. The end of the first five years saw influence on new, aligned frameworks and assessments, as well as the beginning of scale-up efforts through extended professional development, school restructuring, and regional assistance to districts. Competency-based curriculum reform and high school exit examinations adopted in 1979 are influential, but are not aligned with SSI efforts.

Curriculum. Impact on trained teachers' attitudes was high. Change in classroom practice of trained teachers was broad but uneven in depth.

Student outcomes. Students instructed by SSI teachers scored slightly higher on state (non-aligned) fifth grade and seventh grade mathematics tests.

General comment. Judged solely by actual impacts on policy, curriculum, and achievement at the end of the first five years, Louisiana's SSI would have deserved a lower rating. But the reform group has a strong, coordinated influence on policy, as shown in the recent development of new aligned frameworks and assessments and new scaling-up measures for schools, teachers, and districts.

MICHIGAN

Reform. SSI pushed for alignment of technical assistance with existing strong state assessment initiatives and assisted twenty-four "focus districts" with grants. Technical assistance efforts influenced or produced guidelines for mandatory professional development, curriculum and instruction materials on the internet, further alignment of state tests with national standards, and advice to regional assistance centers. But staff was cut more than twenty percent by the governor at the end of SSI funding.

Policy. State assessment and the high school exit examination developed prior to the SSI are the leading policy instruments. The SSI focused on capacity building through the technical assistance described above, all of which became an infrastructure for reform.

Curriculum. Two-thirds of teachers in the focus districts used active learning techniques, all five districts visited by evaluation teams had updated their curricula during the SSI period to reflect the state assessment changes, and textbook selections in focus districts reflect NCTM standards.

Student achievement. Gains of five to nineteen points on state mathematics tests in fourth, seventh, and eleventh grades (but a plateau was reached around 1995, three years after the beginning of the SSI). From 1992-96, there were gains of six and ten points on NAEP mathematics in fourth and ninth grades. From 1996-97, there were seven to ten point gains in the state science test in fifth and eleventh grades, but a decline in the eighth grade. Thirteen percent more African American students were proficient on the fourth grade state mathematics test (but the gap remains the same), and the NAEP eighth grade mathematics gap narrowed by three percent.

General comment. Substantial gains in student achievement appear primarily related to earlier policy changes, classroom changes in the focus districts were uneven, and SSI funding was cut at the state level, thereby threatening sustainability.

CALIFORNIA

Reform. Two teacher networks, in mathematics and science, achieved deep and broad access among teachers, schools, and districts on curriculum and teaching, and each was refunded by NSF under different grants after SSI funding was not renewed. Both networks developed an infrastructure of statewide leadership and regional and school delivery systems.

Policy. California's mathematics and science teacher networks are an interesting example of how a strong "policy" influence can be exerted by intermediate delivery organizations, even when these are no longer supported by state policies. Both networks utilized intensive training sessions in the summer or at other times and academic year follow-up. Both extended their scale on the basis of what appears to be popular demand (the mathematics network expanding from middle school to elementary school, and the science network adding a mathematics component). The mathematics network (Math Renaissance) used a strategy of curriculum replacement units and influenced curriculum design and textbook selection at the district level. The science network developed a strategy of whole school change and curriculum development at the elementary school level. Unfortunately, the turmoil surrounding the state policies leaves the future health of the networks somewhat in doubt.

The good news on the delivery system, however, was matched by bad news in the changes in the policies themselves. A back-to-basics movement in government policy led to revocation of curriculum frameworks, which were placed under new development, and suspension of the state assessment; the statewide textbook approval and funding process has become less aligned; and the governor is pursuing free-standing policy initiatives. Professional reformers in California now have little influence on state policy, but are trying to develop a new consensus.

Curriculum. The breadth and depth of the influence of the networks on the curriculum was strong based on converging evidence: 38,500 teachers from 2,400 schools in fifty percent of the state's districts were trained. A study of reform classrooms found change toward standards-based teaching in a majority of classrooms and, in the science classrooms, an average score of 18.75 on a thirty-point scale of constructivist teaching. An evaluation found that, in a sample of reform schools, reform-based teaching had achieved sustainable implementation. Districts with reformed schools changed their textbook purchasing to match reform goals.

Student outcomes. In science, students in reform classrooms did not do better than the control group on a specially administered test, but students in schools that had been "under reform" for three years did better than those from schools with two years. In mathematics, a special administration of the new standards examination showed that students from reform schools did better in concepts, skills, and problem solving (with the biggest advantage in skills).

General comment. Based on the effectiveness, power, and scale of its teacher networks, and the systemic policies with which it began the 1990s, California's reform would have deserved a higher rating, but its model systemic policies disintegrated, and the absence of supportive state policy threatened the sustainability of the reform. Also, where they were measured, gains in student achievement were not large, which may be attributable to large declines in financial support for education in the state over many years.

ARKANSAS

Reform. The SSI was initially supported strongly by the governor, but support of a new administration is unclear. The SSI has support from departments of both education and higher education. Some aspect of reform reached a large minority of the state's teachers and administrators.

Policy. Most resources were spent on intensive mathematics and science professional development for thirty-five percent of all teachers in kindergarten through fourth grade, twenty-two percent of all mathematics teachers in fifth through twelfth grades, and twenty-two percent of science teachers were trained. Also, 4,000 school administrators were trained in the leadership academy. The strong state assessment and graduation requirements adopted in 1983 are not well aligned, but the SSI is influential in developing new assessments. Three new levels of SMET teacher certification have been added.

Curriculum. There is anecdotal evidence of active learning techniques in classrooms. A science professional development effort developed and trained teachers in seventeen integrated teaching modules. The SSI claims that trained teachers taught seventy percent of the state's students.

Student outcomes. The six- to nine-point increases in NAEP fourth and eighth grade mathematics scores in the 1990s, increased enrollment in advanced courses, and decreases in students taking remedial education in college probably are mostly caused by basic skills reforms in the 1980s. Student scores were "measurably" higher in schools with seventy-five percent or more SSI-trained teachers.

General comment. This state had an extensive professional development program that reached many teachers and changed the culture of teaching in the state. But there was limited influence on policy, limited evidence of and probably small impact on classrooms and student outcomes, and lack of clear continuing political support.

DELAWARE

Reform. The strategy that the SSI began with was judged faulty and heavily revised at the end of five years. The model schools strategy focused on a limited number of schools, lacked a clear vision of goals, produced little change, and was not understood at the district level. The "polished stones" strategy of teachers developing curriculum units was inefficient and was abandoned in favor of adopting NSF-approved curricula. A new state assessment was suspended after a great number of students failed. Summer professional development institutes suffered from lack of a means of incorporating schoolwide change. But strategies adopted at the end of five years looked more promising (a teacher network built around model curricula, a model of professional development that has been adopted in other states, and continuing work on the assessment).

Policy. Few, if any, sustained policy changes were achieved, but the policy profile at the end of five years began to look more powerful (especially the combination of curriculum replacement units, teacher networks, and revised professional development).

Curriculum. There was little evidence of curriculum change, and the evaluation found spotty change in a few schools. Participating teachers' attitudes were favorable.

Student outcomes. There was no evidence of a change in student achievement.

General comment. The SRI evaluation overview seems accurate: the Delaware SSI was just acquiring an effective focus at the end of the grant period and could be rated in a five–stage model of reform developed by the Education Commission of the States as between the third and fourth stages: "transition to a standards-based system, with an emerging infrastructure." The five stages of the ECS model are: (1) non-standards-led system, (2) awareness and exploration of such a system, (3) transition to such a system, (4) emerging new infrastructure to support such a system, and (5) predominance of such a system. Please note: Under our system of ratings, we probably would classify "awareness and exploration" (the second stage) as stage one, while an "emerging infrastructure" (the fourth stage) sounds like stage two under our system unless there happened to be substantial changes across all four components of reform, policy, classroom, and achievement.

NEW YORK

Reform. New York's strategy was to transform twelve urban schools (R&D schools) plus influence state policy. The SSI did pilot new state assessments in the R&D schools, but otherwise had little visibility in state policy. In 1995, in response to an NSF directive, the SSI changed course to emphasize state policy and adopted what appeared to be an unrealistically ambitious plan to transform education in the state.

Policy. Regarding the pilot school strategy, the SSI had difficulty impacting the schools because of complex district bureaucracies, and effects on the districts themselves were minimal. Teachers from these schools attended summer professional development institutes, but the institutes were not integrated clearly with each other. Regarding state policy, massive cuts were made in the department of education, and reorganization of the department made it more difficult to locate technical assistance. New York had a teaching-oriented school quality review based on the British inspectorate, but funding for the program was cut. New assessments and curriculum frameworks were under development, but the SSI had little involvement.

Curriculum. Restructuring progress in the twelve pilot schools was uneven. Only one small elementary school showed deep restructuring. A survey of teachers in the R&D schools showed what appeared to be modest levels of inquiry-based teaching techniques.

Student outcomes. One percent more students in R&D schools reached the proficiency level during third grade on a state mathematics examination (the PEP) than students from other schools. Equivalent gains in the one deeply restructured school were more in the range of ten to twenty percent in both mathematics and science in third and sixth grades. Science scores were not differentially affected in other R&D schools.

General comment. The state of New York has some promising policies recently developed or under development: new curriculum frameworks, a new assessment aligned with national standards, and rigorous teacher certification. But in a sense the SSI chose a "worst of all worlds" strategy: reforming a handful of R&D schools and achieving modest results in that narrow objective, while having little visibility and impact at the state level. It was a good idea to work with urban schools, but the schools and their districts proved difficult to influence, and reform was further impeded by resource deficits at the school level. Professional development was never effectively coupled with the school restructuring strategy. The state department was also rocked by budget cuts.

NOTES

1. The author wishes to thank the following individuals for reading and commenting on earlier drafts of this chapter: Bernice Anderson, Daryl Chubin, Eric Hamilton, Eric Osthoff, Andrew Porter, Senta Raizen, Patrick Shields, Deborah Stewart, Larry Suter, Norman Webb, Paula White, and Andrew Zucker. Their comments were helpful; any errors in this chapter are mine.

2. The case studies were produced by SRI International and include: Nancy Adelman, *A Case Study of Maine's SSI (MAINE: A Community of Discovery), 1992-97* (Menlo

Park, CA: SRI International, 1998); Nancy Adelman, *A Case Study of Delaware's SSI (Project 21), 1995-97* (Menlo Park, CA: SRI International, 1998); John Breckenridge and David Goldstein, *A Case Study of Louisiana's SSI (LASIP), 1991-96* (Menlo Park, CA: SRI International, 1998); Margaret Goertz and Rebecca Carver, *A Case Study of Michigan's SSI (MSSI), 1992-97* (Menlo Park, CA: SRI International, 1998); Margaret Goertz, Diane Massell, and Thomas Corcoran, *A Case Study of Connecticut's SSI (CONNSTRUCT), 1991-96* (Menlo Park, CA: SRI International); Daniel Humphrey and Rebecca Carver, *A Case Study of New York's SSI (NYSSI), 1993-97* (Menlo Park, CA: SRI International, 1998); Daniel Humphrey and Choya Wilson, *A Case Study of Arkansas' SSI (ARSSI), 1993-97* (Menlo Park, CA: SRI International, 1998); Patrick Shields, Julie Marsh, Camille Marder, and Choya Wilson, *A Case Study of California's SSI (CAMS), 1992-97* (Menlo Park, CA: SRI International, 1998); Andrew Zucker and Camille Marder, *A Case Study of Montana's SSI (SIMMS), 1991-96* (Menlo Park, CA: SRI International, 1998).

3. A summary of the case studies can be found in the appendix.

4. Also funded by the National Science Foundation.

5. Marshall Smith and Jennifer O'Day, "Systemic school reform," in Susan Fuhrman and Betty Malen, eds., *The Politics of Curriculum and Testing* (New York: Falmer Press, 1991), pp. 233-267.

6. David Cohen, Milbrey McLaughlin, and Joan Talbert, eds., *Teaching for Understanding: Challenges for Policy and Practice* (San Francisco: Jossey-Bass, 1993); Joel Mintzes, James Wandersee, and Joseph Novak, *Teaching Science for Understanding: A Human Constructivist View* (San Diego: Academic Press, 1998).

7. "Symposium on national math and science standards: Implications and conclusions," *Teachers College Record* 100 (1998) [Special Issue]; "Mathematics articles," *Phi Delta Kappan* 80 (1999), pp. 425-456.

8. Michael Knapp, "Between systemic reforms and the mathematics and science classrooms: The dynamics of innovation, implementation, and professional learning," *Review of Educational Research* 67 (1997): pp. 227-266.

9. William Clune, *Toward a Theory of Systemic Reform: The Case of Nine NSF Statewide Systemic Initiatives* (Madison, WI: University of Wisconsin, National Institute for Science Education, 1998).

10. Andrew Porter, Robert Floden, Donald Freeman, William Schmidt, and John Schwille, "Content determinants in elementary school mathematics," in Douglas Grouws and Thomas Cooney, eds., *Perspectives on Research on Effective Mathematics* (Hillsdale, NJ: Erlbaum, 1998), pp. 96-113.

11. Knapp, "Between systemic reforms and the mathematics and science classrooms."

12. Ibid.

13. SRI International, *Introduction to the SSI Case Studies* (Menlo Park, CA: Author, 1998).

14. For details regarding the idea of "working in the middle" as a genotype for successful standards-based reform, see Uri Treisman, "Response to what have we learned: What do we need to know?" in William Clune, Susan Miller, Senta Raizen, Norman Webb, Dianne Bowcock, Edward Britton, Ramona Gunther, and Ricardo Mesquita, eds., *Research on Systemic Reform: What Have We Learned? What Do We Need to Know?* (Madison, WI: University of Wisconsin, National Institute for Science Education, 1997), pp. 16-21.

15. See "Symposium on national math and science standards."

16. Lauren Resnick, "The role of teaching and learning in systemic reform," in William Clune, Susan Miller, Senta Raizen, Norman Webb, Dianne Bowcock, Edward Britton, Ramona Gunther, and Ricardo Mesquita, eds., *Research on Systemic Reform:*

What Have We Learned? What Do We Need to Know? (Madison, WI: University of Wisconsin, National Institute for Science Education, 1997), pp. 62-64.

17. For earlier, less linear modeling, see William Clune, "The best path to systemic educational policy: Standard/centralized or differentiated/decentralized?" *Educational Evaluation and Policy Analysis* 15 (1993): pp. 233-254; and William Clune, "Systemic educational policy: A conceptual framework," in Susan Fuhrman, ed., *Designing Coherent Education Policy: Improving the System* (San Francisco: Jossey-Bass, 1993), pp. 125-140.

18. For research showing that professional development is more effective when it focuses on content, see David Cohen and Heather Hill, *Instructional Policy and Classroom Performance: The Mathematics Reform in California* (Philadelphia: Consortium for Policy Research in Education, 1998); and Mary Kennedy, *Form and Substance in Inservice Teacher Education* (Madison, WI: University of Wisconsin, National Institute for Science Education, 1998).

19. The author wishes to thank Senta Raizen for input on this point.

20. Alberto Rodriguez, *Equity through Systemic Reform: The Case of Whole-School Mathematics and Science Restructuring in Puerto Rico* (Madison, WI: University of Wisconsin, National Institute for Science Education, 1999).

21. Okhee Lee, *Current Conceptions of Science Achievement in Major Reform Documents and Implications for Equity and Assessment* (Madison, WI: University of Wisconsin, National Institute for Science Education, 1998).

22. Mark St. John, Jeanne Century, Felisa Tibbitts, and Barbara Heenan, *Reforming Elementary Science Education in Urban Districts: Reflections on a Conference* (Inverness, CA: Inverness Research Associates, 1994).

23. See Table 1 for numerical ratings. Please note that this appendix reflects the situation in states as of approximately 1998. See section on methodology.

CHAPTER III

Standards-based Accountability: Horse Trade or Horse Whip?[1]

MARGARET E. GOERTZ

States have historically used accountability policies as a way of monitoring and regulating education in their communities. Traditionally, state accountability policies were designed to ensure a minimum level of educational inputs (for example, the number and type of staff in a school and the number of books in the library), a minimum level of quality in these inputs (for example, the use of certified staff), access to educational programs and services (such as minimum course offerings and programs for students with special needs), and the proper use of education resources. The school district was the primary target of these accountability systems, and states relied on accreditation processes and program monitoring to ensure compliance with these input and process standards. The resulting reports received little public scrutiny.

In the 1970s, states expanded their role to ensure a minimum level of educational outcomes. As state financial support of education increased, policymakers began to question how, and how well, these funds were being used. This interest, coupled with concerns about Johnny's [and Jane's] inability to read and compute, led many states to implement minimum competency testing programs to measure and report student performance and as a requirement for high school graduation. These tests focused almost exclusively, however, on the minimum abilities that students would need to function in society.[2]

The standards-based reform movement redefines both educational outcomes and accountability systems. States establish challenging, rather than minimal, content and performance standards for all students. Then, in what the National Governors' Association[3] called a "horse trade," states give schools and school districts greater flexibility

Margaret E. Goertz is a Professor in the Graduate School of Education, and Co-Director of the Consortium for Policy Research in Education, both at the University of Pennsylvania.

to design appropriate instructional programs in exchange for performance based accountability. States monitor the results rather than the process of education; they hold schools accountable for student achievement rather than for compliance with rules and regulations. Standards set clear expectations for students and schools; accountability systems provide the information (through assessments and other measures of student performance) and the incentives (through rewards and sanctions) for students and schools to work toward these standards.

These changes have been reinforced by revisions in the federal government's two largest education programs: Title I of Improving America's Schools Act (Title I) and Individuals with Disabilities Education Act (IDEA). Title I requires that states establish high standards in at least reading and mathematics, develop high quality assessments to measure performance on these standards, define and measure the progress of schools and districts against these standards, and have local districts identify low performing schools for assistance. IDEA requires that states include students with disabilities in state and district assessment programs with appropriate accommodations, and disaggregate and report their test scores.

With its focus on results and consequences for students and schools, performance based accountability has developed much greater public visibility—and with it, controversy—than more traditional accountability systems. On the one hand, researchers and reporters alike laud the success of states like North Carolina and Texas in raising the academic performance of their students and narrowing the performance gap between White students and students of color.[4] On the other hand, some students in Massachusetts refused to participate in their new state assessment,[5] and civil rights advocates have charged in court that high stakes accountability systems discriminate against poor and minority students (e.g., the Committee for Fiscal Equity in New York and the Mexican American Legal Defense and Education Fund in Texas).

This chapter looks at how schools, school districts, and states are responding to the current push for performance based accountability. Data from a three-year study of ten states, twenty-three school districts, and fifty-seven schools, as well as national surveys of state policies, are used to address two sets of questions. First, what are the key design elements of state accountability systems and how do they vary across states? Second, what do accountability systems look like at the school and district level? What are the similarities and differences in these systems in diverse state policy environments? The chapter begins with a brief overview of the study sample and methodology and concludes with a discussion of emerging policy issues.

Study Design and Methodology

In 1996, the Consortium for Policy Research in Education (CPRE) undertook a multi-year study of standards-based reform in ten states and twenty-three school districts. The purpose of this study was to examine the progress and implementation of standards-based reform, focusing on changes in state and local education policies, the coherence of reforms across levels of government and between governmental and non-governmental influences, and ways in which policies affected practice and built capacity in selected schools and districts. The states—California, Colorado, Florida, Kentucky, Maryland, Michigan, Minnesota, Nebraska, Pennsylvania, and Texas—represent a range in the age, strength,[6] and stability of state accountability policies. Together these states educate about forty percent of the United States public school students. Between 1996 and 1999, researchers collected detailed information on state policies in several areas, including standards, assessment, accountability, Title I, and special education. In spring 2000, CPRE researchers collected data on the assessment and accountability policies of the other forty states, and updated information on the ten case study states.

In the springs of 1998 and 1999, researchers conducted site visits in twenty-three school districts—two in California and three each in Colorado, Florida, Kentucky, Maryland, Michigan, Minnesota, and Texas. They interviewed district staff responsible for accountability and assessment, curriculum and instruction, professional development, low performing schools, and federal programs. These districts were selected for their activism in school improvement and standards-based reform but were demographically diverse.[7] In 1998, the researchers also conducted site visits in thirty-three elementary schools in the California, Kentucky, Maryland, and Michigan districts. The school sample was expanded in 1999 to include twenty-four schools in study districts in Colorado, Florida, and Texas. At least two of the three schools in each district participated in the Title I program. At the school level, site visitors interviewed principals and school improvement committee chairs in both years, and surveyed teachers in second through fifth grades in each building in 1999. The district field work does not reflect changes made after spring 1999 to state accountability policies in California, Colorado, Florida, and Kentucky.

State Accountability Policies

Most states have adopted some form of performance based accountability. They differ, however, in how they address three key design elements: *Who* is held accountable?, for *what* are they held accountable and *how*?, and what *consequences* are attached to the accountability system? These policy decisions determine whom incentives are focused on, the strength of the incentives, and the kinds of information available to educators, the public, and policymakers.

This section begins with an overview of whom states and localities are holding accountable for student performance. It then categorizes state accountability systems by who sets goals for the system and the consequences of not meeting these goals. This grouping sets the context for a discussion of local accountability systems. The section concludes with a description of state-defined accountability structures.

WHO IS HELD ACCOUNTABLE?

State assessment and accountability systems developed in the 1970s typically focused on the performance of individual students and used assessment data to identify students in need of remedial services. They also held districts accountable for educational inputs and process standards, such as the number of certified staff and compliance with federal and state regulations. The new accountability systems that emerged in the 1990s hold schools rather than students or school districts accountable for student outcomes. Two beliefs underlie this shift: student performance is cumulative and influenced by the entire school, and a system of collective responsibility will encourage school staff to work collaboratively to improve student performance.[8] Some reformers also felt that a student based accountability system "blamed the victim," rather than the system, for failure.

When schools are held accountable as a unit, it is not necessary to test students at every grade nor to collect measures of individual student performance. Therefore, states and districts can use matrix sampling to generate reliable measures of group performance on performance based tasks without untenable test burden. In addition, rewards and sanctions are directed at the school, not the student. Many state systems adopted these features in the early years of performance based accountability; only a few states continued to test every student in every grade. Within a few years, however, parents and politicians began clamoring for individual student scores which matrix sampling does not provide. A major criticism of the now-defunct California

Learning Assessment System test was its lack of individual results; subsequent legislation made individual test results a mandatory component of any statewide test. In 1997 on the eve of their tests' implementation, Colorado's political leaders switched their statewide testing design from a matrix sample with district level results to assessing every student in the tested grade level and providing individualized results. Teachers also began looking for systematic ways to measure individual student progress during the school year. The use of local assessments began to proliferate.

At the same time, educators and policymakers began to question the lack of student incentives in state accountability systems. Education is co-produced. Teachers' success is dependent on students' efforts in school, but there is nothing in a school based accountability system to motivate students to take the tests seriously, especially in secondary schools. Nor are there any consequences for students who perform poorly on the tests. Thus several states and school districts have enacted promotion gates: students cannot progress to the next grade (often at transition points like fourth grade) if they do not meet district or state performance standards. Eight states have policies for ending social promotion. California, for example, requires districts to develop standards that students must meet to be promoted at "pivotal" points, such as the third, fifth, and eighth grades. Colorado students who are not reading on grade level by the end of third grade cannot move on to fourth grade reading instruction, while North Carolina requires students to pass state assessments at three "gateway" points— third, fifth, and eighth grades. Twenty-eight states have enacted high school exit examinations, an increase of ten since 1996-97.[9] Another seven states place endorsements on students' transcripts or diplomas if they pass the state examinations. While several states have implemented challenging high school assessments, most of the older graduation tests focus on basic skills. Many of these latter states are in the process of revising their high school assessments so they will measure more rigorous content.

The concept of holding individual teachers directly responsible for student performance is extremely controversial. While most states require school districts to evaluate teachers on a regular basis, teacher compensation, tenure, and licensure are not tied to student achievement or student progress. A few states are taking steps to include student performance in the evaluation of teachers. In Texas, for example, improvement in student achievement is one of approximately fifty criteria in eight domains upon which teachers are evaluated in the state's

Professional Development and Appraisal System (PDAS). The use of the PDAS is optional, however. To be eligible for Florida's School Recognition Program (a fiscal rewards program), districts must include student performance as one component in their salary schedule. Most states, however, limit teacher accountability to ensuring that teachers participate in periodic professional development.

TYPES OF ACCOUNTABILITY SYSTEMS

State accountability systems create incentives for schools and districts to focus on student achievement and continuous progress. The type and strength of these incentives is determined in large part by the design of the accountability system (particularly the measures of adequate progress), who sets what goals for the system, and the consequences of meeting (or not meeting) these goals. State accountability systems vary along all of these dimensions.

We have grouped state accountability systems into three categories based on who sets goals for the system and the extent to which schools and districts are held accountable for student performance. These categories are: public reporting systems, locally-defined accountability systems, and state-defined accountability systems.

Public reporting systems. Public reporting is the most basic form of accountability. Schools give an account of their programs and performance. The public can then use this information to demand improvements in their schools, or possibly to choose alternate schools for their children. While nearly all states report annually on student performance, about a dozen states use public reporting as their primary accountability mechanism.[10] In most of these states, districts must administer and report the results of a statewide assessment. A few states without statewide assessment systems, like Nebraska, require districts to administer norm-referenced and classroom level criterion referenced tests of their choosing. Districts must provide performance reports to their communities that include student achievement and possibly other measures of student performance. In all these cases, states do not rank or rate school or district performance, nor do they identify low performing schools. These tasks are left to the public and to local educators.

Locally-defined accountability systems. A handful of other states have developed accountability systems that emphasize local standards and local planning. States allow districts to establish criteria for school performance, but use strategic plans or district and school improvement plans to hold districts accountable for student performance.

Pennsylvania, for example, requires its districts to develop six-year strategic plans that describe how the locality will help students achieve the state's learning objectives. Districts must align their curriculum, establish specific criteria for measuring student achievement of both locally determined and state-developed graduation outcomes, and establish a student assessment plan that supplements the state test. The strategic plans, which are reviewed by the state, must also include professional development plans for teachers.[11]

State-defined accountability systems. The majority of states set performance goals for students, schools, and/or school systems and hold these individuals and units directly accountable for meeting these goals. These states also establish rewards for meeting or exceeding state goals and/or sanctions for not meeting their target. Districts can exceed or supplement state accountability policies, but not make critical choices or changes. The states' performance goals vary, however, along several dimensions, including how performance is measured and whether the performance goal is fixed or relative. Similarly, the consequences of not meeting state goals can range from school improvement planning to a loss of state accreditation to state takeover.

KEY DESIGN ELEMENTS

Performance measures. States use different mixes of cognitive and non-cognitive measures of student performance. All of the states with state assessments use them as the centerpiece of their accountability systems, but the type of test (criterion or norm-referenced) and the number of subjects and grade levels included in the states' assessment systems varies across the country.

Just under half of the states use only criterion-referenced tests to measure student performance. The other states use only norm-referenced tests, or a combination of the two. All states assess reading and mathematics, while between thirty to thirty-four states test writing, social studies, and science as well. But not all states test all subjects in all grades. Texas, for example, assesses reading and mathematics in third through eighth grades and in tenth grade, while Michigan tests these subjects only in fourth, seventh, and eleventh grades. Some states, like Maryland, include social studies and science in all of their assessment grades, while many other states test these subjects at only one or two points in time. States are beginning to expand their assessment programs to include more grades, however. Florida recently extended its testing program to cover third through tenth grades as a way of measuring student learning from year to year. Kentucky and

Maryland are using norm-referenced tests to "fill in" grades not included in their original assessment system and to provide individual student scores not available from their performance based state tests. These norm-referenced tests are not included in Maryland's accountability measures, however, and account for only five percent of Kentucky's school performance index.

About a quarter of the states include non-cognitive outcomes, generally attendance and dropout rates, in some aspect of their accountability systems. However, states weight the relative importance of cognitive and non-cognitive performance measures differently. For example, non-cognitive outcomes account for only five to ten percent of each school's accountability index in Kentucky while Texas gives "equal" weight to multiple indicators by requiring schools to meet minimum performance standards on each of three indicators: state assessments, attendance, and dropout rates.

Measures of progress. Performance based accountability systems focus not only on the level of student performance, but on the progress of students and schools toward meeting states' standards. Schools or districts that do not make continuous progress toward state goals should receive assistance; those that meet or exceed goals should be rewarded. States tend to use one of three approaches to defining progress: meeting an absolute target, making relative growth, and/or narrowing the gap in the percentage of students scoring in the highest and lowest performance levels.

Florida and Texas are examples of states that use *absolute* targets; that is, they establish a performance threshold(s) that all schools must attain to have made satisfactory progress. Under Florida's A+ Plan for Education, the state grades schools on a scale of "A" to "F." A school earns each grade by meeting specific performance standards. For example, at least sixty percent of a school's students must score at Level Two ("limited success at meeting state content standards") on the state assessments in reading, mathematics, and writing to receive a grade of "C." Schools that do not meet this criterion in *any* of the three tested areas are given a grade of "F" and are judged as not making adequate yearly progress. Texas defines adequate yearly progress as achieving the state's "acceptable" rating. For a school to be rated "acceptable" in 1999-2000, at least fifty percent of students in each subgroup had to pass the state assessment in reading, writing, and mathematics; the dropout rate had to be six percent or less; and the student attendance rate had to be at least ninety-four percent.[12]

The use of *relative criteria* emphasizes continuous improvement. Here states set an annual growth target that is based on each school's past performance and often reflects the school's distance from a state-specified performance target. A school's growth goal can be fixed or can change from year to year. Kentucky's Long-term Accountability Model, for example, establishes the same long-term goal for every school—to achieve an average accountability score of 100 by the year 2014. The state then charts a linear "goal line" for each school between its baseline accountability score for 1999-2000 and the target goal, as well as an "assistance" line based on one standard error of measurement. Every two years, each school is expected to meet or exceed the accountability scores indicated on its goal line. Schools that perform above their assistance line, however, are considered to have made adequate yearly progress.

In contrast, Maryland only requires schools to show "statistically significant" change in their School Performance Indices (SPI). The SPI, however, is recalculated annually to reflect how far the school is from meeting state performance goals, such as having seventy percent of students score "satisfactory" on the state assessment. California has assigned schools individualized annual growth targets that are based on five percent of the difference between their Academic Performance Index baseline score for July 1999 and the statewide interim performance target of 800.

However, the use of either absolute or relative targets raises a potential equity issue. Both of these approaches focus on building level accountability; that is, on the performance of the aggregate student population. Neither approach addresses the gap between the lowest and highest achieving students in a school, nor between the performance of subgroups of students within a school. For example, if Maryland's K-8 goals (seventy percent of students scoring "satisfactory" or above on the state assessment) are met, nearly one-third of a school's students may be left behind with poor scores. Many of these may be minority students.

Some states have addressed the achievement gap issue by defining adequate yearly progress in terms of moving students from one achievement level to the next higher level. Michigan, for example, requires Title I schools to reduce by ten percent the gap in the percentage of students scoring in the highest and lowest performance levels on the state assessments. Schools are held accountable for closing the gap in all subject areas. Rhode Island requires schools to increase both overall performance and the performance of students in the lowest performing category by three to five percent a year. Other states have alternative ways of focusing on the lowest performing students. While Kentucky schools can increase their accountability index primarily by moving students from low to high apprentice, or from apprentice to proficient, they must also reduce the number of students in the novice category of achievement. California provides an incentive for schools to focus on low-achieving students by giving extra improvement points for moving students from the lowest to the next highest performance bands.

Consequences. All of the states with "state-defined" accountability systems identify low performing schools, and all make some provision for assistance, either from the state or from the local school district. This assistance generally takes one of three forms: support in the school improvement planning (SIP) process, funding for the SIP process and for improvement initiatives, and technical assistance. Most of these states also apply sanctions to schools that fail to improve after a specified period of time. A few states, like Michigan and Virginia, withhold accreditation from failing schools. Others have provisions for intervening in the management of failing schools or school districts. Interventions include allowing students to attend other schools, reorganizing or closing a school, reassigning school staff, assigning the management of the school to an external agent, and/or allowing a charter school to be developed. Many states also give schools financial rewards for high levels of performance and/or for the improvement of student outcomes.

The District Role in Accountability

State accountability systems set the parameters for local accountability policies. In states with prescriptive accountability policies, districts must use state criteria at a minimum to hold their schools accountable for student progress and to identify schools in need of improvement. As one respondent noted, "The state [accountability] system is our [accountability] system." When states give school districts discretion to design their own accountability systems, one finds a wide variation in local policy.

"STATE-DEFINED" ACCOUNTABILITY SYSTEMS

All of the study districts in states with "state-defined" accountability systems used the state system as the basis of their district systems. While districts do not have the discretion to interpret state provisions, they may establish criteria and/or procedures that exceed state requirements. A few districts raised performance standards when they viewed state standards as too low. In Texas, all three study districts were rated as "academically acceptable" at the time of our field work, and set higher standards for themselves. The goal in two of the districts was to be rated "recognized;" in the third, to be rated "exemplary."[13]

Districts in states with higher performance standards added performance incentives for schools that make progress but do not qualify for rewards under the state definition. Maryland provides monetary rewards to schools that show substantial, sustained, and statistically significant improvement on the state's School Performance Index. While showing progress, few schools in our three study districts had qualified for the state reward. Two of our study districts, however, provided their own monetary rewards to schools to encourage their reform efforts. One of these districts provided funds to schools that showed improvement on at least one of the state accountability criteria; schools that improved on multiple criteria received larger rewards. The other district rewarded elementary schools that had the largest increases in test scores (taking into account school size and socioeconomic composition).

Several districts created student benchmarking systems mapped against state or district goals to ensure that students in all grades are on track to meet state standards and to focus attention on the lower performing students. The impetus for one Kentucky district's accountability system was the state's new high school graduation standards that require all students to complete algebra and geometry in high school. To ensure that all students will graduate reading and able to do mathematics at the twelfth grade level, this district instituted a "competency assurance plan" that measures student performance against grade level standards throughout his or her career. It holds teachers and principals accountable for documenting the progress of low performing students, currently by assessing them three times a year in mathematics and reading using school-selected assessments. The district was in the process of identifying grade level outcomes and districtwide assessments. Two of the Maryland districts used both district-designed end of unit tests and teacher-generated running records to measure student progress against district goals (which are aligned with state goals). No consequences were tied to these assessments, however, and use of these data varied across the schools. A Texas district in the study created a timeline for teaching the Texas Essential Knowledge and Skills (TEKS) and devised benchmark exams to check student progress on the TEKS twice a year. Results of the benchmark exams were used to help teachers, identify problems and gaps in the district's curriculum timeline, and identify students who need additional assistance.

"LOCALLY-DEFINED" ACCOUNTABILITY SYSTEMS

There was significant variation in the design of local accountability systems in states with "locally-defined" accountability systems. Local accountability systems ranged from highly centralized, sophisticated systems that held schools accountable for student performance on multiple measures ("district-defined" systems) to highly decentralized systems where schools set goals and chose performance measures ("school-defined" systems).

One of our California districts provides an example of a comprehensive, centralized accountability system. At the time of the CPRE field work, California had a voluntary Challenge Initiative that called for districts to agree to meet specific growth targets on multiple measures selected by the district, including the state assessment. The consequences for not meeting these goals were unclear. This district had developed standards (which are being realigned against the revised state standards) and proficiency measures in both literacy (reading and writing) and mathematics. Students were assigned proficiency levels by combining their standardized test results and scores from a set of district performance tests. The district goal was to have at least ninety percent of students proficient in district literacy and mathematics standards. Schools were responsible for improving the global proficiency rating (a combination of four mathematics and reading tests) of all students and meeting the other goals of their school improvement plans. The district had developed a program of rewards and technical assistance for improving and struggling schools, respectively.

In contrast, schools set their own goals in the Colorado study districts. One district, for example, required that schools measure progress using district assessments, and the district accountability committee reviewed schools' plans. The district did not set performance targets, however, and there were no formal consequences if schools did not meet their own goals. This district was "flirting" with the idea of setting an acceptable range of performance gains for schools if the state implemented its accreditation program.[14] In another district, schools' foci for school achievement goals varied dramatically. Schools chose different areas of achievement to address and used different metrics to determine achievement, including the number of students at the proficient level, a year's worth of improvement, or improvement by the lowest performers.

This variation reflects differences in district culture, leadership, and capacity. Our two California study sites viewed standards-based reform as a critical strategy for raising student performance. They had spent several years developing district systemic change strategies comprised of standards, and assessments, accountability, and professional development aligned to district (and state) standards. These high capacity districts, which are among the larger school systems in California, were generally ahead of the rest of their state. A study of a larger and more representative sample of California districts conducted in spring 1999 found that most districts were in the early stages of developing their local standards-based accountability systems.[15]

The actions of the Colorado districts reflected both a strong tradition of decentralized management and a limited capacity to support or monitor school actions. Although the districts were developing assessments keyed to local standards and creating accountability plans in anticipation of state action, school level accountability had not become a central strategy for engendering reform. Indeed, some respondents felt that state reporting of assessment results would foster a feeling of competition among the schools, threatening collaborative efforts within their districts. The superintendent in one of these districts was trying to regain some authority over her schools, but her local school board staunchly defended school site autonomy. Stagnation in state education funding, coupled with increases in enrollment and districts' needs (e.g., English language learners), had led to cutbacks in district staff in all three districts. This, in turn, limited the ability of central office staff to work with the schools.

The Effects of Performance Based Accountability Systems

Accountability systems create incentives for school and school system improvement by focusing attention on student outcomes and progress, providing data for decision making, and creating a press for instructional change. This section looks at how educators in the twenty-three study districts responded to their state and district accountability systems.

Performance based accountability systems and policies did provide a clear focus to teachers and principals regarding the attainment of student outcomes. Respondents in one Florida district reported, for example, that the state assessment system coupled with sanctions for low performance focused district attention on the three tested areas of reading, writing, and mathematics. Educators in the Colorado study districts noted that state assessments and student promotion policies in literacy had increased their focus on reading and writing. One district, for example, focused on language arts for three years, phasing in a new reading series and emphasizing English/language arts topics in professional development. The state accountability system focused educator attention on state standards (the TEKS) in all three Texas study districts. It drove the selection of curriculum, prompted professional development, initiated the development of interim assessments, and drove the identification of schools and students needing additional help. Local accountability systems in the two California districts emphasized literacy and mathematics instruction. Respondents in the Maryland districts stressed that the persistence of that state's accountability program and its consistent focus are a major incentive for changing practice.

Yet educators generally faced few formal consequences for not meeting school, district, and/or state performance goals beyond those imposed by the state. Districts used performance data to provide support rather than to impose sanctions. When formal consequences existed, they fell more heavily on students and principals than on teachers. The stakes were the highest for students, particularly those in states and/or districts with high school graduation and/or promotion requirements. In Minnesota, for example, respondents in all three study districts mentioned that the *only* stakes in their systems were for students who have to pass a state basic skills test to graduate from high school.

At the school level, the principal was the primary focus of accountability. But principal accountability was generally ill defined. Few districts had set formal performance goals or consequences for principals, and some respondents spoke of consequences in hypothetical terms.[16] Typically, principals whose schools were posting low scores would be called in to explain their past actions, were required to submit new improvement plans, and were closely monitored. If their school was identified as "in crisis," media coverage was intensive. These principals might be shifted to another school or placed on a different type of assignment. They were rarely fired or demoted as the result of low student achievement.

Some superintendents, however, did move or remove principals from low performing schools. One superintendent replaced nine principals in his first year in office. The new superintendent of a district in another state demoted thirteen principals and two vice principals. The superintendent of a highly decentralized district in a third state used a focus on data-driven decision making to communicate her expectations about improved performance. These actions sent strong signals to principals that districts would hold them accountable for student performance.

Looking across the study sites, it appears that the strength of principal accountability policies varied more across sites within states than across accountability contexts. Four factors explain some of this variation. The first is the philosophy of the district. Some local school boards and district administrators stressed school autonomy. When there were problems in student performance, the central office staff met with principals and developed strategies to address the problems. Other school systems communicated their expectations more directly through principal evaluations. One Kentucky superintendent, for example, used his authority to evaluate and potentially fire principals, and held them accountable for student performance and for developing and implementing school plans that will improve performance.

A second factor is the size of the performance gap and the urgency of change. The Kentucky district cited above had seen test scores plateau after steady growth, and schools were not meeting their state-defined growth targets. As a result, respondents noted that was probably the first time that principals had feared being held accountable for tangible data. Another study district has a large number of low performing schools (with some under state sanctions) and has increased both the level of oversight and support to these buildings. Data is an element of principal evaluations and this district has removed principals in chronically low performing schools.

Third, the political and contractual environment of the districts varied. Union contracts forbid the use of performance data in principal evaluations in at least one of our study districts. The local board of education in another district rejected a performance based evaluation system for administrators and teachers. A few states are beginning to include student test data in their evaluation policies. But even districts that consider student achievement in their evaluation of principals look at other measures of principal performance. Principals continue to be held responsible for a multiplicity of responsibilities, including the evaluation and development of their teaching staff, the maintenance of a positive school climate and good parent and community relationships, and the overall management of their building.

Finally, the urban districts in our study faced a shortage of principals—qualified or not. One respondent commented that hypothetically his district could transfer a principal to another school for failure to support school improvement, but principal turnover is so high they usually leave before the district can move them against their will.

Teachers, on the other hand, faced few consequences for poor student performance. Many of the teachers in our study reported that their districts and states held schools more accountable for student performance than teachers. While some districts looked at student performance, teachers were generally held accountable for the delivery of their instruction and for meeting their professional development goals. As with principals, some union contracts or school board policies forbid the inclusion of student test scores in teacher evaluations. While several districts in the study were looking more closely at instructional practice, few had clear performance standards or consequences linked to these evaluations. Consequences for poor performance appeared limited to professional development, coaching, and mentoring. And urban districts could not afford to fire many teachers. Unfilled vacancies, uncertified teachers, and staff teaching out of field plague them. A respondent in one urban district reported that teachers leave their system on average after three years.

Issues

State accountability policies represent variations on the theme of performance based accountability. Although state accountability systems have common elements—assessments, standards, performance reporting and, in most cases, consequences for performance—states have found different ways to define what it means for schools to succeed, what indicators to include in that definition of success, and the consequences of success or failure. These variations reflect differences in state demographics, political culture, educational governance structures and policies, and educational performance.

In the CPRE study districts, the incentives embodied in state and local accountability systems motivated educators to focus on state and local goals and on the performance of their schools and students, and to redirect curriculum and professional development. The incentives were not necessarily sufficient to change instructional practice in classrooms, however.[17] Consequences fell more heavily on students and schools than on individual educators. The impact of accountability policies on school principals and teachers reflected differences in district philosophy and leadership, the political and contractual environment, capacity, and the urgency of change.

States need to address this seeming imbalance between student and adult accountability. States also face issues of alignment, equity, and capacity.

BALANCING STUDENT AND ADULT ACCOUNTABILITY

The intent of standards-based accountability was to hold schools and their staff accountable for student performance as a way of focusing attention and effort on the reform of teaching and learning. States that were early implementers of standards-based reform generally designed such school based accountability systems, limiting student based accountability to high school graduation examinations that tested only basic skills. Increasingly, states are raising the stakes for students by enacting promotion policies at the elementary and middle school grades and developing rigorous high school exit examinations as a way of motivating students to achieve. Some of these states are implementing strong student accountability policies before putting school accountability mechanisms in place. This is unfair to students, however. States must hold adults accountable and responsible for student performance before applying consequences to the students themselves.

LACK OF ALIGNMENT

Two alignment issues emerged from the CPRE study. The first concerns the alignment of state and Title I accountability policies within a state. Supporters of the 1994 Title I amendments hoped that this federal legislation would serve as an impetus for states to develop an integrated set of education reform policies that applied equally to all students and schools. Title I schools and students would be brought under the larger umbrella of state standards-based reform; states would no longer have different expectations for Title I students or requirements for Title I schools. However, this vision has not been realized in a majority of states. In these states, Title I schools are subject to different measures of adequate yearly progress, consequences, and support systems.

The second issue concerns how well states have aligned their standards and assessments. In some cases, the lack of alignment is a necessary consequence of the evolution of reform. There is normally a time lag between the promulgation of new or revised state standards and the development and implementation of an assessment to measure performance on these standards. In other cases, states use norm-referenced tests that are designed to measure the knowledge and skills of students across the country, rather than the knowledge and skills embodied in specific state standards. Some educators and researchers question whether and how well norm-referenced tests are aligned with state standards and whether they are appropriate measures of student performance on challenging standards. Yet these tests provide something that parents, policymakers and the public want—a way to compare the performance of their students to students in other states.

EQUITY

A primary goal of standards-based reform is high standards and improved achievement for all students, particularly those students who have been denied access to challenging educational programs. Accountability programs can help address the achievement gap between students of different socioeconomic, racial, ethnic, and language backgrounds, and between students with different educational needs by providing information on the nature of the gap and creating incentives for educators to narrow these differences. For this policy to work, however, states must assess all students on the content of the standards-based curriculum, disaggregate and report their scores, and include their scores in accountability measures. And assessments must generate valid information about their knowledge and skills.

Unfortunately, large-scale assessments currently do not provide valid and comparable measures of performance for all students. The federal government requires states and school districts to assess all students with appropriate accommodations, modifications, and alternate assessments. These assessment changes, however, do not always yield accurate and reliable information on students' mastery of state standards, particularly if they alter the content of the test or the construct the test is measuring. And some testing conditions inhibit test score comparability. As a result, states either exclude some students from their state assessment programs (generally English language learners) or exclude student test results from reporting and accountability systems if these scores are not valid measures of what students know and/or are not comparable to the scores of students tested under regular conditions.

In addition to having valid performance data on students, schools and districts need incentives to address the educational needs of the lowest performing students and of special needs populations. A growing number of states are making school level data on subgroup performance readily available to educators and the public. Fewer states require schools to narrow the gap between the lowest and highest performing students as part of their accountability systems. Only two states hold schools accountable for having all groups of students meet the same performance standards. Thus many schools and/or districts can meet state performance goals without narrowing achievement differences.

Closing the achievement gap also requires addressing inequities in students' opportunities to learn to high standards. Ensuring that all students have comparable learning opportunities is perhaps the most politically challenging issue that states face. The courts have established the principle that a high stakes graduation test should be a fair measure of what students are taught; students should receive adequate advanced notice and sufficient educational opportunities to prepare for the test.[18] It was easier for states to meet these requirements when students were held accountable for mastering only basic skills. As students are expected to meet more challenging standards, they need access to an academic program that addresses these standards. They need access to teachers who have the content knowledge and pedagogical skills to teach this curriculum to a diverse group of learners. And they need access to supplemental help as they move through the system.

CAPACITY

The concept of opportunity to learn applies to all levels of the education system, not just students. Research on school based performance awards programs shows that clear goals and incentives are necessary, but not sufficient, to motivate teachers to reach their school's student achievement goals. Teacher motivation is also influenced by the presence of various capacity-building conditions, such as leadership from the principal and district office around standards-based instruction, feedback on student assessment measures and results, meaningful professional development related to program goals, and structured teacher collaboration. Teacher knowledge and skills related to improved instruction are also important.[19]

The unanswered question in the performance based accountability movement is whether states and districts can ensure that these conditions exist, particularly in struggling and failing schools. States and districts need knowledge, human resources, and financial resources to turn around poorly performing schools. Research on capacity-building activities in the CPRE study states and districts has identified some promising strategies. At the state level, these include creating decentralized support systems involving individuals and organizations that work directly with schools, nurturing professional networks of teachers and other education experts, providing curriculum frameworks and other curricular materials that include examples of standards-based instruction, and developing professional development and training standards.[20] District strategies include enhancing teacher professionalism, curriculum reform aligned to state standards, data-driven decision making, and assistance targeted on low performing schools.[21]

The optimum mix and level of support is unknown, but states and districts report having insufficient resources to help the number of schools that have been (or should be) identified as in need of improvement. California, for example, designated 3,144 schools as underperforming in 1999-2000, but included only 430 of these schools in the first year of its Immediate Intervention/Underperforming Schools Program. Many states rely primarily on federal funds, particularly from the Title I program, to support program improvement initiatives. Sufficient capacity is critical to making the "horse trade" work. Without it, performance based accountability is reduced to a "horse whip."

NOTES

1. The research reported in this chapter was conducted by the Consortium for Policy Research in Education (CPRE). Funding for this work was provided by the United States Department of Education's National Institute on Educational Governance, Finance, Policymaking, and Management (Grant #OERI-R308A60003); the Annie E. Casey Foundation; and The Pew Charitable Trusts. Opinions expressed in this chapter are those of the author and do not necessarily reflect the views of the National Institute, the Office of Educational Research and Improvement, the United States Department of Education, The Pew Charitable Trusts, the Annie E. Casey Foundation, or the institutional partners of CPRE. Kirsty Brown, Anne Burns, and Mark Duffy of CPRE provided invaluable assistance in analyzing the state and local level interview data.

2. Walt Haney and George Madaus, "Making sense of the competency testing movement," *Harvard Educational Review* 48 (1978): pp. 462-484; Robert Linn, "Assessments and accountability," *Educational Researcher* 29 (2000): pp. 4-16.

3. National Governors' Association, *Time for Results* (Washington, DC: Author, 1986).

4. David Grissmer and Ann Flanagan, *Exploring Rapid Achievement Gains in North Carolina and Texas* (Washington, DC: National Education Goals Panel, 1998); David Grissmer, Ann Flanagan, Jennifer Kawata, and Stephanie Williamson, *Improving Student Achievement: What State NAEP Test Scores Tell Us* (Santa Monica, CA: RAND, 2000).

5. Jacques Steinberg, "Blue Books Closed, Students Protest State Tests," *New York Times*, Thursday, 13 April 2000, p. A28.

6. The strength of an external accountability system can be gauged by many factors, including: the kinds of consequences (rewards and sanctions) attached to the accountability system, its prescriptiveness—to what extent the state gives local districts discretion in the accountability design, the rigor of the measures used, and its scope—what the system includes in its purview.

7. The districts ranged in size from 2,600 to more than 300,000 students, and from less than one percent to more than ninety-five percent students of color. Six of the districts had fewer than thirty percent of their students participating in the free and reduced school lunch programs; nine had more than sixty percent of their students enrolled in this program.

8. Jennifer O'Day, *One System or Two? Title I Accountability in the Context of High Stakes for Schools in Local Districts and States* (Washington, DC: United States Department of Education, 1999).

9. Linda Bond, Edward Roeber, and Selena Connealy, *Trends in State Student Assessment Programs, 1996-97* (Washington, DC: Council of Chief State School Officers, 1998).

10. Many of these states have developed performance targets for their Title I schools and some have enacted input-based accreditation policies.

11. Legislation enacted in May 2000 gives Pennsylvania the authority to identify, assist, and potentially intervene in low performing school districts.

12. The assessment threshold was raised over time in increments of five percentage points each year, from a twenty-five percent passing rate to the current fifty percent passing rate.

13. A district is rated as "recognized" if at least eighty percent of all students and students in each group pass each subject area on the state assessment and schools have lower dropout rates, and "exemplary" if at least ninety percent of all students and students in each group pass each subject area and schools have still lower dropout rates. In addition, a district cannot be rated "recognized" or "exemplary" if it has one or more low performing schools.

14. The Colorado legislature subsequently instituted a state system of school ratings. Failing schools that do not improve after two years can be chartered as an independent charter school.

15. WestEd/MAP. *Evaluation of California's Standards-Based Accountability Systems: Final Report. Executive Summary* (available online at http://www.wested.org/wested/news.html, 2000).

16. WestEd/MAP found this as well in its evaluation of local accountability policies in California.

17. See Floden and Wilson's chapter in this volume.

18. *Debra P. v. Turlington*, 644F.2d 397, 5th (cir. 1981).

19. Carolyn Kelley, Allan Odden, Anthony Milanowski, and Herbert Heneman III, "The motivational effects of school based performance awards," *CPRE Policy Briefs* (Philadelphia, PA: Consortium for Policy Research in Education, 2000).

20. Diane Massell, "State strategies for building local capacity: Addressing the needs of standards-based reform," *CPRE Policy Briefs* (Philadelphia, PA: Consortium for Policy Research in Education, 1998).

21. Diane Massell, "The district role in building capacity: Four strategies," *CPRE Policy Briefs* (Philadelphia, PA: Consortium for Policy Research in Education, 2000).

Section Two
ASSESSING REFORM
IMPLEMENTATION AND EFFECTS

CHAPTER IV

Are Content Standards Being Implemented in the Classroom? A Methodology and Some Tentative Answers

ANDREW C. PORTER AND JOHN L. SMITHSON

Arguably the most notable trend in education policy in the past ten years has been the movement toward a standards-based approach to ensuring the quality of education provided to all children. Standards have been set by professional organizations—such as the National Council of Teachers of Mathematics, the American Association for the Advancement of Science, and the National Council of Teachers of English—by the states and strongly encouraged by the federal government. Title I of the ESEA legislation requires all states to adopt challenging content and performance standards in at least reading, language arts, and mathematics.

The question is whether standards-based reform is making a difference in the type and/or quality of instruction experienced by students. This chapter focuses on the issues that must be addressed and the challenges that must be overcome to provide a credible answer to questions regarding the impact of standards on the quality of instruction received by students. Results from some preliminary investigations are reported herein.

Andrew C. Porter is the Director of the Wisconsin Center for Education Research, Director of the National Institute for Science Education, and a Professor of Educational Psychology at the University of Wisconsin-Madison. John L. Smithson is an Assistant Researcher in the Wisconsin Center for Education Research.

Determining the impact of standards on classroom practice can be viewed as a three-part problem. First, one needs a description of the relevant educational practice that permits comparison to the standard or goal being targeted. Second, one must establish the target (i.e., just what *are* the standards of concern, and how will one know if they have been met?). Third, it is necessary to have an explanatory model by which to attribute the practice described as a result of the standards established.

Establishing causal relations between indicators of education processes and school outputs is complicated, and the results always tentative, especially from correlational studies such as an indicator system would support. Although there are differences of opinion about how useful such analyses can be in diagnosing the relative utility of different types of educational practices, most agree that such indicator data are better than no information at all.

Because the number of potential school process variables is large, some criteria are needed for deciding which to measure. If what is wanted is an index of opportunity to learn, then the criterion for establishing priority should be utility for predicting gains in student learning (achievement). The best predictors of student achievement gains are the properties of instruction as it occurs in schools, what content is taught, how effectively, to which students, and to what levels of achievement. Our discussion will focus on descriptions of instructional content as these descriptions seem best suited to explaining student achievement.

In what follows, a framework for attributing instructional practices to standards-based reform is offered as a context for examining how such analyses might proceed. Examples are given of recent work describing the content of practice, followed by a discussion on determining the content implications of standards-based policy instruments. Procedures for measuring alignment are developed and illustrations given for assessing alignment between policy instruments (e.g., standards, assessments) and instruction as well as illustrations of alignment between instruction and gains in student achievement. The chapter concludes with consideration of the issues that must be addressed in measuring the content of instruction.

Attributing Causality

While it is true that education presents an exceptionally complex system with numerous steps in the causal chain between policy tool and student effects,[1] for the purpose of this discussion we simplify the causal chain into three key components: the *intended* curriculum, the *enacted* curriculum, and the *learned* curriculum (i.e., student outcomes). The logic behind this chain of causality suggests that the *intended* curriculum—as represented by policy tools such as content standards, curriculum frameworks/guidelines, and state assessments—influences teacher practice (the *enacted* curriculum), which in turn impacts student learning as measured by state assessments. The necessary evidence to attribute changes in student outcomes to policy initiatives can be divided into two parts. One part of such an explanation is to provide evidence that policies have changed practice in desirable ways, while the second part of the explanation seeks to make the link between practice and outcomes. Both parts are necessary in order to draw the link between policy initiative and student achievement. Kennedy's critique on this point that researchers' focus on one or the other of the explanations is perhaps not surprising as each of the two explanatory pieces to the overall causal puzzle require different types of evidence, reasoning, and theory.

LINKING THE INTENDED AND ENACTED CURRICULA

Assuming for the moment that one has comparable, quantifiable descriptions of the intended curriculum or "target" and the enacted curriculum, a measure of agreement or alignment between the intended and enacted curricula can be calculated. Such an alignment measure is much like a correlation in that it suggests a relationship but is insufficient to support a causal connection. Thus if the resulting alignment measure was high (indicating strong agreement between the intended and enacted curricula), one would still need more information, as well as a theoretical framework, to argue causality. For example, one useful additional piece of information would be longitudinal data indicating change in practice over time. If such data were available, and those data indicated the direction of change over time was toward greater alignment with the intended curriculum, one would have a stronger case, but still insufficient to be confident about cause and effect. In addition, one needs a theoretical model in which to set the explanation for policy influence.

Porter[2] has offered an example of one such model. In this model, policy tools are described on the basis of four characteristics: prescriptiveness, consistency, power, and authority. *Prescriptiveness* indicates the extent to which a policy instrument specifies desired practice. *Consistency* describes the extent to which policy instruments are mutually reinforcing (i.e., aligned). One important measure of consistency is the extent to which the content standards and assessments of a given state present a common message about the intended content of instruction. A curriculum policy instrument has *power* to the extent that rewards and sanctions are tied to compliance with the policy. High stakes tests are one notable example of a curricular policy with power. *Authority* refers to the extent to which policies are persuasive in convincing teachers that the policy is consistent with notions of good practice.

The hypothesis is that the more a curriculum policy reflects these four characteristics the stronger the influence that policy will have on curricular practice. Thus if a specific policy or set of policies is shown to be strong on several or all of these characteristics, if descriptive data reveal substantial agreement between descriptions of the intended and enacted curricula, and if this level of agreement has increased over time as the policy has had an opportunity to exert an influence, one can begin to make claims of attribution.

LINKING THE ENACTED CURRICULUM TO STUDENT OUTCOMES

Having sufficient evidence to attribute instructional practice to the influence of policy instruments (such as content standards and state assessments) still falls short of explaining student outcomes. To stretch the causal chain to include outcomes, evidence is necessary to make the link between instructional practice and gains in student learning. Note here the reference to "gains" rather than achievement. While achievement scores alone provide some indication of the level of knowledge students have attained, they say nothing about when and how that knowledge was acquired. To measure the contribution of instructional practice to a student's score, a more narrow measure of achievement is necessary. By focusing on gains in student achievement, rather than simple test scores, it is possible to examine the contribution of classroom experience to student achievement over specified periods of time. This is essential if one is trying to demonstrate the effects of recent changes in policy and instruction on achievement.[3]

In addition to controlling for prior achievement (accomplished by the use of learning gain measures), one must also control for the socioeconomic status (SES) of students' families. In a recent analysis of results from the *Prospects* study (a large-scale nationally representative study), Rowan[4] found that prior achievement and SES accounted for as much as eighty percent of the variance in mean achievement among classrooms. Rowan estimated the percentage of variance among classrooms to be eleven percent after controlling for prior achievement and

SES. This suggests that the extent to which the classroom experience of students in a given year contributes to their overall achievement score is relatively small compared to these other factors. However, Rowan also notes that the percentage of variance attributable to classroom differences may be significantly higher when the alignment between the test and instruction is taken into account.

If one has comparable descriptions of the content of instruction and the assessment being utilized, an alignment variable can be calculated. This measure, used in conjunction with controls for prior achievement and SES, may be suitable for attributing achievement gains to instruction, particularly if alignment succeeds in predicting student achievement above and beyond the control variables.

Recent Efforts at Describing Instructional Practice

The largest and best known effort of recent years to describe instruction has been the *Third International Mathematics and Science Study* (TIMSS). Though perhaps best known for its national rankings of student achievement scores on the TIMSS assessments, substantial information was also collected on instructional practice, using teacher surveys and videotaped observations of classroom practice.[5] Analyses of textbooks conducted as part of the TIMSS revealed a characteristic of mathematics and science instruction in the United States that has since become a familiar refrain among mathematics and science educators. The description of mathematics and science curricula in the United States as being "a mile wide and an inch deep" is now commonly offered as an explanation for the mediocre performance of United States students on the TIMSS assessments.[6]

Another example of the uses to which descriptions of classroom practice have been put is provided by the *National Evaluation of the Eisenhower Professional Development Program*, in which researchers conducted a longitudinal study of the effects of professional development activities on teacher practice in the classroom. In this study, researchers used descriptions of classroom practice and instructional content collected over a period of three years to track changes in practice as a result of professional development. Results from this study suggest that professional development activities with a clear content focus lead toward increased emphasis on those topics during instruction. Researchers identified several other characteristics of professional development that also appear effective in changing teacher practice. These included the use of active learning strategies as part of the professional development activity, collective participation by a group of teachers from the same school or grade level, linking professional development opportunities to other activities, and designing activities that build on teachers' prior knowledge.[7]

A third example concerns the development of a set of survey instruments as part of a multi-state collaborative to provide a set of practical tools for collecting consistent data on mathematics and science teaching practices and instructional content. The surveys define a comprehensive set of indicator data on instructional processes for elementary, middle, and high school classes in mathematics and science. Both teacher and student surveys have been developed. The teacher surveys for each subject and grade level consist of two distinct instruments. One instrument, the Survey of Instructional Practices, focuses on instructional activities, teacher opinions, characteristics and background, professional development, and school and student characteristics. The other instrument, the Survey of Instructional Content, collects detailed information on content using a two-dimensional content matrix design developed by Porter and Smithson and based on previous work.[8] Together these instruments are referred to as the Surveys of the Enacted Curriculum (SEC). The SEC instruments are currently being employed in at least three separate studies of mathematics and science reform. One of these studies (funded by the eleven participating states and the National Science Foundation) is exploring the efficacy of the SEC instruments as a tool for states and researchers to use in monitoring reform and in evaluating the efficacy of reform efforts on classroom practice.[9] Data collected from this eleven-state study indicate differences in teaching styles and instructional content that emerge between grade levels and between teachers that are and are not involved in pursuing reform strategies. The results are being shared with states and the participating schools to provide them descriptive information about practice, professional development, and teacher opinions for use in monitoring reform and evaluating improvement efforts.

In addition to this state-initiated study, two independent evaluations of the urban systemic initiatives (USI) program are being conducted utilizing the SEC instrumentation. Both studies, one conducted by Kim, Blank, Noyce, and Richardson, *How Reform Works: An Evaluative Study of NSF's Urban Systemic Initiatives*,[10] and the other by Borman and Kersaint at the University of South Florida, *Assessing the Impact of the National Science Foundation's Urban Systemic Initiatives*,[11] are using the SEC instruments in conjunction with in-depth case studies, observations, and interviews to examine the effectiveness of USI programs currently funded in forty urban school districts. The use of a standard set of instruments across research studies, now occurring in these studies, provides a unique opportunity to examine descriptions of practice across studies.

Selecting the Target

Though an essential piece of the educational puzzle, descriptions of practice alone are insufficient to determine the extent to which standards are being implemented. What is necessary is some target against which to compare those descriptions. This "target" needs to be set in terms of what one should see happening in classrooms. Ideally, the target would be described using the same language used to describe practice. There are at least three potential targets: a state's content standards, curriculum guides or framework, and assessments.

One obvious choice for a target would be a state's content standards, or possibly the content and pedagogy standards set forth by one or another professional association (e.g., the National Council of Teachers of Mathematics). The challenge with such sources is translating the language contained in documents describing the standards into a clear picture of desired classroom practice. Many states have vague and visionary statements of practice incorporated into the language of their standards. This leaves a good deal of room for interpreting just how instruction should look in a specific classroom on a day-to-day basis. If the target is fuzzy, determining the extent of standards implementation will also be fuzzy.

For this reason, one might turn instead to curriculum guides or frameworks. These tend to be more specific than standards, though curriculum guides also leave considerable ambiguity about exactly what unit is to be taught when. As with standards, the more prescriptive the curricular materials are, the better (for the purpose of content analysis and according to our theory).

Yet another potential source for establishing a description of the target against which to compare practice are state assessments. Assessments have the advantage of presenting clear indications of what content is considered important as well as the level of knowledge expected of students with regard to that content. In that sense, assessments are prescriptive in that they specify particular topics and the depth of knowledge considered most important. Perhaps more importantly, since student outcome measures are often the basis for rewards and sanctions (whether for students, teachers, or schools), using the assessment as a target can be useful in diagnosing why students succeed or fail on assessments.

On the other hand, assessments are not prescriptive in the sense of defining well what *should* be taught, since the items on an assessment represent only a sample from the content domain the assessment is intended to represent. As a result, one problem with using assessments to describe the intended curriculum is that any particular form of an assessment will necessarily represent only a sample of items from the domain of interest. Thus where multiple test forms exist, content analyses of the assessments should include all items across all forms to capture a more complete picture of the content message embedded in the assessment instruments.

Ideally, assessments will be aligned to the standards; i.e., they are intended to convey the same content message as the standards. With descriptions of practice, and comparable descriptions of the target for successful standards implementation in hand, it is possible to measure the degree of alignment between instruction and the target. The higher the degree of alignment between instruction and the target, the greater the extent to which standards can be said to have been implemented in the classroom.

Of course measured for only a single point in time, alignment is only correlational, and thus not strong evidence of cause and effect (though low levels of alignment make clear that standards are not being fully implemented). Stronger evidence can be developed through investigation into whether alignment increases over time after standards have been put in place.

Measuring Alignment Between Assessments and Instruction

As part of the eleven-state study mentioned earlier, six states participated in a sub-study to analyze alignment between instruction and assessments. To the extent that instruction is aligned to a state's assessment, one link in the complex causal chain necessary to connect policy initiatives and student outcomes can be established. Presumably, if standards-based reform is having an effect, instruction in a state will be more aligned to that state's test than to tests given by other states.

The assessments analyzed were mathematics and science tests in third, fourth, or fifth grade at the elementary level, and seventh or eighth grade at the middle school level (depending on the grade level assessed in a given state). The majority of assessments analyzed were for fourth and eighth grades, which coincided with the grade level at which teacher descriptions of practice were collected. For some states, multiple forms were analyzed (which was the goal). In addition, NAEP mathematics and science assessments were content analyzed. All fourth and eighth grade NAEP test items were included in the content analysis of the NAEP assessments.

Tests were content analyzed, item-by-item, using the same language and distinctions for describing content (topics by cognitive demand) as employed in the teacher surveys described earlier. Six state mathematics representatives, six state science representatives, three university mathematics educators, and four science educators were involved in the content analyses that were conducted during a two-day period in the summer of 1999.

Descriptions of practice were based on survey results from 503 teachers across eleven states. These included elementary and middle school teachers reporting on their science or mathematics instruction for the then current school year (the surveys were administered in the spring of 1999) using the SEC instruments. The participating teachers do not offer a representative sample, particularly at the state level, as sampling was neither random nor sufficiently robust to warrant generalizations. Therefore, the alignment measures described below are presented for illustrative purposes only.

These data allow investigation of assessment-to-assessment alignment (including state assessment alignment with NAEP), instruction-to-assessment alignment, and instruction-to-instruction alignment (state by state), at each grade level for each subject. For each test, the average degree of emphasis on a topic (e.g., linear equations) by cognitive demand (e.g., solve novel problems; see Table 6) intersection, across content analyzers, was calculated. The result was a matrix of proportions, with dimensions topic-by-cognitive-demand. Similar topic-by-cognitive-demand matrices of content emphasis were calculated for instructional content based on teacher reports. An alignment index with a range from zero to one was created and calculated to describe the degree of alignment between assessments and instruction.[12] As can be seen from Table 1, state tests were generally more aligned with each other (.32 to .45) than they were with NAEP (.24 to .34), though the differences are not large. For each subject and grade level, state test to state test alignment is, on average, higher than is state test to NAEP alignment. At the same time these data establish that each state test presents a unique target for instruction. State tests are not interchangeable.

TABLE 1

AVERAGE ALIGNMENT
TEST TO TEST

	STATE TO STATE	NAEP TO STATE
Math 4	0.41	0.35
Math 8	0.33	0.30
Science 4	0.33	0.29
Science 8	0.28	0.20

Instruction in a state was, in general, no more aligned to that state's test than it was aligned to the tests of other states, suggesting that standards-based reform has not yet brought instruction into alignment with these states' tests. In mathematics, instruction was at least as aligned with NAEP than with state tests. In science, the opposite was true (see Table 2). Two caveats are important. First, recall that the data on instruction are illustrative only. The samples of instruction from each state cannot be taken as representative of that state since the samples are neither random nor sufficient in size for such inferences. Second, to the extent that a state's test is not aligned to the state's content standards, one might not want instruction to be highly aligned to the state test. For example, if the state assessment is a basic skills test, one would hope that instruction would still get beyond the basics. Nonetheless, to the extent a state test is used in an accountability program, it may have an influence on instructional practice. While only illustrative, these analyses and results do provide some indication of the utility that such measures would hold if based on a more representative sample.

TABLE 2

AVERAGE ALIGNMENT
INSTRUCTION TO TEST

	TARGET STATE	OTHER STATES	NAEP
Math 4	0.42	0.33	0.41
Math 8	0.33	0.24	0.22
Science 4	0.37	0.28	0.23
Science 8	0.33	0.23	0.14

The data suggest that instruction in one state is quite similar to instruction in another state. Average instruction-to-instruction alignment indicators ranged from .64 to .80 (see Table 3). However, one should be careful not to interpret this as an indication that there is little variation in practice across teachers. When individual teacher reports of content are compared within a state, and even within a school, the degree of alignment drops considerably.

TABLE 3

AVERAGE ALIGNMENT
INSTRUCTION TO INSTRUCTION

	STATE TO STATE
Math 4	0.80
Math 8	0.68
Science 4	0.70
Science 8	0.64

It is also possible to use the alignment index to measure the level of inter-rater agreement in the content analysis of the test items. Illustrative results are reported for elementary and middle school mathematics and science (see Table 4). In these inter-rater agreements, any one item may assess several different types of content. Raters were limited to selecting only three topic-by-cognitive-demand combinations per item. This limit undoubtedly forced some disagreements among raters. When raters made distinctions at the finest grain (i.e., topics by cognitive demand), alignment was in the neighborhood of .40 to .50. Alignment is obviously better when comparisons are made at a larger grain size (such as algebra or geometry) by cognitive demand. Since assessments were described as the average across raters, and each form was content analyzed by at least four experts, the validity of the descriptions of the tests is high.

TABLE 4

AVERAGE INTER-RATER AGREEMENT
ON ASSESSMENT ANALYSES

	FINE GRAIN	MEDIUM GRAIN	LARGE GRAIN
Elementary Math	.47	—	.70
Distinctions Possible	*(438)*	*(N/A)*	*(36)*
Middle School Math	.47	—	.70
Distinctions Possible	*(504)*	*(N/A)*	*(36)*
Elementary Science	.40	.50	.56
Distinctions Possible	*(396)*	*(84)*	*(30)*
Middle School Science	.38	.56	not available
Distinctions Possible	*(876)*	*(150)*	*(36)*

Recent Efforts at Linking Instruction to Student Outcomes

What about the second link in the causal chain? At least two recent studies, one in mathematics[13] and one in science[14] have utilized sophisticated quantitative modeling tools[15] to demonstrate the power of classroom measures of instructional content in predicting achievement gains among students. Because the mathematics study utilized an approach to instructional alignment similar to the one discussed above, it is described in more detail here.

The study looked at the efficacy of transition mathematics courses in California (Mathematics A) and New York (Stretch Regents) in bridging the gap between dead-end, basic mathematics courses and college preparatory courses for low-achieving, low-income students. The sample consisted of two schools from each of four districts, two in California, and two in New York. Two schools were then selected from each of the four districts. Within each school, the sample included at least one traditional low level course (e.g., general mathematics or pre-algebra) and at least one college preparatory course (e.g., Regents One, algebra, or geometry). In one district, all lower-level mathematics courses had been eliminated, representing an exception to this design. In total, fifty-six classrooms from seven schools participated in the study.

Using a combination of survey, observation, and interview and pre/post-test data, researchers constructed comparable descriptions of practice and assessment content to describe the relationship between different course types. Since all students in the participating classes were administered the same test (drawn from public release NAEP items), it was also possible to look at gains in student achievement across the differing course types to compare the differential effects of instruction in the college preparatory, transition, and basic mathematics courses.

Several indicators were formed for investigating the relationship between the content of instruction delivered in the classroom as reported by the teacher and student gains on the achievement test constructed from NAEP public release items. One indicator of content coverage of tested material is the proportion of instructional time spent covering tested content (level of coverage). Another indicator is the match of relative emphases of types of content between instruction and the test (configuration of coverage). The mean proportion of instructional time that addressed one or more types of content tested (level of coverage) was .07 with a standard deviation of .02. The mean for configuration was .58 with a standard deviation of .08.[16]

Alignment can be defined based on topics (the rows in the content matrix), cognitive demand (the columns), or at the intersection of topics by cognitive demand (the cells in the matrix). The highest correlations with student achievement gains occur when content is defined at the intersection of topics by cognitive demand (see Table 5). The correlation for class gains is .48 and for student gains is .26. These are substantial correlations for predicting student achievement gains.

TABLE 5

INDICATORS OF INSTRUCTIONAL ALIGNMENT CORRELATIONS
WITH ACHIEVEMENT GAINS

MULTIPLE REGRESSION USING LEVEL AND CONFIGURATION	R CLASS GAINS	R STUDENT GAINS
Topics Only	.260	.245
Cognitive Demand Only	.106	.166
Topics by Cognitive Demand	.481	.260

Issues in Defining Indicators of the Content of Instruction

There are several problems that must be solved in defining indicators of the content of instruction.

DO WE HAVE THE RIGHT LANGUAGE?

Getting the right grain size. One of the most challenging issues in describing the content of instruction is deciding upon the level of detail of description that is most useful. Either too much or too little detail presents problems. For example, if description were at the level of distinguishing mathematics from science, social studies, or language arts, then certainly all mathematics courses would look alike. Nothing would have been learned beyond what was already revealed in the course title. On the other hand, if content descriptions make distinctions that essentially identify the particular exercises on which students are working, then surely all mathematics instruction would be unique. At that level of detail, no two courses with the same title cover the same content because trivial differences are being distinguished.

An issue related to grain size is how to describe instruction that does not come in nice, neat, discrete, mutually exclusive pieces. A particular instructional activity may cover several topics and involve a number of cognitive abilities. The language for describing the content of instruction must be capable of capturing the integrated nature of scientific and mathematical thinking.

Getting the right labels. The labels that are used to denote the various distinctions being made when describing the content of instruction are extremely important. Ideally, labels can be chosen that have immediate face validity for all respondents so that questionnaire construction requires relatively little elaboration beyond the labels themselves. What is needed to have valid survey data is instrumentation language having the same meaning across a broad array of respondents.

Some have reviewed our languages and suggested that the terms and distinctions should better reflect the reform rhetoric of the National Council of Teachers of Mathematics' mathematics standards[17] or the National Research Council's science standards.[18] But the purposes of the indicators described here are to characterize practice as it exists, and to compare that practice to various standards. For those purposes a reform-neutral language is appropriate. Still, one might argue that the language described here is not reform neutral but rather status quo. Ideally the language utilized should be translatable into reform language distinctions so comparison to state and other standards is possible.

Another criterion for determining the appropriateness of the content language is to ask educators. As instruments have been piloted with teachers, the feedback has been surprisingly positive. Teachers often found completing the questionnaires to be an engaging, although challenging, task. They report that all too rarely are they engaged in conversations about their goals for instruction and the content of their enacted curriculum. When teachers have been provided descriptions of their practice (as in the case of the *Reform Up Close* study), these descriptions have caused them to reflect. In many cases, they were surprised by what they saw despite having provided the data themselves. This surprise is probably a function of the analytic capacity of the language to describe not only what is taught and with what relative emphasis, but also what is not taught. As described earlier, these procedures are being offered by the Council of Chief State School Officers' State Collaborative on Assessment and Student Standards as tools for schools to use in self-study and reflection, tools which they believe will help schools pursue their reform agenda. Once again, educators are attracted to the kinds of data these types of instruments can provide.

Getting the right topics. Do we have content broken up into the right sets of topics? An alternative framework is in its beginning stages of development, under the auspices of the Organisation for Economic Co-operation and Development (OECD), as part of its plan for a new international comparative study of student achievement. In that framework, big ideas are distinguished (e.g., chance, change and growth, dependency and relationships, and shape). Clearly, the OECD has a very different and interesting way of dividing up mathematical content than that taken here. Still, practice is currently organized along the lines of algebra, geometry, measurement, etc. not in terms of big ideas. Perhaps practice should be reformed to better reflect the big ideas, but that has not happened yet.

Getting the right cognitive demand. When describing the content of instruction with a goal of building an indicator with a strong predictive value for gains in student achievement, content must be described not only by the particular topics covered (e.g., linear algebra, cell biology), but also by the cognitive activities that students are to be engaged in with those topics (e.g., memorize facts, solve real world problems). A great deal of discussion has gone into how many distinctions of cognitive demand should be made, what the distinctions should be, and how they should be defined. In the earliest work focusing on elementary school mathematics, just three distinctions were made: conceptual understanding, skills, and applications.[19] In the *Reform Up Close* study of high school mathematics and science,[20] nine distinctions were made for both mathematics and science: (1) memorize facts/definitions/equations; (2) understand concepts; (3) collect data (e.g., observe, measure); (4) order, compare, estimate, approximate; (5) perform procedures: execute algorithms/routine procedures (including factoring, classify); (6) solve routine problems, replicate experiments/replicate proofs; (7) interpret data, recognize patterns; (8) recognize, formulate, and solve novel problems/design experiments; and (9) build and revise theory/develop proofs.

Later, in yet another generation of the survey instruments (with funding from the National Center for Education Statistics), student cognitive activities were defined by the categories: (1) memorize: facts, definitions, formulas; (2) understand or explain concepts/ideas; (3) complete computations, follow detailed instructions; (4) solve equations that are given; (5) solve routine problems (e.g., stories/word problems); (6) solve novel/non-routine or real world problems; (7) design experiments/empirical investigations; (8) collect, analyze, and/ or report on data; (9) build/revise theory, develop proofs; and (10) explain solutions/answers to any type of problem.

Then, in the national evaluation of Eisenhower Program,[21] performance goals for students were defined as: (1) memorize; (2) understand concepts; (3) perform procedures; (4) generate questions/ hypotheses; (5) collect, analyze, and interpret data; and (6) use information to make connections. Each of these distinctions was further defined using descriptors. For example, "generate questions/hypotheses" had as descriptors, brainstorm, design experiments, and solve novel/non-routine problems. "Use information to make connections" was elaborated by use and integrate concepts, apply to real world situations, build/revise theory and make generalizations (see Table 6). The goal is to have distinctions on a questionnaire that are understood in the same way by each respondent. Obviously, with the types of distinctions made for cognitive demand, perfect clarity is not achievable.

TABLE 6

PERFORMANCE GOALS FOR STUDENTS

Memorize	**Collect Data**
Facts	Make observations
Definitions	Take measurements
Formulas	
	Analyze and Interpret Information
Understand Concepts	Classify/order/compare data
Explain concepts	Analyze data, recognize patterns
Observe teacher demonstrations	Infer from data, predict
Explain procedures/methods of science	Explain findings, results
and inquiry	Organize and display data in tables,
Develop schema, or frameworks of	graphs, or charts
understanding	
	Use Information to Make Connections
Perform Procedures	Use and integrate concepts
Use numbers in science	Apply to real world situations
Do computation, execute procedures	Build/revise theory
or algorithms	Make generalizations
Replicate (illustrative or verification)	
experiments	
Follow procedures/instructions	
Generate Questions/Hypotheses	
Brainstorm	
Design experiments	
Solve novel/non-routine problems	

Note: The preceding list identifies key descriptors for each category of cognitive demand. Refer to this list in considering your responses for each category of cognitive demand on those topics covered as part of science instruction.

One language or several? A related issue is whether a different language for describing the content of instruction is needed within a subject area at different grade levels or within a grade level for different subjects. In the *Reform Up Close* study,[22] cognitive activities were described the same for both high school mathematics and high school science. Obviously, the topics differed between mathematics and science and were largely unique for each subject area. When describing the content of elementary school instruction, however, many of the mathematical or science topics are different from the mathematical or science topics in high school courses. Different grade levels may require different languages for describing the content of instruction. It also may be that, when describing the content of language arts instruction or social studies instruction, the cognitive activities and instructional mediums will be sufficiently distinct from those in mathematics and science that new languages are required.

The possibility of a third dimension. Throughout the development of questionnaires to survey teachers on the content of their instruction, a third dimension of the content matrix has been entertained. In *Reform Up Close*, this third dimension was referred to as mode of presentation. The distinctions were exposition (verbal and written), pictorial models, concrete models (e.g., manipulatives), equations/formulas (e.g., symbolic), graphical, laboratory work, and field work. At various times, differing categories of modes of presentation have been tried. However, mode of presentation has not been a powerful addition to the descriptions provided by topics and cognitive demand. Mode of presentation has not correlated well with other variables or with student achievement gains. Perhaps the problem is with its definition. Perhaps the problem is that mode of presentation really isn't an attribute of the content of instruction.

WHO DESCRIBES THE CONTENT?

In most efforts to describe the enacted curriculum, teachers have been used to self-report on their instruction. For *Reform Up Close*, independent observers from the research team also reported on selected days of instruction. Comparisons were made between observers' descriptions and those from teacher self-reports. There was strong agreement between the teachers and observers.[23]

From the perspective of policy research, teachers are probably the most important respondents, since it is teachers who make the ultimate decisions about what content gets taught to what students, when, and to what standards of achievement. Curriculum policies, if they are to have the intended effect, must influence teachers' content decisions. Since the period of instruction to be described is long (i.e., at least a semester), teachers and students are the only ones likely to be in the classroom for the full time. Since content changes from week to week if not day to day, a sampling approach such as would be necessary for observation or video simply won't work. While it is true that video and observation have been used to good effect in studying pedagogical practice, they have only worked well when those practices have been so typical that they occur virtually every instruction period. However, some pedagogical practices are not sufficiently stable to be well studied even with a robust sampling approach[24] such as the sampling methods used in the *Third International Mathematics and Science Study*.

Students could also be used as informants reporting on the content of their instruction. An advantage of using students is that they are less likely than teachers to report on intentions rather than actual instruction. A risk with using students as respondents is that students' ability to report on the content of their instruction may be confounded with their understanding of that instruction. For students struggling in a course, their reporting of instructional content might be incomplete and inaccurate due to their own misunderstandings and lack of recall. We conclude that it is more useful to look to teachers for an accounting of what was taught and to students for an accounting of what was learned.

RESPONSE METRIC

When having respondents describe the content of instruction, not only must the distinctions in type of content be accurately presented as discussed above but also respondents need an appropriate metric for reporting the amount of emphasis placed on each content alternative. The ideal metric for emphasis is time: how many instructional minutes were allocated to a particular type of content? This metric facilitates comparisons across classrooms, types of courses, and types of student bodies being served. But reporting number of instructional minutes allocated to a particular type of content over an instructional year is not an easy task. Other response metrics include number of hours per week (in a typical week), number of instructional periods, how frequently the content is taught (e.g., every day, every week), and percent of instructional time per year or per semester. The issue is how to get a response metric as close to the ideal as possible and still have a task that respondents find manageable and that they can use with accuracy.

HOW FREQUENTLY SHOULD DATA BE COLLECTED?

There is a tension between requiring frequent descriptions to get accuracy in reporting, which is expensive, versus less frequent descriptions covering longer periods of instruction (say, a semester or full school year), which is less expensive and less burdensome but may be less accurate as well. The issue is what frequency of reporting has an acceptable cost and still provides acceptable accuracy. We have used daily logs, weekly surveys, biannual surveys, and a single survey at the end of the year. When comparing daily logs to a single end-of-year survey, the results were surprisingly consistent.[25]

In addition to cost and teacher burden, determining the instructional unit of time that should be described could also affect decisions about the frequency of reporting. At the high school level, the unit might be a course, but some courses are two semesters long while others meet for only a single semester. Alternatively, the unit might be a sequence of courses to determine, for example, what types of science a student studies when completing a three-year sequence of science courses. At the elementary school level policymakers are typically interested in a school year or a student's entire elementary school experience (or at least the instruction experienced up to the state's first assessment).

Summary and Conclusions

There are a number of important uses to be made of good quantitative information about the content of the enacted curriculum. There are, however, a number of issues in defining such indicators: grain size, language, response metric, period of time to be described, and appropriate respondent. Several illustrations were provided of past efforts to measure the content of the enacted curriculum. Examples came primarily from high school mathematics and science, though similar work has been done at the elementary and middle school levels. The primary method used to collect the information is teacher self-report using survey instruments including daily class logs, although observations have been used as well.

While teacher log data have been shown to agree quite well with accounts from observations by researchers, and teacher questionnaire data have been a good predictor of teacher log data,[26] perhaps the best indicator of the quality of survey data comes from using teacher self-reports to predict gains in student achievement. The *Upgrading Mathematics Project*[27] reported the correlation at the class level to be about .5 and about .25 at the student level.

The language given to teachers for describing the content of their instruction can also be used for content analyses of standards and tests, and alignment between the enacted curriculum and tests or standards can be determined. This process was illustrated by content analyzing state tests as well as the National Assessment of Education Progress, and by determining alignment between teacher self-reports of their instruction and tested content. A great deal of attention is being given to alignment in standards-based reform, and these methodologies appear to be useful tools for determining where alignment exists and where it does not.

Teachers have also found the instruments to be useful in helping them to reflect upon their practice. In that sense then, teachers have provided validation for decisions made about grain size, language, response metric, and period of time to be described. Finally, as a standards-based approach to reform continues to be utilized by states as a key feature of educational improvement efforts, interest in and need for useful descriptions of practice, assessments, and standards will become increasingly important for answering questions about the implementation of standards in the classroom.

NOTES

1. Mary Kennedy, "Approximations to indicators of student outcomes," *Educational Evaluation and Policy Analysis* 21 (1999): pp. 345-363.

2. Andrew Porter, "Creating a system of school process indicators," *Educational Evaluation and Policy Analysis* 13 (1991): pp. 13-29.

3. Robert Meyer, "Value-added indicators of school performance: A primer," *Economics of Education Review* 16 (1997): pp. 283-301.

4. Brian Rowan, *Assessing Teacher Quality: Insights from School Effectiveness Research* (unpublished manuscript, 1999).

5. Lois Peake, *Pursuing Excellence: A Study of United States Eighth-grade Mathematics and Science Teaching, Learning, Curriculum, and Achievement in an International Context: Initial Findings from the Third International Mathematics and Science Study* (Washington, DC: National Center for Education Statistics, 1996).

6. William Schmidt, Curtis McKnight, Leland Cogan, Pamela Jakwerth, and Richard Houang, *Facing the Consequences: Using TIMSS for a Closer Look at United States Mathematics and Science Education* (Boston: Kluwer, 1999).

7. Andrew Porter, Michael Garet, Laura Desimone, Kwang Suk Yoon, and Beatrice Birman, *Does Professional Development Change Teachers' Instruction? Results from a Three-year Study of the Effects of Eisenhower and Other Professional Development on Teaching Practice* (Washington, DC: American Institutes for Research, 2000).

8. Andrew Porter, Robert Floden, Donald Freeman, William Schmidt, and John Schwille, "Content determinants in elementary school mathematics," in Douglas Grouws and Thomas Cooney, eds., *Perspectives on Research on Effective Mathematics Teaching* (Hillsdale, NJ: Erlbaum, 1988), pp. 96-113; Andrew Porter, Michael Kirst, Eric Osthoff, John Smithson, and Steven Schneider, *Reform Up Close: An Analysis of High School Mathematics and Science Classrooms* (Madison, WI: University of Wisconsin-Madison, Consortium for Policy Research in Education, 1993).

9. Council of Chief State School Officers, *Using Data on Enacted Curriculum in Mathematics and Science: Sample Results from a Study of Classroom Practices and Subject Content* (Washington, DC: Author, 2000).

10. "How Reform Works: An Evaluative Study of NSF's Urban Systemic Initiatives" is funded by the National Science Foundation (REC98724344). The principal investigators are Jason Kim, Rolf Blank, Pendred Noyce, and Lloyd Richardson.

11. "Assessing the Impact of the National Science Foundation's Urban Systemic Initiatives" is funded by the National Science Foundation (NSF#9980509). The principal investigators are Kathryn Borman and Gladis Kersaint.

12. Alignment between pairs of topic-by-cognitive-demand matrices of content emphasis were calculated as, $I = 1 - (\sum |x\text{-}y|)/2$, where x is the cell proportion for one matrix (representing an assessment or instruction) and y is the corresponding cell proportion for the other matrix (representing an assessment or instruction).

13. Adam Gamoran, Andrew Porter, John Smithson, and Paula White, "Upgrading high school mathematics instruction: Improving learning opportunities for low-achieving, low-income youth," *Educational Evaluation and Policy Analysis* 19 (1997): pp. 325-338.

14. Jia Wang, "Opportunity to learn: The impacts and policy implications," *Educational Evaluation and Policy Analysis* 20 (1998): pp. 137-156.

15. Anthony Bryk and Steven Raudenbush, *Hierarchical Linear Models: Application and Data Analysis Methods* (Newbury Park, CA: Sage Publications, 1992).

16. To form the configuration of coverage index, first the proportion of instructional time for each type of content tested relative to the total amount of instructional time spent on tested content was determined. Second, the proportion of test items in each tested area was determined. The absolute value of the difference between these proportions was summed, and the sum re-scaled by dividing by 2.0 and subtracting the result from 1.0, to create an index that ranged from 0.0 to 1.0.

17. National Council of Teachers of Mathematics, *Principles and Standards for School Mathematics* (Reston, VA: Author, 2000).

18. National Research Council, *National Science Education Standards* (National Academy of Sciences. Washington, DC: National Academy Press, 1996).

19. Porter, Floden, Freeman, Schmidt, and Schwille, "Content determinants in elementary school mathematics."

20. Porter, Kirst, Osthoff, Smithson, and Schneider, *Reform Up Close*.

21. Michael Garet, Beatrice Birman, Andrew Porter, Laura Desimone, and Rebecca Herman, with Kwang Suk Yoon, *Designing Effective Professional Deveopment: Lessons from the Eisenhower Program* (Washington, DC: American Institutes for Research, 1999).

22. Ibid., pp. 2-10.

23. Porter, Kirst, Osthoff, Smithson, and Schneider, *Reform Up Close*.

24. Richard Shavelson and Paula Stern, "Research on teachers' pedagogical thoughts, judgments, decisions, and behavior," *Review of Educational Research* 51 (1981): pp. 455-498.

25. Porter, Kirst, Osthoff, Smithson, and Schneider, *Reform Up Close*.

26. Smithson and Porter, *Measuring Classroom Practice*.

27. Gamoran, Porter, Smithson, and White, "Upgrading high school mathematics instruction: Improving learning opportunities for low-achieving, low-income youth."

CHAPTER V

Translating Teaching Practice into Improved Student Achievement

JONATHAN A. SUPOVITZ

Introduction

Educators have learned a lot over the past decade about what comprises effective, standards-based professional development and have demonstrated repeatedly that these principles of professional development can change teachers' practices. However, there is minimal evidence that the resulting changes in teaching practice translate into substantial gains in student performance. This chapter explores the puzzle of why effective methods for changing teaching practices do not appear to translate into higher levels of student performance.

In this chapter I first develop a conceptual model for the relationship between professional development and student achievement. Next I relate what we know makes for effective professional development, with a focus on what we have learned from research on standards-based professional development in mathematics and science. Third, I examine the evidence on the relationship between effective teaching practices and student achievement, again drawing mostly from research in mathematics and science. Finally, I explore five possible reasons why professional development may be effective at changing teaching practice but less successful in raising student achievement.

The Logic of Professional Development

The implicit logic of focusing on professional development as a means for improving student achievement is that high quality professional development will produce superior teaching in classrooms, which will, in turn, translate into higher levels of student achievement.

Jonathan A. Supovitz is a Senior Researcher with the Consortium for Policy Research in Education and a Research Assistant Professor in the Graduate School of Education at the University of Pennsylvania.

This chain of logic is graphically represented at the core of Figure 1. Several factors mediate this hypothesized chain of events and are depicted around this core. First, the context within which teachers operate, the school environment, has a powerful influence on core activities. For example, if a different method of teaching practice is predominant in a school, the incentives to conform to this overriding culture can mute or counteract the effects of even the most powerful professional development for individual teachers. Further, school environments that are strife-ridden or unsafe are likely to distract teachers from their prime teaching and learning mission. Second, district and state policies are also powerful mediators of the core sequence. For example, assessment practices that are not aligned with reforms in teaching practice create powerful disincentives for teachers to change their teaching practices.

FIGURE 1
MODEL DEPICTING THEORETICAL RELATIONSHIP BETWEEN
PROFESSIONAL DEVELOPMENT AND STUDENT ACHIEVEMENT

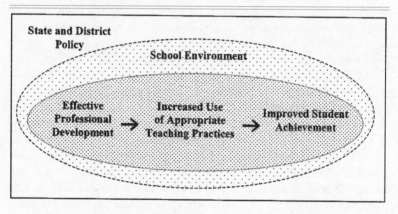

What We Know About Effective Professional Development

Over the past decade, researchers and educators have forged a remarkable level of national consensus about what may constitute effective professional development. They posit that professional development is most likely to be of high quality if it includes six critical components.

First, professional development must show teachers how to connect their work to specific standards for student performance.[1] Work in cognitive development suggests that more complex knowledge and problem solving skills require more sophisticated teaching strategies,[2] and that this kind of teaching can be achieved through setting higher learning goals.[3] One of the major findings from the Third International Mathematics and Science Study was that common, high standards for student performance are strongly related to national achievement.[4]

Second, effective professional development must immerse participants in questioning and experimentation and therefore model inquiry forms of teaching.[5] Little[6] argues that such reforms "constitute a departure from canonical views of curriculum and from textbook-centered or recitation-style teaching" and represent "a substantial departure from teachers' prior experience." Marek and Methven[7] found that the programs that modeled scientific reasoning have a greater influence on student achievement than did programs that taught teachers to use specific curricula.

Third, reformers argue that professional development must be both intensive and sustained.[8] The National Council for Teachers of Mathematics[9] and National Science Education Standards,[10] for example, call for more long term, coherent professional development plans. Evidence on the effectiveness of this component, however, is mixed. In a review of science and mathematics professional development programs that had evidence of impact on student achievement, Kennedy[11] found little relationship between professional development contact time and student learning.

Fourth, staff development must engage teachers in concrete teaching tasks and be based on teachers' experiences with students.[12] Studies have shown that staff development undertaken in isolation from teachers' ongoing classroom duties seldom have much impact on teaching practices or student achievement.[13] Lieberman[14] argued that the definition of professional development must be expanded to include "authentic opportunities to learn from and with colleagues *inside* the school."

Fifth, professional development must focus on subject matter knowledge and deepen teachers' content skills.[15] For example, the National Science Education Standards call for professional development to emphasize essential science content.[16] Kennedy[17] concluded that "programs that focus on subject matter knowledge and on student learning of particular subject matter are likely to have larger positive effects on student learning than are programs that focus on teaching behaviors."

Finally reform strategies must be connected to other aspects of school change.[18] One of the most persistent findings from school improvement research is the intimate relationship between staff development and school improvement. As Fullan[19] states, "staff development cannot be separated from school development." According to Lieberman,[20] reform plans that have a chance to succeed must create a "culture of inquiry," which is an "ongoing part of teaching and school life." Marsh and LeFever[21] also find that school leadership is critical to school reform.

What We Know about the Relationship Between Professional Development and Teaching Practice

Empirical evidence confirming the first link in the hypothesized chain relating effective professional development to student achievement is growing. Several recent studies have found a strong relationship between professional development and teaching practice. In a study of teachers who participated in Ohio's Statewide Systemic Initiative in science and mathematics, Supovitz, Mayer, and Kahle[22] found that intensive, standards-based professional development conducted in the context of systemic reform significantly increased teachers' attitudes toward reform, their preparation to use reform-based practices, and their use of inquiry-based teaching practices. Further, they found that these changes persisted several years after teachers concluded their experience.

Cohen and Hill[23] studied the implementation of the Mathematics Framework in California in the 1980s and conducted a survey in 1994 of a representative sample of 1,000 second through fifth grade teachers. Part of their work investigated the relationship between teachers' professional development opportunities and teaching practice. The professional development opportunities ranged from content-focused workshops ranging from two to six days in length, one-day special issues workshops (Family Mathematics and cooperative learning), and ongoing formal networks between teachers. They found that the teacher learning opportunities that were grounded in the curriculum that students study connected to several elements of instruction (curriculum and assessment) and occurred over time were associated more of the kind of practice supported by the Mathematics Framework.

In another study, Supovitz and Turner[24] investigated the teaching practices of 3,464 science teachers in 666 schools from twenty-four localities that participated in a National Science Foundation Teacher Enhancement program called the Local Systemic Change initiative. They employed hierarchical linear modeling to examine the relationship between professional development and standards-based teaching practice in science. Although there was clearly variation in implementation, for the most part, the professional development used in local sites contained many of the qualities described earlier in this chapter as comprising high quality experiences. The findings from this study indicated that the quantity of professional development in which teachers participated was strongly linked to teaching practices. In fact, after adjusting for differences between teachers and schools, the results indicated that, on average, teachers with no professional development were predicted to employ standards-based practices four-tenths of a standard deviation less frequently than that of the average teacher in the sample. It was only after approximately eighty hours of professional development that teachers reported using standards-based teaching practices significantly more frequently—about two-tenths of a standard deviation—than the average teacher.

The above studies are based upon self-report survey data. The self-report nature of these studies may shake our confidence in their conclusion as self-report data can overestimate impacts because teachers can genuinely believe they are changing practice while not actually doing so. The classic example of this phenomenon is Cohen's analysis of Mrs. Oublier,[25] a teacher who believed she had revolutionized her mathematics teaching but observations of her teaching revealed that "innovations in her teaching have been filtered through a very traditional approach to instruction." However, a separate Consortium for Policy Research in Education (CPRE) study using observation data confirms the findings of the self-report studies described above. A CPRE[26] evaluation of a partnership between the Merck Institute for Science Education (MISE) and four school districts conducted classroom observations by trained raters of a stratified random sample of ninety-two teachers of mathematics and science who participated in different amounts of high quality (similarly defined to our definition) professional development. They found statistically significant differences in the ratings of the teachers' practice dependent on their participation in the program's professional development. The importance of this observational study is that it supports the findings of studies done with teacher self-report survey methods.

The fact that the results of these studies are replicated across different contexts and involve different methods strengthen our confidence in their veracity. Together, these studies provide a solid basis of evidence for concluding that professional development that is connected to specific standards for student performance, based upon intensive and sustained training around concrete tasks, focused on subject matter knowledge, and embedded in a systemic context is likely to be effective.

What We Know about the Relationship between
Teaching Practice and Student Achievement

In contrast to the evidence of the relation between high quality professional development and changes in teachers' practices, relatively few studies have documented a link between science and mathematics teaching practices and student achievement. Kennedy[27] combed the peer-reviewed literature on professional development programs in mathematics and science and reported that "although the literature on inservice programs is voluminous, the volume subsides quickly when you limit yourself to studies that include evidence of student learning." In fact, she found just seven studies in mathematics and five studies in science that documented a relationship between professional development and student achievement.

The few studies that have reported a relationship between teaching practice and student achievement found the impacts to be small. For example, CPRE's evaluation of MISE[28] examined the link between inquiry-based teaching practices and student achievement on the open-ended portion of the Stanford-9 achievement test. The authors identified a statistically significant, but substantially small, relationship between standards-based teaching practice and fifth grade student achievement. Each full standard deviation increase in the frequency of teacher use of standards-based teaching practice was associated with a four percent increase in student test performance. They did not detect any association between teaching practice and student achievement in the seventh grade. This was due, they argued, to more concerted implementation in the elementary school grades.

Cohen and Hill's study of teacher learning opportunities in California[29] also directly examined the relationship between professional development and fourth grade student achievement on the California Learning Assessment System (CLAS). Because the state only reported achievement data at the school level, they were forced to compute school averages of teacher practice to make their comparisons. They found a modest relationship between schools in which teachers reported classroom practices more oriented to the Mathematics Framework and school average student scores on the CLAS after controlling for demographic characteristics of schools.

A RAND study of eleven sites from around the country that were emphasizing reform in mathematics and science examined the relationship between instructional practice and student achievement.[30] Because each site had its own measure of student achievement, the study attempted to look at the relationship in each context and build a "mosaic" of evidence. Based upon pooled results, they concluded that "the consistency of the findings across sites provide some (albeit weak) support for the hypothesis that the reform practices are associated with improved student achievement."[31] In sum, there is some evidence, although it is relatively hard to detect, and modest when detected, that increased use of standards-based teaching practices results in higher levels of student achievement.

Why Teaching Practice May Not Translate into Student Achievement Gains

How are we to explain the relative paucity of evidence of the effectiveness of standards-based professional development programs on improving student achievement when they seem to be so successful in changing teachers' practices? Some of the scarcity of results can be attributed to the difficulty of collecting the data to link professional development to student achievement and the technical challenges inherent in detecting the effects of such a relationship. As any researcher who has attempted to do so will confirm, gaining access to student achievement data, linking it to specific teachers, and then linking that data to professional development experiences is an arduous and complex task. The additional challenge of conducting the appropriate analyses for examining the relationship between two different levels of data—students and teachers—is both delicate and daunting. But these barriers are only technical obstacles that should not dissuade determined researchers and therefore are only part of the reason for such a meager evidence base.

In the rest of this chapter I identify and discuss five major arguments as to why successfully changing teaching practices may not translate into gains in student achievement. First, testing instruments themselves are often inconsistent with the pedagogy of reform-oriented professional development programs and thus not sensitive to effects. Second, the content of what is taught is often poorly related to the content that is tested and therefore is less likely to detect effects. Third, our preoccupation with instant results leads us to seek effects before we should reasonably expect them to appear. Fourth, models that relate teaching practice to student achievement may not include key state and local policy environment characteristics that may be important contributors to student performance. And finally, the content of professional development may not yet be fine-tuned and powerful enough to influence student achievement.

POOR ALIGNMENT BETWEEN WHAT IS TAUGHT AND THE
FORM BY WHICH IT IS TESTED

Many researchers and program directors contend that the influence of reform-oriented professional development programs that change teaching practice are not visible on standardized tests because the measures used to assess student learning are not aligned with the form and goals of the programs and thus are not sensitive to their impacts. They contend, for example, that it would be inappropriate to assess the impact of an inquiry-oriented initiative with a multiple choice standardized test. Essentially, they argue, the measures used are not sensitive to the initiatives.

What is the evidence about the sensitivity of student performance to the instruments used to measure it? Here I will discuss the findings of three studies that have examined the relationship between student performance on standardized tests as well as student performance on alternative assessments. The results suggest that there is some sensitivity in student performance to the measures used, but that changes in instrumentation do not dramatically change student performance rankings.

Baxter, Shavelson, Goldman, and Pine[32] examined the association between fifth grade student performance on a cognitive ability test, the Comprehensive Tests of Basic Skills (CTBS) in science, and a science performance assessment developed by the British Assessment of Performance Unit which asked students to determine which of three paper towels holds the most water. The study consisted of ninety-six students from two school districts. The correlation between the CTBS and the performance assessment (.40) was moderate. Interestingly, after removing the proportion of student performance associated with the cognitive ability test, the correlations between the CTBS and the performance assessment plummeted to .16. The authors concluded that the modest correlation between the two measures indicated that the performance task and the standardized test were measuring overlapping, but somewhat different, things. The small sample size and use of only one performance task makes this study vulnerable on its own, but it is included here because, as you will see, its results reflect the broader trend.

In a larger scale study of 5,264 first and second grade students in Rochester, New York, Supovitz and Brennan[33] compared students' language arts portfolio performance and their scores on the districtwide multiple choice standardized tests. First graders also took the California Achievement Test (CAT), a multiple choice test of reading and writing skills. Second graders were tested with Degrees of Reading Power (DRP), a criterion-referenced test that focused on reading and reading comprehension skills. In the study, the authors found that the correlation between the CAT and the Language Arts portfolio for first graders was .55 and the correlation between the DRP and the Language Arts portfolio for second graders was .58. This confirms the moderate relationship between standardized tests and performance assessments indicated in the Baxter, Shavelson, Goldman, and Pine study.

Burger and Burger[34] analyzed the relationship between student performance on the subtests of the Fourth Edition of the Comprehensive Tests of Basic Skills (CTBS-4), a reading performance assessment of the Michigan Educational Assessment Program (MEAP), and a locally developed performance writing assessment. The assessments were given to 6,176 students in second through tenth grades in a small city in the western United States. The results indicated high correlations (ranging from .58 to .94) between the subtests of the CTBS-4. The correlations between the MEAP reading performance assessment and the local writing assessment were substantially lower (ranging from .37 to .61). Finally, the correlations between the CTBS-4 subtests and the performance assessments were moderate, ranging from .39 to .65. According to the authors, "this finding supports the argument that performance assessment provides different kinds of information about student abilities than does normative assessment."[35]

These three studies show a clear and consistent pattern. First, the correlations across different forms of assessment, even when they are assessing performance in the same general domain (reading, writing, science, etc.), are moderate, in the .40 to .60 range. This indicates that the forms of assessment have substantial overlap but are measuring different things. Thus while we would expect student performance to vary to some extent across different assessment formats, which may mute effects in some cases, we would also expect that, should they exist, patterns of effect across multiple studies would be evident.

POOR ALIGNMENT BETWEEN THE CONTENT
OF WHAT IS TAUGHT AND WHAT IS TESTED

The second contention is that the measures that are used to assess particular programmatic reforms are rarely tightly linked to the curricula and pedagogy being advocated, but are rather more generic, "off the shelf" instruments that are used indiscriminately. For example, consider a fourth grade science class where the teacher has participated in standards-based professional development and consequently covers fewer content areas in greater depth. The assessment used to measure the impact of this teacher's professional development experience is the multiple choice component of the Stanford-9 achievement test. On one side of this argument are those who say that if the reform is effective, any measure that broadly assesses fourth grade science should be able to detect whether, on average, students exposed to the reform are more knowledgeable and skillful than students who take science from more traditional instructors. On the other side are those who contend that if the reform focuses on developing teachers' knowledge and pedagogy in a particular content area which the teacher then adopts in her classroom, then a fair assessment would cover that particular domain. Otherwise, the assessment is just testing general knowledge not related to the instruction of interest. In other words, is it reasonable to ask students to transfer knowledge from one domain to another and skills from one type of task to another? Should assessments be curriculum independent or curriculum dependent?

Underlying this contention is the issue of transfer, which cuts to the heart of our knowledge of what it means to learn. Since Thorndike and Woodworth[36] investigated the relationship between improvement in one mental function and performance in other cognitive areas, educational psychologists have been studying the way that people transfer knowledge of specific content to new situations. Thorndike and Woodworth were sanguine about the possibilities, concluding that "The mind is a machine for making particular reactions to particular situations."[37] Researchers since have tried to find evidence for transfer with sporadic success. In a recent book entitled *Transfer on Trial*, Detterman and Sternberg[38] argue that "most studies fail to find transfer" and "those studies claiming transfer can only be said to have found transfer by the most generous criteria." Transfer is hard to find and difficult to replicate.

An alternative view comes from proponents of "situative cognition" who contend that learning is a combination of context specific knowledge and general problem solving abilities.[39] In this view, learning is an inextricably connected action in the world and is constructed from sociocultural exchanges. As an example of how this relates to the connection between instruction and assessment, Perkins and Solomon[40] asked the question, "Is skillful thought-demanding performance relatively context-bound, or does it principally reflect use of general abilities of some sort?" They concluded that "general heuristics that fail to make contact with a rich domain-specific knowledge base are weak. But when a domain-specific knowledge base operates without general heuristics, it is brittle—it serves mostly in handling formulaic problems."[41]

However, the debate between situated cognitionists and transferites is far from over. Bransford and Schwartz[42] argue that the traditional view of transfer is too narrow and that "evidence of transfer is often difficult to find because we tend to think about it from a perspective that blinds us to its presence." They argue that the conception of transfer should be broadened to include people's preparation for future learning by which they mean general considerations that shape future learning but may not be visible in on-demand tasks.

Before dipping our madeleine too deeply into the tea of this debate, let it suffice to say that how people learn is still an uncertain process. But it seems that we are on fairly stable ground to conclude that traditional transfer—our ability to apply behaviors to new situations—is weak. And this suggests that assessments should be somewhat closely related to the content of what is taught if the intent is to measure the effects of teaching practice.

LACK OF SUFFICIENT TIME

Most efforts to measure impacts on students do so at the end of one year of an intervention. This is problematic for two reasons. First, the timeframe may be too short and second, education is a cumulative process not the product of nine months of a student's experience. As my financial advisor reminds me, "Compounding is a wonderful thing." The same may be true in educational research as small effects compounded over multiple years may translate into much larger impacts. This may both explain the moderate student impact effects and raise our hopes about their meaningfulness.

American educators are notorious for their impatience in expecting results. Often new programs are subjected to student impact assessments even before the program has been fully implemented. Teachers who are learning new instructional methods are supposed to magically master them and implement them competently in their classroom. Further, students are supposed to pliably unlearn old ways of schooling and instantly adopt new forms of learning. When student impacts are nil or small in the first few years of a heretofore promising reform, the initiative is relegated to the dustbin of educational reforms. No wonder recycling is such a popular educational convention.

Now this is not to say that many educational reforms do not deserve to end up in the scrap heap, but what this impatience obscures is the fact that the really powerful effects of educational reform are sometimes found only over time. What students successfully know and are able to do is a product of their collective experiences, not just their understanding from a single subject class in a single year. While we often acknowledge this in terms of the important roles of outside school factors such as family life and socioeconomic status, we less often take this into account when we are studying the effects of educational experiences.

Several pieces of research hint at the promise of looking at cumulating effects of teaching practices to more adequately judge impacts on students. The importance of looking longitudinally is most apparent in the work of William Sanders.[43] According to his findings, consistent sequences of highly effective teachers over time (as measured by students performing above average in comparison to those of similar socioeconomic status) had the most powerful effects on students' achievement. By contrast, students who had multiple years of ineffective teachers fell further and further behind.

As another example, in CPRE's evaluation of the Merck Institute for Science Education,[44] the authors found that both fifth and seventh grade students who took science classes over several years with teachers who had professional development in standards-based science instruction performed significantly better than students with multiple years in the classes of teachers who did not have standards-based science training. What is especially germane to this discussion is that these differences were most visible, and statistically significant, when comparing students whose teachers had multiple years of professional development to students whose teachers had no professional development. In other words, if we had looked solely at a single point in time, we would have been a lot more likely to miss the trend, which was only visible as a cumulative effect.

UNDERSPECIFICATION OF THE MODEL RELATING
TEACHING PRACTICE TO STUDENT ACHIEVEMENT

Attempts to relate professional development to student achievement via teaching practices may also fall short because most fail to capture important policy factors that contribute to the environment in which teaching practice occurs. At the beginning of this chapter I posited a model (Figure 1) depicting the theoretical relationship between professional development and student achievement. In the model, professional development, teaching practice, and student achievement are embedded in a school context which is, in turn, surrounded by a district and state policy context. State and local standards, curriculum frameworks, curriculum materials, high stakes assessment systems, and teacher evaluation systems all undoubtedly contribute to the environments within which teachers practice their craft. Most studies occur within a specific district or state, and are not able to look at variation across contexts. No study of which I am aware has included state and district policy factors as independent variables in investigating the relationship between professional development, teaching practice, and student achievement.

In their chapter in this volume entitled "Are Content Standards Being Implemented in the Classroom?" Andrew Porter and John Smithson describe a useful way of thinking about the links between policy initiatives and student outcomes. They envision a causal chain that starts with what they call the "intended curriculum," or the state and local policy environments (made up of content standards, curriculum frameworks and guidelines, and high stakes assessments). In their model, the intended curriculum comprises the environment that influences teaching practices (the enacted curriculum) which, in turn, influences student achievement (the intended curriculum). They offer intriguing evidence from an eleven state study of the common misalignment within states of different policy instruments. It is easy to imagine the resulting conflicting messages sent to teachers about what and how to teach. Therefore, models that do not specify policy factors may be missing critical environmental variables that play important intermediary roles in explaining the relationship between professional development, teaching practice, and student achievement.

THESE MAY NOT BE THE KINDS OF PRACTICES WHICH CHANGE STUDENT ACHIEVEMENT

Another reason that practice may change without affecting student achievement is that the intended practices simply may not be powerful enough to impact student achievement. Two particular areas that may be underspecified in our current formulations are teacher content knowledge and the linkages between standards, instruction, and student work.

Implicit in this realm of research is the notion that the instructional style and supporting materials (i.e., curricula) are the cornerstones for changes in achievement. What is becoming increasingly recognized is that teacher content knowledge is also a powerful element of practice. It makes sense that teachers well versed in their content area are more able to take the flexible approach to instruction implicit in the inquiry-oriented environment underlying the mathematics and science standards-based reform movement. Research supports this notion. In their analysis of the NSF Local Systemic Change data, Supovitz and Turner[45] found that teachers' content preparation was the most powerful predictor of their teaching practice. A twenty percent increase in teacher reported content preparation was associated with twenty-two percent more frequent use of inquiry-oriented teaching practices. Further, in CPRE's evaluation of the partnership between the Merck Institute for Science Education and four school districts,[46] the authors found that each additional semester of college science coursework was associated with a statistically significant .11 of a standard deviation increase in science teaching practice. Each additional semester of college mathematics coursework was associated with a statistically significant .08 of a standard deviation increase in mathematics teaching practice.[47] In both subject areas, content knowledge was far more influential than other teacher characteristic. Both studies also point to the important influence of content knowledge in affecting teaching practice. Kennedy's[48] investigation of the relationship between inservice and student achievement supports the importance of content. She concluded that "programs that focus on subject matter knowledge and on student learning of particular subject matter are likely to have larger positive effects on student learning than are programs that focus on teaching behaviors."[49]

Finally, but not least importantly, distinctions between interpretations of what embodies powerful standards-based professional development intimate that our understanding of the relationships between the standards, professional development, and student learning is still rudimentary. In our work at CPRE we have had the opportunity to research several different forms of standards-based reform activities. Through these experiences we have noted several different incarnations of standards-based professional development. One distinguishing characteristic is the tightness between the links among the standards, curriculum, and instruction that teachers apply in the classroom, and the resulting student work. Some standards-based professional development programs, like the Standards in Practice training sponsored by the Education Trust and the America's Choice comprehensive school design of the National Center for Education and the Economy, employ a more concentrated emphasis on these links than is characterized by many of the NSF-sponsored professional development programs. The effectiveness of this content formulation is by no means proven but forms a powerful alternative vision of content within the same structural paradigm of high quality professional development.

Conclusion

Abundant evidence exists that powerful professional development structures can effectively change teachers' practices. By contrast, we have little compelling evidence that the particular types of practices embodied in the current science and mathematics standards-based reform movements are powerfully impacting student learning. Moving student achievement is a bigger boulder to budge. In this chapter I offer five possible reasons why this may be so. First, there are often incompatibilities between standards-based reform practices and the assessment instruments used to measure their impact. Second, there is often poor alignment between the content of what is taught and what is tested. Third, our impatience for results leads us to look for impacts too soon, rather than allowing effects to accumulate. Fourth, our models relating teaching practice to student achievement may not include crucial environmental specifications. Finally, reformers' specifications of professional development may not be precise enough to powerfully impact student achievement.

The solution to this complicated puzzle probably does not lie in any one of these areas alone, but rather is likely some combination of these reasons. Based on the evidence, I find the lack of alignment between the professional development and the form of the assessment to be the least persuasive of these arguments. The studies presented here indicate that this type of misalignment may dampen the magnitude of any effects, but is unlikely to obscure major impacts. On the other hand, loosely coupled linkages between the content that is taught by teachers and what is covered on the tests may result in assessments which are measuring no more than general student subject matter knowledge rather than what is learned in a specific course. Because we do not know what it means to learn, it follows naturally that we are unsure about the best method to assess. Furthermore, our haste to identify professional development that works may be working against us. While it is certainly reasonable to expect professional development to influence teachers' practices almost immediately (in one way or another), we may be asking too much for students who have learned in a particular form all of their school careers to immediately absorb and act upon new forms of instruction, particularly when these are often introduced in isolated subjects.

The fourth argument poses a challenge for researchers to develop measures and specify models that better capture the broader environments within which teachers are trained and instruct students. Finally, the fifth possibility pushes professional developers to further explicate the content of their offerings. While it appears that we have mastered the *form* of professional development necessary to change practice, we still do not know enough about the *content* of instruction that produces student learning. The recipe for producing student learning through teacher professional development still lacks important ingredients.

NOTES

1. Willis Hawley and Linda Valli, "The essentials of effective professional development: A new consensus," in Gary Sykes and Linda Darling-Hammond, eds., *Handbook of Teaching and Policy* (New York: Teachers College Press, 1999); National Research Council, *National Science Education Standards* (Washington, DC: National Academy Press, 1996).

2. Hilda Borko and Ralph Putnam, "Expanding a teacher's knowledge base: A cognitive psychological perspective on professional development," in Thomas Guskey and Michael Huberman, eds., *Professional Development in Education: New Paradigms and Practices* (New York: Teachers College Press, 1995), pp. 35-66.

3. Lauren Resnick and Leopold Klopfer, "Toward the thinking curriculum: An overview," in *Toward the Thinking Curriculum: Current Cognitive Research* (Alexandria, VA: ASCD, 1989), pp. 1-10.

4. William Schmidt (Untitled paper presented at the annual conference of the National Center for Education and the Economy, San Diego, January 1999).

5. Roger Bybee, *Reforming Science Education: Social Perspectives and Personal Reflections* (New York: Teachers College Press, 1993); Lillian McDermott, "A perspective in teacher preparation in physics and other sciences: The need for special science courses for teachers," *American Journal of Physics* 58 (1990); Arnold Arons, "What science should we teach?" in *A BSCS Thirtieth Anniversary Symposium: Curriculum Development for the Year 2000* (Colorado Springs, CO: Biological Science Curriculum Study, 1989), pp. 13-20.

6. Judith Warren Little, "Teachers' professional development in a climate of educational reform," *Educational Evaluation and Policy Analysis* 15 (1993): p. 130.

7. Edmund Marek and Suzanne Methven, "Effects of the learning cycle upon student and classroom teacher performance," *Journal of Research in Science Teaching* 28 (1991): pp. 41-53.

8. Hawley and Valli, "The essentials of effective professional development"; Mark Smylie, Diane Bilcer, Rebecca Greenberg, and Rodney Harris, *Urban teacher professional development: A portrait of practice from Chicago* (Paper presented at the annual meeting of the American Educational Research Association, San Diego, April 1998).

9. National Council for Teachers of Mathematics, *Curriculum and Evaluation Standards for Teaching Mathematics* (Reston, VA: Author, 1989).

10. National Research Council, *National Science Education Standards* (Washington, DC: National Academy Press, 1996).

11. Mary Kennedy, *The relevance of content in inservice teacher education* (Paper presented at the annual meeting of the American Educational Research Association, San Diego, April 1998).

12. Milbrey McLaughlin and Linda Darling-Hammond, "Policies that support professional development in an era of reform," *Phi Delta Kappan* 76 (1995), pp. 597-604.

13. Patricia Zigarmi, L. Betz, and D. Jennings, "Teachers' preferences in and perceptions of inservice," *Educational Leadership* 34 (1977): pp. 545-551.

14. Ann Lieberman, "Practices that support teacher development," *Phi Delta Kappan* 76 (1995): p. 591.

15. David Cohen and Heather Hill, *State Policy and Classroom Performance: Mathematics Reform in California* (Philadelphia: Consortium for Policy Research in Education, University of Pennsylvania, 1998).

16. National Research Council, *National Science Education Standards.*

17. Kennedy, *The relevance of content in inservice teacher education.*

18. Tom Corcoran and Margaret Goertz, "Instructional capacity and high performance," *Educational Researcher* 24 (1995): pp. 27-31; Jennifer O'Day and Marshall Smith, "Systemic reform and educational opportunity," in Susan Fuhrman, ed., *Designing Coherent Education Policy: Improving the System* (San Francisco: Jossey-Bass, 1993), pp. 250-312; Michael Fullan, *The New Meaning of Educational Change* (New York: Teachers College Press, 1991).

19. Fullan, *The New Meaning of Educational Change*, p. 331.

20. Lieberman, "Practices that support teacher development."

21. David Marsh and Karen LeFever, *Educational leadership in a policy context. What happens when student performance standards are clear?* (Paper presented at the annual meeting of the American Educational Research Association, Chicago, 1977).

22. Jonathan Supovitz, Daniel Mayer, and Jane Kahle, "Promoting inquiry-based instructional practice: The longitudinal impact of professional development in the context of systemic reform," *Educational Policy* 14 (2000): pp. 331-356.

23. Cohen and Hill, *State Policy and Classroom Performance.*

24. Jonathan Supovitz and Herbert Turner, "The influence of standards-based reform on classroom practices and culture," *Journal of Research in Science Teaching* 37 (2000): pp. 1-18.

25. David Cohen, "A revolution in one classroom: The case of Mrs. Oublier," *Educational Evaluation and Policy Analysis* 12 (1990), p. 311.

26. Consortium for Policy Research in Education, *A Close Look at Effects on Classroom Practice and Student Performance: A Report of the Fifth Year of the Merck Institute for Science Education 1997-98* (Philadelphia: Author, 1998).

27. Kennedy, *The relevance of content in inservice teacher education.*

28. Consortium for Policy Research in Education, *A Close Look at Effects on Classroom Practice and Student Performance.*

29. Cohen and Hill, *State Policy and Classroom Performance.*

30. Stephen Klein, Linda Hamilton, Daniel McCaffrey, Brian Stecher, Abby Robyn, and Delia Burroughs, *Teaching Practices and Student Achievement: Report of the First-Year Findings from the "Mosaic" Study of Systemic Initiatives in Mathematics and Science* (Santa Monica, CA: RAND, 2000).

31. Ibid., p. xxiv.

32. Gail Baxter, Richard Shavelson, Susan Goldman, and Jerry Pine, "Evaluation of procedure-based scoring for hands-on science assessment," *Journal of Educational Measurement* 29 (1992): pp. 1-17.

33. Jonathan Supovitz and Robert Brennan, "Mirror, mirror on the wall, which is the fairest test of all: An examination of the equitability of portfolio assessment relative to standardized tests," *Harvard Educational Review* 67 (1997): pp. 472-506.

34. Susan Burger and Donald Burger, "Determining the validity of performance based assessment," *Educational Measurement: Issues and Practice* (1994): pp. 9-15.

35. Ibid., p. 13.

36. Edward Thorndike and Robert Woodworth, "The influence of improvement in one mental function upon the efficacy of other functions," *Psychological Review* 8 (1901): pp. 247-261.

37. Ibid., p. 249.

38. Douglas Detterman and Robert Sternberg, eds., *Transfer on Trial: Intelligence, Cognition, and Instruction* (Norwood, NJ: Ablex, 1993), p. 15.

39. Lauren Resnick, Roger Saljo, and Clotilde Pontecorvo, *Discourse, Tools, and Reasoning* (Germany: Springer, 1997).

40. David Perkins and Gavriel Solomon, "Are cognitive skills context-bound?" *Educational Researcher* 18 (1989): p. 16.

41. Perkins and Solomon, "Are cognitive skills context-bound?", p. 23.

42. John Bransford and Daniel Schwartz, "Rethinking transfer: A simple proposal with multiple implications," *Review of Research in Education* 24 (1999): pp. 61-100.

43. William Sanders and June Rivers, *Cumulative and residual effects of teachers on future student academic achievement* (Knoxville, TN: Value-Added Research and Assessment Center, University of Tennessee, 1996); William Sanders and Sandra Horn, "Research findings from the Tennessee value-added assessment system (TVAAS) database: Implications for educational evaluation and research," *Journal of Personnel Evaluation in Education* 12 (1998): pp. 247-256.

44. Consortium for Policy Research in Education, *Deepening the Work: A Report of the Sixth Year of the Merck Institute for Science Education, 1998-99* (Philadelphia: Author, 1999).

45. Supovitz and Turner, "The influence of standards-based reform on classroom practices and culture."

46. Consortium for Policy Research in Education, *A Close Look at Effects on Classroom Practice and Student Performance.*

47. Consortium for Policy Research in Education, *Deepening the Work.*

48. Kennedy, *The relevance of content in inservice teacher education.*

49. Ibid., p. 11.

Section Three
DISTRICT RESPONSE TO REFORMS

CHAPTER VI

Big Isn't Always Bad: School District Size, Poverty, and Standards-based Reform[1]

JANE HANNAWAY AND KRISTI KIMBALL

For most of the twentieth century, school districts in the United States exercised tremendous power, determining financial resource levels and expenditure patterns, hiring and supervising teachers and other staff, and designing the education program. The traditional power of districts in the United States is striking in comparison to other countries, many of which have no local governance bodies.[2] But some analysts think the days of school districts in the United States are numbered. Elmore,[3] for example, has suggested that the continued "push toward state-to-school accountability measures" may leave districts in a "spectator" role. Others go farther and view school districts, especially large ones, as part of the problem of education in the United States. Guthrie,[4] for example, argues that centralizing authority in larger and larger school systems and effectively disenfranchising individual local schools is the main reason "America has lost its way in education."[5] Still other analysts implicitly question the role of districts by doubting the value of expenditures outside the classroom.[6]

Low expectations for the contribution of school districts to improving student performance should not be surprising. School districts historically have not focused heavily on matters of teaching and learning, tending to focus more on procedural and accounting matters.[7]

Jane Hannaway is Director and Principal Research Associate in the Education Policy Center at The Urban Institute, and a senior researcher with the Consortium for Policy Research in Education. Kristi Kimball, formerly a Research Associate at The Urban Institute, is a graduate student at Princeton University.

Increased accountability from state and federal agencies for higher standards of student performance and the limited capacity of many individual schools to meet the challenges of higher standards, however, may shape a new focus for district level efforts.[8] In short, viewing state-local relations as a zero-sum game may be misplaced.[9] School districts may be particularly well positioned to advance state reforms and to facilitate their school level implementation, and the bigger the district, the more it may have to offer. Indeed, an expanded state role may lead to an expanded district role.

We examine issues related to the district role in education reform by drawing on data from two companion national surveys as well as national archival files. The first survey, conducted by The Urban Institute, collected data from a national sample of school districts.[10] The purpose of the survey was to assess the progress of standards-based reform by asking districts about (1) the progress they were making in particular aspects of reform (e.g., establishing standards, aligning professional development with standards) and (2) the sources of information and assistance that they find helpful in their efforts. We incorporated data from the Agency File, Common Core of Data (CCD), on district size and from the decennial census on poverty in the district. The second survey, conducted by Westat, collected data from a national sample of schools using similar questions.[11]

The two samples—the district sample and the school sample—were designed independently. That is, while the two surveys were conducted within the same timeframe, the schools surveyed are not nested within the districts surveyed. Using data from the CCD, however, we are able to assign to schools the characteristics of the districts in which they reside. We can then determine the extent to which district characteristics that are related to progress reported at the district level are also related to progress reported at the school level. The samples and the data we use from each of these surveys are described more fully later.

Conceptual Background

The primary focus here is the relationship between district size and the progress in standards-based reform efforts reported by districts and schools. We are particularly interested in the effect of district size on reform in high-poverty school districts. This interest stems from policy concerns as well as a theoretical puzzle.

From a policy perspective, while the largest school districts (those with enrollments over 25,000) account for a small fraction of the school districts in the United States (1.3 percent), they account for a large fraction of the student population (thirty percent).[12] Thus reforms that occur in these relatively few districts affect a large number of students in the United States. For this reason alone, an analysis of reform in large districts is important. Big districts are also under attack. Large district size is often blamed for low school productivity,[13] and proposals for breaking up large districts, for example in Philadelphia and Los Angeles, have generated considerable support. Large districts, especially urban ones, often also have a large fraction of students from poor families and typically face serious performance problems. Distinguishing the effect of poverty and the effect of size, as well as understanding their combined effect is, thus, important.

In the organizational literature, the benefits and costs of large organizational size are the subject of much analysis. The conventional wisdom is that large size leads to bureaucratization and heavy administrative costs,[14] but empirical findings examining this relationship are inconsistent. Two effects of large organizational size work against each other: the increased differentiation typically associated with large size leads to a more elaborated administrative structure (e.g., for purposes of coordination), but economies of scale leads to decreased proportionate administrative costs.[15] Many observers also presume that large size leads to increased centralization, but again the empirical findings do not necessarily support this supposition. Larger organizations generate more rules and regulations, but also exhibit more decentralized decision making.[16] Larger organizations also tend to be more highly differentiated with more specialized positions and specialized sub-units. And though differentiation produces coordination costs, it also yields efficiencies to the extent that specialization promotes expertise in important areas.

When we turn to school districts, the picture becomes more complicated. Attempts to determine the efficiency advantages and disadvantages of larger size have been largely inconclusive, though larger districts are generally viewed to be less efficient in enhancing student outcomes.[17] Concern about the possibly negative consequences of size has focused on both extremes of the size distribution—the largest districts and the smallest ones.

The relationship between district size and student performance appears to be not a simple one. Friedkin and Nocochea,[18] for example, found the relationship between district size and student achievement depends on the socioeconomic characteristics of students in the district. Among low SES school systems, the relationship between district size and student performance is strongly negative, but this relationship weakens and, indeed, is eliminated among higher SES school systems. The authors reason that large size presents districts with both opportunities and constraints. The opportunities are in the form of additional resources produced through economies of scale; the constraints are in the form of significant numbers of students with social needs producing service units that detract attention from the core instructional focus of the district. Hannaway and Talbert[19] similarly find differences between urban and suburban districts in the effect of district size on school process measures commonly presumed to affect school productivity; larger size appears to benefit suburban districts, but poses problems for urban districts, perhaps because large urban districts are generally politically more complex and contentious than large suburban districts.[20]

A limitation of all these studies, for our purposes, is that they are concerned with the relationship between district size and educational productivity during "steady state." In this study, we are concerned with the effect of size on reform (i.e., we are interested in the effect of district size on adaptation and change). The question, however, can be framed similarly to earlier research; large size may well have advantages for advancing reform under some conditions, but disadvantages under other conditions as discussed below.

On one hand, larger districts, as a consequence of economies of scale, are likely to have slack resources available that could be directed to facilitating the reform process. While such resources might indicate inefficiency during "steady state," the classic analysis of Cyert and March[21] features organizational slack as a critical element for successful organizational adaptation to a changing environment. These resources might be deployed, for example, to analyze new demands on the district, plan district responses, allow for investments of various types, and overall resulting in a smoother and better informed change process. Differentiation and specialization within large organizations, to the extent that they relate to important dimensions of change, are also likely to facilitate reform. School districts, for example, with an assessment unit are probably better able, and more likely, to monitor developments in accountability policies, effectively evaluate how they might affect assessment strategies, and have the skills and knowledge to respond appropriately and in a timely manner.

On the other hand, we might expect larger districts, constrained by regulations and bureaucracy, not to be as nimble as smaller districts in responding to pressures for change. To the extent that differentiation and specialization are entrenched and not related to areas of change, they could generate a "drag" on the system or, at best, have no effect (other than consuming resources). And if larger size is associated with more special interest groups, a cumbersome, and perhaps contentious, decision making process might impede reform. While we do not have data to explore fully the processes by which size may facilitate or impede reform, we are able to assess the effects, on average, of district size on reports of reform progress by administrators at both the district and the school level.

Study Design

SAMPLE, DATA, AND METHODS

District Survey. The district survey resulted from a congressional mandate for the United States Department of Education to report on the implementation of federal educational reforms, including Goals 2000 and the 1994 reauthorization of the Elementary and Secondary Education Act (ESEA), designed to support state and local efforts to raise academic standards in schools. It represents the first systematic attempt to assess the progress of standards-based reform. A random sample of school districts was chosen from the CCD.[22] The sample was designed to be nationally representative of school districts, stratified by whether the district was located in an "early reform" state,[23] by the poverty level in the district (percentage of children five to seventeen years in poverty as reported in the census), and by district enrollment (from the CCD).[24] The final sample includes 2,700 districts, representing a response rate of eighty-three percent.

The district survey was sent by mail to the district superintendents in the spring and summer of 1996, but superintendents were told they could pass it on to someone else in the district that might be more knowledgeable about the topics covered in the survey. Eighty-six percent of the surveys were completed by superintendents, or directors or assistant superintendents in charge of curriculum and instruction in the district.[25]

Responses to questions about district progress in different areas of reform implementation are central to our analysis. Specifically, the survey asked respondents to report on a four-point scale their progress ("have not begun," "little progress," "some progress," and "a great deal of progress") on the following six elements of standards-based reform:

- Establishing high content and performance standards for all students;
- Aligning curricula and instructional materials with standards;
- Developing or adopting assessments linked to standards;

- Linking professional development to standards;
- Linking school/district accountability to student performance; and
- Building partnerships with parents/community.

School Survey. The school survey was administered by mail, with follow-up phone calls, to 1,360 principals in a nationally representative sample of public schools in the United States in the spring of 1996, and asked questions about the extent to which various elements of standards-based reform were being implemented in the school. The sample was stratified by instructional level (elementary, middle, high school), enrollment, and poverty (percent of students receiving free/reduced lunch). High-poverty schools were over sampled. Responses were received from 1,216 schools for a response rate of eighty-nine percent. To make the sample correspond to the district sample, we excluded from our analyses thirty-nine schools located in districts with enrollments less than 300. Thus the analyses are based on responses of 1,177 schools.[26]

Two questions from the school survey are used to gauge progress in implementation. (See Appendix for survey items.) The first question asked principals to report on a four-point scale ("not at all," "small extent," "moderate extent," and "great extent") the extent to which their school was using content standards in four areas: reading/language arts, mathematics, science, and history/social studies. The second question, using the same four-point scale, asked the extent to which eight reform strategies were being implemented in their school: strategic planning, professional development, instructional materials, innovative technologies, linking assessments to standards, using assessments for school accountability, parent involvement, and restructuring the school day.

Two major sections of results follow. The first examines the extent to which different characteristics of school districts are associated with reports of progress on various elements of reform. The second moves to the school level and examines the extent to which district characteristics that are related to reports of progress at the district level—district size, district poverty, and early reform status—are also associated with reports of progress at the school level.

We should note that we have no measures of *actual* progress in school districts and schools since survey data consist only of *reports* of progress. The presumption is that administrators in schools/districts moving ahead with reform are more likely to report progress than administrators in schools/districts unmoved by reform, resulting in district and school level reports varying systematically with the progress they are actually experiencing. The data also suggest reasons to have reasonable confidence that the reports of progress are correlated with actual progress. First, patterns of responses make sense as a qualitative picture. For example, larger districts not only report greater progress, but also more extensive networks of support and assistance than smaller districts.[27] Second, reports from both the district level and the school level are associated with many of the same factors. In a sense, the school level findings provide an independent test of the relationships shown in district level findings. In addition, the large district and school samples used here allow us to obtain reasonably accurate estimates of the associations of interest.

We should also note that the surveys were completed in the spring of 1996 and there has likely been further progress in reform since the data were collected. Our purpose here is not to provide an up-to-date snapshot of the state of reform, but rather to examine factors related to reports of progress at the early stages of organizational adaptation. The findings suggest characteristics of districts able to move quickly with reform and the characteristics of those moving more slowly. Subsequent studies can assess whether the early movers maintain their advantage.

District Size and Reform Progress: District Level Analysis

DESCRIPTIVE RESULTS

Most districts reported making progress in standards-based reform, although the percent reporting different levels of progress varies with the particular element of reform. Districts nationally reported the *greatest* progress in "establishing content and performance standards" and the *least* progress "linking school/district accountability to student performance" and "developing or adopting assessments linked to standards." Indeed, at the time of the survey, about one-third of the districts reported making "little" or "no" progress in areas of assessment and accountability. (See Figure 1.)

Our analyses focus on respondents' reports of making "a great deal" of progress since such reports most clearly suggest districts are making good headway. Table 1 shows how reports of progress differ for districts in different size ranges. As can be seen, the likelihood of reporting "a great deal" of progress increases with the size of the district. The smallest districts, those with enrollments between 300 and 2,500, are the least likely to report high levels of progress in any reform elements.

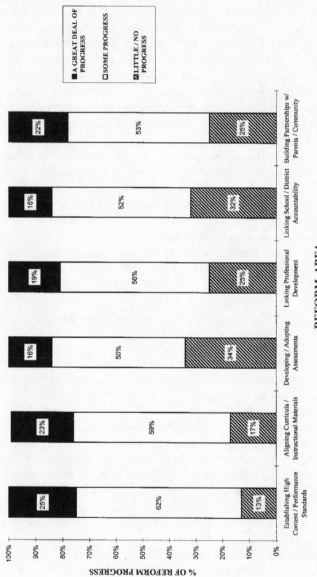

FIGURE 1

Percent of Respondents Reporting Progress in Reform Areas

District Level Reports

For "building partnerships with parents/community" and "linking school/district accountability to student performance," the benefits of larger size are particularly pronounced. For example, only thirteen percent of the smallest districts report making a great deal of progress in accountability, but more than a third of the largest districts do. For other elements of reform, the benefits of larger size appear to taper off at earlier size levels. The step-like relationship between reported progress and district size is shown in Figure 2.

Factors beyond district size, of course, are likely to affect reform progress. For example, districts with large fractions of children in poverty, spurred by reform-oriented provisions in Title I, may be particularly likely to make good reform headway. Conversely, we might expect progress in these districts to lag since they typically deal with more demanding educational problems and often more complex political environments. Progress in districts in different policy contexts might also vary. For example, districts receiving Goals 2000 funding, support designed to facilitate the reform process,[28] and districts in "early reform" states, which aggressively pursue reform, might report greater progress than other districts. We examine these possibilities below.

Table 1 shows that low-poverty districts,[29] not high-poverty districts, reported greater progress across most areas of reform, though only statistically significant for "establishing high content and performance standards" and "building partnerships with parents/community." Both the highest and the lowest poverty districts reported making significantly more progress in "linking school/district accountability to student performance" than districts in the moderate-poverty category (twenty percent versus fourteen percent).

As expected, districts in "early reform" states reported significantly more progress than the average district in the United States in many areas of reform. (See Table 1.) The biggest differences were in "developing assessments" (thirty-one percent versus sixteen percent), "linking school/district accountability" to student performance (thirty percent versus fifteen percent), and "linking professional development to standards" (thirty-four percent versus eighteen percent). Since assessments and accountability are an integral part of the reform agendas of these states, these findings should not be surprising. It would also not be surprising if the pressure of the assessment led directly to more focused professional development efforts. These findings show the considerable influence that state level policies have on reform at the local level. Districts that received federal Goals 2000 funding were

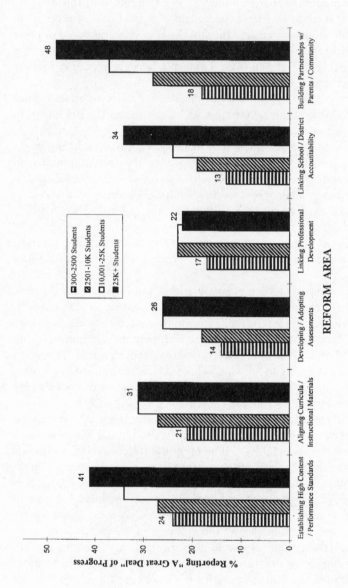

FIGURE 2

Percent of Respondents Reporting "A Great Deal" of Progress in Reform Areas by District Size

District Level Reports

TABLE 1

Percent of Respondents Reporting "A Great Deal" of Progress in Reform Areas
District Level Reports

Reform Area	All	District Size[a]				District Poverty[b]			Early Reform		Goals 2000	
		300–2500	2501–10K	10,001–25K	25K+	<5%	5 = <25%	>25%	Early Reform	Other	Goals 2000	Other
Establishing Content/ Performance Standards	25	24	27	34**	41	35***	24	22	30	25	24	27
Aligning Curricular/ Instructional Materials	23	21	27**	31	31	27	23	23	34***	23	25	24
Developing/Adopting Assessments	16	14	18*	26***	26	17	15	18	31***	16	17	16
Linking Professional Development	19	17	23***	23	22	22	18	20	34***	18	22	18
Linking School/District Accountability	16	13	19***	24	34**	20**	14	20**	30***	15	15	17
Building Partnerships w/ Parents/Community	22	18	28***	37**	48**	29**	22	19	26	22	26**	20

*** = p < .001
** = p < .01
* = p < .05
[a] tests difference with preceding size category
[b] tests difference with adjacent poverty category

significantly more likely to report "a great deal" of progress in only one area of reform—"building partnerships with parents/community."

MULTIVARIATE RESULTS

In this section, we examine simultaneously the effect of district size, poverty, location in an "early reform" state, and being a recipient of a Goals 2000 grant on reports of reform progress.[30] (See Table 2.)

TABLE 2

REGRESSION RESULTS-EFFECTS OF DISTRICT SIZE, POVERTY, GOALS 2000, EARLY REFORM STATE LOCATION ON REFORM PROGRESS

DISTRICT LEVEL RESULTS

VARIABLE	INTERCEPT	DISTSIZE	DISTPOV	GOALS	EARLY REFORM	DISTSIZE*DISTPOV
Establishing high standards	.271	.034**	-.003*	-.043	.033	-.001
Aligning curriculum and instruction w/ standards	.235	.035**	-.002+	.001	.079+	-.002+
Developing assessments linked to standards	.161	.035**	.001	-.007	.119**	.000
Linking professional development to standards	.185	.028**	.000	.016	.113**	.000
Linking accountability to student performance	.168	.036**	.001	-.033	.112**	.000
Building partnerships w/ parents & community	.205	.058**	-.002*	.039	.006	.000

*** = p < .001
** = p < .01
* = p < .05
+ = p < .10

The results show that even when we include this full set of district level variables, district size shows significant positive effects on all areas of reform. (See Table 2.) Being in an "early reform" state shows significant and generally large positive effects on three of the six areas, and approaches significance on a fourth area. It is interesting that the areas in which location in an "early reform" state has its greatest effect—developing assessments, linking professional development to standards, and linking accountability to student performance—are those areas where districts nationally, on average, report the least progress. The findings for poverty and Goals 2000, where we might expect to pick up possible federal program and policy effects, are insignificant or slightly negative. We should be careful interpreting this result, however, since these districts are also likely to face the greatest educational challenges and, thus, the least likely to show much progress in the short run. A different picture might emerge over time. We also examined whether there was an interaction effect between district size and poverty (i.e., whether large districts that had high poverty rates were different from large districts with low poverty rates). In general, no significant interactions were evident, though one area of reform—aligning curriculum and instruction with standards—approached significance, suggesting that districts serving students from poor backgrounds may benefit less from large size in making reform progress.

The above analysis shows the relationship between district level characteristics and district level reports of progress. Given possibly loose linkages between levels in education organization,[31] we cannot assume that factors associated with reports of progress at the district level are also associated with progress at the school level. The next section examines the extent to which significant predictors of district level progress are also associated with reports of reform progress at the school level.

District Size and Reform Progress: School Level Analysis

While the school level data are not nested within the particular districts about which we have data, they provide reports on the progress of reform at the school level for a nationally representative sample of schools, though the survey items in the district and the school surveys are not identical. (See Appendix.) Principals reported the extent to which their schools were implementing various aspects of reform. We examine the relationship between district level characteristics and reports of progress at the school level by assigning to each school in the sample its district size (enrollment) which is, as we have seen, significantly related to reports of progress by district level administrators and which is available from the Common Core of Data.

DESCRIPTIVE RESULTS

Like district level administrators, a large fraction of principals reported their schools were implementing many aspects of reform to "a great extent." For example, over half (fifty-six percent) of the schools reported they were using content standards in mathematics to "a great extent," and about half of the schools reported the same for reading.

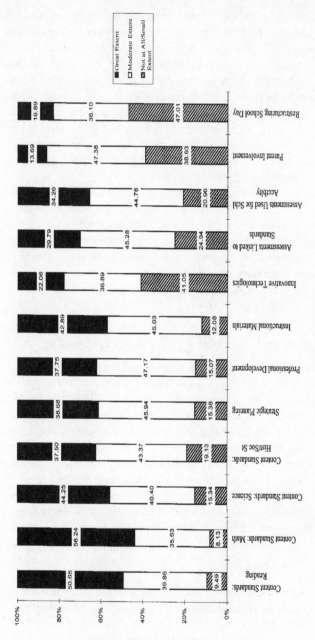

REFORM AREA

FIGURE 3

Percent of Respondents Reporting Progress in Reform Areas
School Level (Principal) Reports

Smaller fractions of schools, however, reported that they were implementing other aspects of reform to "a great extent." For example, only fourteen percent of the principals reported using "parent involvement activities to help parents work with their children to achieve high standards" to a great extent and less than thirty percent reported having assessments linked to standards. (See Figure 3.)

Similar to the district level results, principals of schools in larger districts were more likely to report "a great extent" of progress in implementing aspects of reform than principals of schools in smaller districts. (See Figure 4.) Some of the differences are large. For example, about one-third of schools in smallest districts (enrollment $300 \leq 2,500$) reported "using content standards in reading" a great deal while sixty-three percent of schools in the largest districts (enrollment 25,000+) reported doing the same. Schools in the largest districts reported using a strategic plan at more than twice the rate of those in the smallest districts (fifty-four percent versus twenty-four percent). And while only twenty-three percent of schools in the smallest districts reported using assessments for school accountability to "a great extent," forty-three percent of schools in the largest districts did. The only areas where there does not appear to be a clear district size relationship is in the use of "instructional materials" and "innovative technologies."[32] Table 3 also shows that while reported progress tends to be greater in each successive size category, the largest jump most often occurs between the smallest districts (300-2,500) and districts of the next size.

Again, similar to the findings for school districts, schools in the lowest poverty (most affluent) districts tend to report somewhat higher levels of progress in implementing reform, though the differences were not usually significant.[33] (See Table 3.) Schools in the highest poverty districts, however, were significantly more likely than schools in districts of moderate poverty to report "a great extent" of progress in "strategic planning," "assessments used for accountability," "professional development," and "restructuring the school day."

The school sample was not stratified by early reform status so a relatively small number of schools (fifty-eight) from these states were included in the sample.[34] Some of the differences appear large and in the expected direction, for example, forty-six percent of the schools in the "early reform" states report that "assessments (are) used for school accountability" to "great extent" and only one-third of other districts report the same; but with such a small sample in the "early reform" states, the standards errors are too large for differences to be statistically significant.

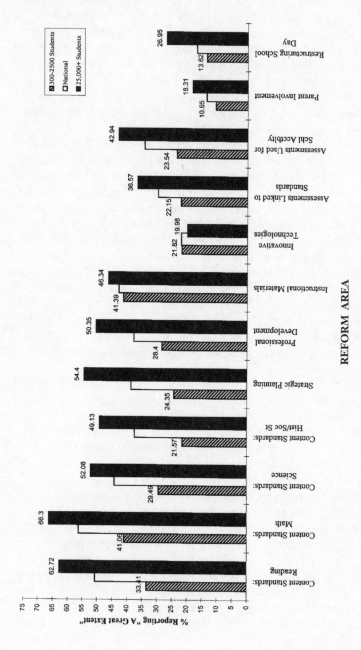

FIGURE 4

Percent of Respondents Implementing Reform Areas to "A Great Extent" by District Size
School Level (Principal) Reports

TABLE 3
PERCENT OF RESPONDENTS IMPLEMENTING REFORM AREA TO "A GREAT EXTENT"
SCHOOL LEVEL (PRINCIPAL) REPORTS

Reform Area	All	District Size[a]					District Poverty			Early Reform	Other
		300-2500	2501-10K	10,001-25K	25K+	<5%	5>=25%	>25%		
Content Standards: Reading	50.65	33.41	53.77***	60.52	62.72	53.71	49.68	52.08	43.90	51.07
Content Standards: Math	56.24	41.06	59.04**	65.43	66.30	66.67	54.02	56.19	48.26	56.73
Content Standards: Science	44.25	29.49	49.14***	51.39	52.08	52.13	43.87	40.38	43.95	49.13
Content Standards: Hist/Soc St	37.50	21.57	41.64***	43.31	49.13	41.39	37.56	35.06	37.25	41.57
Strategic Planning	38.68	24.35	43.23***	34.86	54.40**	43.32	35.27	46.31*	31.62	39.12
Professional Development	37.75	28.40	37.72	38.18	50.35	43.59	34.65	43.77*	33.68	38.00
Instructional Materials	42.89	41.39	41.32	44.35	46.34	60.64	39.23**	41.69	28.28	43.80
Innovative Technologies	22.06	21.82	22.18	25.09	19.98	24.85	22.32	18.08	22.10	22.06
Assessments Linked to Standards	29.79	22.15	31.80	30.95	36.57	39.01	27.05	31.15	30.34	29.75
Assessments Used for Schl Acctblty	34.26	23.54	37.93*	35.05	42.94	41.20	30.95	39.60*	46.19	33.52
Parent Involvement	13.69	10.65	12.83	14.87	18.31	16.42	12.37	15.99	24.16	13.04
Restructuring School Day	16.89	13.62	12.61	18.07	26.95	7.63	16.76*	24.16*	24.08	16.44

*** = p < .001
** = p < .01
* = p < .05
a tests difference with preceding size category

MULTIVARIATE RESULTS

As with the district level results, we examined the effect of district size, poverty, and location in an "early reform" state simultaneously on the school level reports of progress. Controlling for whether the school is a middle or high school, separate models for each aspect of reform are run in order to provide a detailed picture of effects. The possibility of an interaction effect of district size and district poverty as well as the interaction of district size and school poverty is also examined.

Table 4 shows regression results for reported progress in each area of reform. As can be seen, larger district size is positively and significantly associated with reports of progress in eight of the twelve reform areas examined. District poverty often shows negative effects and in two cases ("content standards: science" and "content standards: history/social studies"), the associations are negative and significant. The only reform area which is positively and significantly associated with poverty is "restructuring the school day." Table 4 also shows that associations with location in an "early reform" state tend to be insignificant, with the exception of a negative association with "instructional materials." The lack of effects here is likely a consequence of the small number of schools in the sample in these states.

TABLE 4

REGRESSION RESULTS-EFFECTS OF DISTRICT SIZE, POVERTY,
DISTRICT SIZE*DISTRICT POVERTY ON REFORM PROGRESS
SCHOOL LEVEL RESULTS[a]

REFORM AREA	INTERCEPT	DISTSIZE	DISTPOV	EARLY	DISTSIZE*DISTPOV
Content Standards: Reading	.558	.074***	-.002	-.142+	-.003**
Content Standards: Math	.613	.068***	-.003+	-.157+	-.003***
Content Standards: Science	.447	.065***	-.004*	-.004	-.002*
Content Standards :Hist/Soc St	.382	.071***	-.003*	-.015	-.002*
Strategic Planning	.421	.055***	.001	-.180	.000
Professional Development	.413	.043**	.001	-.067	.001
Instructional Materials	.492	.008	-.003	-.173*	.000
Innovative Technologies	.210	.100	-.002	-.012	-.001+
Assessments Linked to Standards	.326	.029+	-.001	-.021	-.001
Assessments Used for Schl Acctblty	.323	.042***	.001	.105	.000
Parent Involvement	.152	.015	.000	.104	.001
Restructuring School Day	.136	.026*	.004**	.067	.000

*** = p < .001
** = p < .01
* = p < .05
+ = p < .10
[a] Results control for whether the school is a middle school or high school

Most importantly for the purposes of this chapter, the results show significant negative interactions of district size and district poverty on reports on the extent of use of content standards in all four content areas: reading, mathematics, science, and history/social studies.

The results of the district level and the school level analyses are remarkably similar. In larger districts, both district level and school level administrators report greater progress in a number of dimensions of standards-based reform than administrators in smaller districts. In addition, administrators in higher poverty districts, at both the district and the school level, report less progress than administrators in low-poverty districts. While district level results suggest the effects of size may be moderated in high-poverty districts, the school level results are stronger, showing the beneficial effects of larger size are significantly reduced when the district is also poor.[35]

The overall picture strongly suggested by independent reports at the district and the school level is that, at least during a time of reform, large district size has important advantages that facilitate change. We suspect these effects may be partly due to the greater capacity of larger districts to retrieve and utilize information and assistance from external resources as discussed below.

Networks of Information and Assistance

A likely reason larger districts have progressed farther and faster in reform than smaller districts is that they are better connected to helpful sources of information and assistance. Indeed, our findings suggest that, at least in the early days of reform, smaller districts were left to sort out standards-based reform more or less on their own. (See Figure 5.) For example, the largest districts (those with enrollments above 25,000) are about twice as likely as small districts (enrollments less than 2,500) to report finding "subject matter associations" very helpful in their reform efforts (fifty-two percent versus twenty-six percent).[36] They are also more than twice as likely to find education periodicals and publications helpful (fifty-six percent versus twenty-six percent). Similarly, nearly one-third (thirty-two percent) of the largest districts find "contacts with federal officials" very helpful compared to only nine percent of the small districts. Larger districts, of course, have the specialized staff available, referred to as "boundary-spanning" staff in the organizations' literature, which enables them to take fuller advantage of external resources.

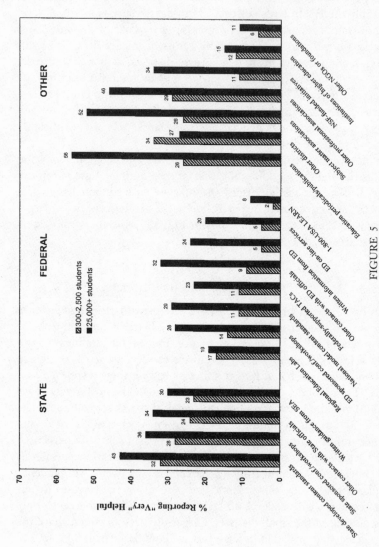

FIGURE 5

Percent of Respondent Reporting Sources of Information/Assistance "Very" Helpful by District Size

Summary and Implications

This study was concerned with the question of whether districts make a difference in advancing standards-based education reform. It addressed the question by examining the relationship between district characteristics and reports of reform progress at the district level and at the school level. District size and district poverty were of particular interest. The results showed that reports of progress varied systematically with district size and to a lesser extent with district poverty. Larger district size appears to contribute to reform progress in significant ways and the results are evident at both the district and school level. Districts and schools with higher levels of poverty (i.e., districts serving larger fractions of students from poverty backgrounds) appear to be making less progress than those with lower poverty levels (i.e., districts serving students from more affluent backgrounds). The results suggest further that the beneficial effects of large size are significantly lower when the district is also poor. According to reports at the district level, states assertively seeking reform also appear to promote reform progress in very significant ways.

The findings suggest that districts are important players in standards-based reform. Moreover, larger districts may not be part of the education problem; they may, in fact, be part of the solution. They appear to be better able to promote or facilitate reform than smaller districts, probably because they have greater specialized areas of expertise, such as dedicated units for assessment and professional development, slack resources available to direct to reform due to economies of scale, and better access to technical assistance. As a consequence, larger districts may be better structured as "learning organizations" than smaller districts. They have the capacity to link to various outside agencies and take advantage of information and assistance that these sources provide. At the same time, the findings draw attention to the special challenges of reform faced by small districts and call for targeted technical assistance to these districts or collaborative strategies that would allow these districts to pool resources and acquire specialized help when needed, and access to information so as not to be left behind. In addition, the findings show that aggressive state action has significant effects on progress at the district level and suggest similar effects at the school level.

The findings also have equity implications. Higher poverty districts appear to be lagging in some areas of reform, and poverty appears to diminish significantly the advantages of large district size. In short, the strategies that appear to work well in many districts do not appear to work as well in districts with large poverty populations. Until and unless we are able to identify ways to facilitate reform in these districts, one consequence of current efforts—to the extent that they improve student performance—might be increased performance disparities, even though districts of all types appear to be making reform headway.

APPENDIX

Reports of progress (part (c) of question 1) from the district survey

1. The Goals 2000: Educate America Act (Goals 2000) and the reauthorization of the Elementary and Secondary Education Act (ESEA) support comprehensive standards-based education reform . . . Report (a) the extent to which you UNDERSTAND what it means to implement each of the following components of reform in your district; (b) how much CHANGE will be required in your district to implement each component; and (c) your district's actual progress in IMPLEMENTING each component. (Circle your responses.)

c. **Progress Implementing**

	Have Not Begun	Little Progress	Some Progress	A Great Deal of Progress
Establishing high content and performance standards for all students.	1	2	3	4
Aligning curricula and instructional materials with standards.				
Developing or adopting assessments linked to standards.				
Linking school/district accountability to student performance.				
Building partnerships with parents/community.				

Reports of progress—from the school survey

1. **To what extent does your school use content standards to guide curriculum and instruction in:**

	Not at All	Small Extent	Moderate Extent	Great Extent
Reading/language arts	1	2	3	4
Mathematics				
Science				
History/social studies				

4. **Various strategies are being proposed and developed to support comprehensive reform. In Column A, indicate the extent to which the following strategies are being implemented in your school.** (1 = not at all, 2 = small extent, 3 = moderate extent, 4 = great extent)

1   2   3   4

a. A strategic plan for enabling all
students to achieve to high levels of
performance.
b. Professional development to
enable staff to teach the content
students are expected to learn.
c. Instructional material such as
textbooks that expose students to the
content they are expected to learn.
d. Innovative technologies such as
the Internet and telecommunications-
supported instruction that expose
students to the content they are
expected to learn.
e. Assessments that measure
performance against the content
students are expected to learn.
f. Assessments that are used for
school accountability and continuous
improvement.
g. Parent involvement activities that
help parents work with their children
to achieve to high levels of performance.
h. Restructuring the school day to
teach content in more depth.

Notes

1. This research was supported by a grant to Policy Studies Associates and subcontracted to The Urban Institute. The research reported here does not necessarily represent the views of The Urban Institute, Policy Studies Associates, or the United States Department of Education.

2. Kenneth Travers and Ian Westbury, *The IEA Study of Mathematics I: Analysis of Mathematics Curricula* (New York: Pergamon, 1989).

3. Richard Elmore, "The politics of education reform," *Issues in Science and Technology* 14 (1997), pp. 41-49.

4. James Guthrie, "Organizational scale and school success," *Educational Evaluation and Policy Analysis* 1 (1979), p. 34.

5. In the last fifty years, school district consolidation has resulted in a dramatic decrease in the number of school districts—from 101,382 in 1945 to 14,772 in 1995, a decline of eighty-five percent—and a concomitant increase in district size. Indeed, approximately thirty percent of United States students now attend schools in districts with more than 25,000 students.

6. E.g., Eric Hanushek, "Outcomes, costs, and incentives in schools" in Eric Hanushek and Dale Jorgenson, eds., *Improving America's Schools: The Role of Incentives* (Washington, DC: National Academy Press, 1996).

7. Jane Hannaway and Lee Sproull, "Who's running the show: Coordination and control in educational organizations," *Administrator's Notebook* 27 (1979), p. 9; Jane Hannaway, *Managers Managing: The Workings of an Administrative System* (New York: Oxford University Press, 1989).

8. Richard Elmore and Susan Fuhrman, "The national interest and the federal role in education," *Publius* 20 (1990), pp. 149-163; James Spillane, "Districts matter: Local

educational authorities and state instructional policy," *Educational Policy* 10 (1996); Michael Kirst, "Recent research on intergovernmental relations in education policy," *Educational Researcher* 24 (1995), pp. 18-22; Thomas Corcoran and Margaret Goertz, "Instructional capacity and high performance schools," *Educational Researcher* 24 (1995), pp. 27-31; David Cohen and James Spillane, "Policy and practice: The relation between governance and instruction," *Review of Research in Education* 18 (1992), pp. 3-49; Nancy Jennings and James Spillane, "State reform and local capacity: Encouraging ambitious instruction for all and local decision making," *Journal of Education Policy* 11 (1996), pp. 465-482; James Spillane, "A cognitive perspective on the LEA's role in implementing instructional policy: Accounting for local variability," *Educational Administration Quarterly* 34 (1998).

9. Elmore and Fuhrman, "The national interest and the federal role in education."

10. Jane Hannaway with Kristi Kimball, *Reports on Reform from the Field: District and State Survey Results* (Washington, DC: The Urban Institute, 1997).

11. United States Department of Education, *Final Report: Fast Response Public School Survey on Education Reform* (Washington, DC: Author, 1997).

12. A sizable fraction of the student population also attends schools in small districts. Districts, for example, with less than 2,500 students account for almost seventy-five percent of the districts in the United States and twenty percent of the student population (National Center for Educational Statistics, *Digest of Educational Statistics*, 1995).

13. Herbert Walberg and William Fowler, "Expenditure and size efficiencies of public school districts," *Educational Researcher* 16 (1987), pp. 5-13.

14. E.g., Cyril Northcote Parkinson, *Parkinson's Law and Other Studies of Administration* (Boston: Houghton Mifflin, 1957).

15. Peter Blau, "A formal theory of differentiation in organizations," *American Sociological Review* 35 (1970), pp. 201-218.

16. For a review, see W. Richard Scott, *Organizations: Rational, Natural, and Open Systems* (Englewood Cliffs, NJ: Prentice-Hall, 1992).

17. Charles Bidwell and D. John Kasarda, "School district organization and student achievement," *American Sociological Review* 40 (1979), pp. 55-70; Lawrence Kenny, "Economics of scale in schooling," *Economics of Education Review* 2 (1982), pp. 1-24; Richard Butler and David Monk, "The cost of public schooling in New York State," *Journal of Human Resources* 20 (1985), pp. 361-380; Walberg and Fowler, "Expenditure and size efficiencies of public school districts."

18. Noah Friedkin and Juan Necochea, "School system size and performance: A contingency perspective," *Educational Evaluation and Policy Analysis* 10 (1988), pp. 237-249.

19. Jane Hannaway and Joan Talbert, "Bringing context into effective schools research: Urban-suburban differences," *Educational Administration Quarterly* 29 (1993), pp. 164-186.

20. Jane Hannaway, "Political pressure and decentralization in institutional organizations: The case of school districts," *Sociology of Education* 66 (1993), pp. 147-163.

21. Richard Cyert and James March, *A Behavioral Theory of the Firm* (Englewood Cliffs, NJ: Prentice-Hall, 1963).

22. The sampling frame was restricted to those districts with at least 300 students resulting in a universe of 11,143 districts.

23. The "early reform" states, identified by a panel of national experts as states moving ahead with systemic efforts to raise academic standards, are Kentucky, Oregon, and Maryland.

24. Appropriate corrections were made to standard errors in the analysis to take into account the sampling design.

25. Seven percent were completed by Title I or Federal Program Coordinators and the remainder were completed by principals (2.7 percent), generally in small districts, or were "missing values."

26. Weights were used in the analyses to correct for biases introduced by the sampling plan and standard errors were corrected accordingly.

27. Hannaway with Kimball, *Reports on Reform from the Field*.

28. Goals 2000: Educate America Act was passed in 1994. In 1995, over $400 million was awarded to states, and states were obligated to pass ninety percent along to school districts. The amount of Goals 2000 funding and the precise purposes to which this funding was put varies from district to district.

29. For creating these figures, districts were grouped into the following poverty categories based on the census data: low poverty (< 5 percent of children five to seventeen years in poverty), moderate poverty (5-25 percent of children in poverty), and high-poverty (≥ 25 percent of children in poverty).

30. Poverty and district size (log) are entered in the regression as continuous variables. We standardize each of these variables by subtracting its respective mean so that the intercepts are estimates for districts with mean poverty and mean district size for the total sample. "Early reform" status and "Goals 2000 sub-grantee" are dummy variables.

31. Karl Weick, "Educational organizations as loosely coupled systems," *Administrative Science Quarterly* 21 (1976), pp. 1-19; James March and Johannes Olsen, eds., *Ambiguity and Choice in Organizations* (Bergen, Norway: Universitetsfarlaget, 1976); Hannaway and Sproull, "Who's running the show."

32. The following are the correlations between (log) district size and the various aspects of reform progress reported at the school level: reading/language arts content standards (.21***), mathematics content standards (.19***), science content standards (.16***), history/social science content standards (.19***), strategic planning (.19***), professional development (.15***), instructional materials (.04), innovative technologies (-.00), assessments for student performance (.10***), assessments for school accountability (.13***), and parent involvement (.08**) . [***< .0001; **< .001]

33. The only correlations between poverty and the measures of reported progress that were significant at < .05 were: strategic planning (.06*) and instructional materials (-.06*).

34. The only correlations between being in an "early reform" state and measures of reported progress that were significant at < .05 were: instructional materials (-.07*), assessments for school accountability (.06*), and parent involvement (.08*).

35. These same results hold when we substitute school level measures of poverty rather than district level measures.

36. These reports are based on the responses of districts that had contact with these various sources of assistance.

CHAPTER VII

The District Role in State Assessment Policy: An Exploratory Study[1]

JANET C. FAIRMAN AND WILLIAM A. FIRESTONE

There has been relatively little exploration into the role of the district in the implementation of centrally-mandated reforms, and what there is, has been somewhat mixed.[2] The district is important for the implementation of state standards because it is the legal entity responsible for delivering education. Yet districts are accountable not only to the state but also to the local community which may have interests different from the state. Moreover, given past research on teacher autonomy in the classroom,[3] the impact of the district may be limited.

In this chapter, we report on one study that examined the district's role in mediating the effects of state standards and assessments on teaching practice. We conclude that:

1. State standards (and related assessments) can influence districts to attend to certain aspects of content and pedagogy when supported by other policies (e.g., professional development, district size, and governance); and

2. Where districts attend to state standards, they can influence the content of instruction. They are less successful to date in influencing pedagogy. Districts have been able to get teachers to adopt isolated activities and strategies. With additional support and professional development, such activities could lead toward more far reaching change in teachers' basic instructional approaches.

Movement toward more standards-based instruction requires both will and capacity on the part of individuals and organizations. As the

Janet Fairman conducts research in mathematics and science education at the elementary level through Rutgers University. William Firestone is a Professor; Chair of the Department of Educational Theory, Policy, and Administration; and Director of the Center for Educational Policy Analysis, all in the Graduate School of Education at Rutgers University.

data presented here suggests, districts vary greatly on these two dimensions and in their approaches to developing teachers' will and capacity to acquire new knowledge and skills. State policies can support and encourage the considerable effort needed by districts and teachers to align curricula and instruction with state and national standards.

This study took place within the context of a larger exploration of how standards and state assessment policy affect the teaching of middle school mathematics. After reviewing current thinking about reform-by-assessment, we describe the study's research methods. Then we describe the policy approaches in the two states studied (Maine and Maryland), how districts mediated state policies, and the efforts teachers made to respond to new state standards and assessments.

Standards and Assessment

Many reformers have changed their opinions about the contribution of state testing policies to instructional reform. Only a few years ago, minimum competency tests—especially the high-stakes versions—were decried for dumbing down the curriculum, deskilling teachers, pushing students out of school, and generally sowing fear and anxiety among both students and educators.[4] These critiques contributed to the rise of performance based assessment in state testing. These new assessments are supposed to offer a technology for assessing higher order skills and deeper understanding of content areas. They do so by requiring students to construct responses rather than respond to multiple-choice items.[5] Expectations for performance based assessment are quite high. As a part of the standards movement more generally,[6] assessment reform is seen as a likely intervention to break the established pattern of American instruction. This pattern features teacher-led recitation where students, working alone, are expected to remember and reproduce a wide range of specific facts (and in mathematics, discrete operations), but not to think deeply or creatively about them.

The last decade has seen several challenges to the main paradigm of teaching. At the macro level, the standards movement seeks to orchestrate a variety of policy tools, including assessment, to promote teaching more rigorous content to all children.[7] One leader in the effort to promote more demanding standards is the National Council of Teachers of Mathematics (NCTM) whose standards have been emulated in other subject areas. Central to these standards is the concept of "mathematical power," a notion based on the recognition of mathematics as more than a collection of concepts and skills to be mastered. Students need to calculate accurately, but they also need to be able to hypothesize, abstract mathematical properties, explain their reasoning, and validate their assertions about mathematics.[8]

Insight into teaching methods that can promote a more thoughtful approach to mathematics comes from the Third International Mathematics and Science Study (TIMSS) videotape study, which compared the practices of eighty-one eighth grade teachers in the United States with fifty in Japan and 100 in Germany.[9] American mathematics lessons began with an acquisition phase where teachers demonstrated how to solve a sample problem and clarified the procedures students should follow on their own. This was followed by an application phase where students practiced the procedures they had been taught.

In Japan, mathematics lessons had only one or two problems. Teachers did not tell students how to solve problems first. Instead, students worked on problems in teams and then explained their solutions to the class. Teachers sometimes suggested alternative approaches, and they summarized the mathematical principles behind these methods. Generally, Japanese classrooms were more conceptual and pushed students to invent procedures. Stigler and Hiebert[10] summarize these differences on a number of dimensions. For instance, they note that American teachers have their children practice mathematical procedures almost exclusively while their Japanese counterparts give children much more opportunity to apply and even invent procedures.

While the broad differences between standards-based and conventional teaching are clear, observers who analyze how policies encourage instructional change point out that teachers do not revise their practice all at once. Cohen and Ball[11] describe a number of teachers in the process of changing their teaching. Several had adopted new materials aligned with the reforms but used them in a drill-based manner more congruent with earlier direct instruction models than what was intended by the standards in question. More recent studies suggest that a variety of standards-based and restructuring reforms are relatively successful at changing the kinds of assignments teachers use, or content of lessons (i.e., the tasks given students, the materials used, and sometimes even the intended products). However, these reforms are less successful in modifying how teachers conduct lessons in terms of introducing the topic, asking questions, offering feedback, and fostering student discourse about concepts.[12]

Thus the evidence to date suggests that most teachers incorporate only some aspects of the standards into their practice and that the changes they make typically center on the content of lessons more than on the instructional strategies or goals for student learning.

Methods

Data reported here come from a qualitative study of administrative and teacher responses to testing policies in states that recently adopted performance based middle school assessments. We chose Maryland and Maine as these two states both had mathematics assessments for eighth grade and they represented contrasting approaches in testing policy: Maryland linked formal sanctions to test performance while Maine did not. The Maryland School Performance Assessment Program (MSPAP) was somewhat more mature than the Maine Educational Assessment (MEA) and that state had a longer history of mandated state assessment. We observed teachers in the fifth year of administration of the MSPAP (1995-96) and in the first year that the MEA had gone to a fully open-ended format.

Since the main purpose of this study was to examine how state policies were locally interpreted, we chose an embedded case study design that allowed us to look at teachers within districts within states.[13] We studied two middle schools from each of two districts in Maryland and a total of six middle schools or junior high schools from three Maine districts (five districts, ten schools in all). District selection allowed for comparison between low/middle income and rural/suburban districts.

During the first field visit, interviews were conducted with seventeen district administrators, eleven principals, one board member from each of the five districts, and twenty-four department heads for mathematics and language arts. In two subsequent field visits, twenty-five mathematics teachers were observed teaching and interviewed each time on topics which included: teachers' goals for the lesson, district policies and instructional practices, teachers' views of state standards and assessments, teachers' professional development experiences, and teachers' beliefs about mathematics and student learning.

To examine the kinds of activities teachers used and the way teachers implemented those activities, we coded the ninety-one classroom observations on two dimensions of mathematics teaching that came from the TIMSS video study and that clearly separated Japanese from American teaching practice. The first dimension was whether students practiced procedures they had been taught or applied procedures to new situations; the second dimension was whether teachers described procedures to students or developed mathematical concepts. Stigler and Hiebert's[14] discussion of these two dimensions suggests that the first item of each pair represents conventional American teaching, while the second item of each pair more closely approximates standards-based teaching. We divided some lessons into segments if the teacher's instructional style diverged significantly or if student activities were so different that the segments had to be coded separately. As a result, we coded ninety-nine separate lesson segments.[15]

Throughout this chapter, we refer to will and capacity both at the organizational and individual levels. Districts are most likely to attend to state policy directives when they have both the *will* and *capacity* to do so and likewise at the level of classroom teachers.[16] Will refers to the motivational dimension of implementation. Capacity is a more ambiguous concept. As people consider the amount of learning required to implement deep changes in instruction, this concept is receiving more attention in the research literature.[17] Broadly speaking, capacity denotes knowledge, personnel, money, or other materials and resources necessary to carry out decisions.[18] Spillane and Thompson[19] equate district capacity with three types of "capital" that are important for instructional reform: human capital (which includes knowledge and dispositions of people), social capital (the relations among individuals within a group or between a group and the outside world including both networks and norms or habits of trust and collaboration), and financial capital (that which buys staffing, time, and materials). These constructs provide a useful way for understanding the conditions under which new educational goals are communicated and assimilation or change takes place.

State Policy

The state typically communicates its will to reform educational goals through new standards, assessments, and/or teacher certification requirements. State policies can influence district will to respond through the mobilization of stakes or sanctions, including both public comparisons and formal sanctions for educators.[20] Much attention has been given to the stakes—i.e., rewards or punishment that are linked to assessment.[21] Most analysts of state policy assume that changing incentives can influence district will to respond, and there is evidence that high stakes can shape district will. However, the use of high stakes as a state policy approach is often expected to work against standards-based teaching, in part, by focusing educators' efforts on test performance over depth of student learning.[22] Comparisons can influence educators by causing a personal sense of embarrassment. Smith[23] sees this as a major motivator for teaching to the test.

The state helps to build capacity for reform at the local level by providing materials and new knowledge either directly or indirectly to districts and teachers by fostering the growth of consortia, teacher networks, or summer institutes for ongoing teacher professional development. Some states involve teachers in developing and scoring assessment tasks. These types of professional development policy contribute to the human and social capital of educators by providing opportunities for district supervisors and teachers to learn more about new content and instructional approaches, and by providing opportunities for collaboration among educators across districts.[24] State educational finance decisions contribute to the financial capital districts need to purchase new textbooks, offer high quality inservice programs, or to develop district assessment programs aligned with state standards.

Generally, Maryland districts (Chesapeake and Frontier) responded to state tests more directly than did Maine districts. Differences in the policy approaches of the two states only partly explain these differences. Differences in district will and capacity mediated the impact of the state policies. Here we discuss the policy approaches both states used to influence districts.

STATE POLICY AND DISTRICT WILL

With regard to testing stakes, district test scores were published in both states. Yet embarrassment from comparison of district performance did not create the stress suggested by Smith.[25] When asked what repercussions stemmed from test scores, administrators referred to "possible embarrassment." More significant than embarrassment is the threat of school "reconstitution" that exists in Maryland but not in Maine. Reconstitution is a form of state intervention that may include removing teachers and the principal. Schools where performance is low and declining on a set of indicators that features, but is not limited to, MSPAP scores are eligible for reconstitution. Before the state reconstitutes a school, the district has an opportunity to remediate it.

Reconstitution in Maryland had more impact on district performance than did public comparison, but its effect alone was still limited. That threat seemed remote to our respondents. By 1997, fifty-two Maryland schools had been declared eligible for reconstitution, fifty of them in Baltimore City. Chesapeake's test scores were in the middle quintile of the state's distribution, and Frontier's were in the fourth. Many schools would have to be reconstituted before the state would get to any schools in this study. Thus the policy for school reconstitution represented a somewhat abstract threat to the schools we visited, even for the poor, rural district, and had only a modest influence on district will to focus on the state's standards.

In addition to testing stakes, other state mandates can be used to increase the accountability of districts. In Maryland, the state required each school to create a School Improvement Team (SIT), comprised of teachers, administrators, board members, and parents. The team was obligated to submit an improvement plan each year, addressing specific changes in curricula or instruction to improve students' test scores. These documents were read by the superintendents of the two Maryland districts we studied and forwarded to the state educational agency. In Frontier, principals stated that the superintendent used the school improvement plans in his evaluation of principals. The state policy requiring SITs appeared to be an important mechanism to increase district accountability by pushing districts to attend to state educational goals and to move toward change. Maine had no such requirement.

In general, the political culture of Maryland differs from Maine[26] in that Maryland traditionally has had a longer history of state policies governing education.[27] Such policies include: the state assessments, high school graduation requirements, school improvement plans, and reconstitution of school systems failing to perform well on state tests. This level of state involvement in local education did not exist in Maine, nor would it likely be tolerated given the persistent desire for local control, which characterizes the political culture of that state.

THE ASSESSMENTS

Maine and Maryland used different approaches to assessment to communicate their educational goals and standards. In general, more publications and data were produced by the state educational agency in Maryland to communicate the goals, structure, and test results of the MSPAP than were published in Maine for the MEA. These included sample test items and scoring guides, and detailed test performance data for each tested grade by district. The number of people working in the assessment division of the state educational agency to communicate with districts and the public in Maryland was greater by far, and district administrators in Maryland spoke of more frequent communication with state assessment people.

In both states, the performance assessments were developed under the strong influence of the NCTM standards.[28] For instance, both assessments de-emphasize pure computation by allowing students to use calculators on at least parts of the test. Both tests include problems in probability, statistics, and geometry—topics for which NCTM recommends greater attention. On both tests, students must show their mathematical work and explain their reasoning to obtain the highest scores on a rubric system.[29] Yet careful examination of how well these assessments align with the NCTM standards[30] shows a somewhat mixed picture. There are important differences in the structure of the tests that make Maryland's a somewhat better model.[31] The MEA uses shorter problems that focus on mathematics (with a heavier emphasis on calculation), while MSPAP problems tend to be longer, or to include linked parts, and may be scored for two or more subject areas such as mathematics and science.

An older testing program in Maryland, the Maryland Functional Tests, confused the state's message to educators about what types of skills and knowledge students would need in the twenty-first century. The older test represents a more basic skills definition of standards and is now given one year before the eighth grade MSPAP. It creates considerable dissonance for teachers who have to figure out how to prepare students to pass both tests.[32] In this regard, the articulation of state educational goals and standards was more clearly expressed by Maine's testing program.

STATE POLICY AND CAPACITY BUILDING

In both states, the effort to build educators' human capital centered on the performance assessments themselves. State assessment developers hoped that by administering the tests and preparing students for the tests, teachers would understand what content and skills to emphasize. The experience of writing tasks or scoring them might also build teachers' knowledge of the standards. Yet only a handful of the twenty-four teachers in our study had ever administered the test, and only one teacher had helped to score tasks for a pilot test in Maryland. Thus important opportunities for developing teacher knowledge of the tests and standards were not available to most teachers in our study.

Both states took advantage of federal programs, most notably the Eisenhower program, to support teachers' professional development. Teachers in both states spoke of participating in these programs. In addition, Maryland created the Maryland Assessment Consortium (MAC) which provided workshops to help teachers develop instructional approaches better aligned with the conception of challenging standards represented in the MSPAP. However, when compared to the imaginative, aggressive approaches to professional development used in a few other states,[33] considerably more could have been done.

How districts are organized in terms of size and governance can be an important factor influencing the power of the state to influence district will and may determine the level of response from district personnel. Both recent restructuring advocates[34] and early twentieth century, good government progressives[35] share the view that larger units are less responsive to public pressures, although the former group objects to this isolation while the latter group welcomed it. Rural communities have fought district consolidation, viewing schools as instruments for maintaining communities and a valued way of life.[36] This work suggests that smaller, more responsive districts may not support new visions of teaching and achievement that come from professional reformers. More recent work suggests that large size is not necessarily an impediment to implementing standards-based reform; it can actually enhance districts' capacity to respond.[37]

The form of district governance is also debated. One view is that small governmental units and ward- or town-based elections are presumed to increase sensitivity to local interests and to undermine the influence of professionals committed to efficiency and a more "progressive" understanding of education. Another view holds that larger units and at-large elections were supposed to increase the influence of professionals.[38] So-called good government progressives argued through the late 1950s that bigger is better.[39] Large organizations were supposed to promote economies of scale and large districts could offer more differentiation in programs and employ more specialists to supervise teachers.[40] These views contributed to disputes about school and district consolidation through the 1970s.[41]

In Maine and Maryland, districts differ substantially in their size, governance, and linkage to the state. The two states have very different district sizes. While Maine has about one-fourth the total population of Maryland (1.2 million versus 4.8 million), it has almost eight times as many entities for governing its schools. Maryland only has twenty-four districts (twenty-three county districts plus Baltimore City), serving about 33,000 students each. By one way of figuring, Maine has 188 entities (including independent cities, community school districts, supervisory unions, School Administrative Districts, and special districts), with an average of about 1,200 students each. Looked at another way, Maine has 264 K-12 governing units alone.

Clearly, it is more cumbersome for state educational agency staff to communicate or meet with district administrators in Maine than in Maryland. While the Maryland State Department of Education organized job-alike meetings throughout the year for district personnel to meet with their counterparts at the state level, district administrators in Maine said they had little contact with Maine assessment staff and didn't know whom they would call if they wanted guidance.

The two Maryland districts we studied were considerably smaller than most but they were still almost six times larger than the three Maine districts (see Table 1). One correlate of these size differences was in central office staff. Including curriculum directors, subject matter specialists, and testing directors, the Maryland districts had many more curriculum specialists than those in Maine (about twelve people compared to one). In proportion to enrollment size, the Maryland districts had, on average, one curriculum staff person for every 1,063 students while the Maine districts had one person for all 2,250 students (on average) in the district. Thus a larger and more specialized district staff in Maryland provided more human capital to attend to testing, curriculum revision, supervision of teachers, provision of teacher professional development, and communication with the public. District size also influenced social capital as the Maryland districts organized events that strengthened internal networks for teachers: schoolwide inservice days and subject based inservice days. By contrast, two of the three districts in Maine offered no system-wide inservice at all.

TABLE 1
District Configuration

District	Enrollment	Curriculum Staff	Governance
Factory Town	1,500	0.5	3 towns each have separate school boards. One central office for all 3.
Farm Town	2,250	1	15 member board with members elected by town.
River City	3,000	1	7 member board: 4 elected by ward, 3 at-large.
Frontier	11,250	10	5 member board elected at-large.
Chesapeake	14,250	14	5 member board appointed by Governor.

The two states also differed in how governance arrangements linked districts to their communities. School boards in Maine were more closely linked to their constituencies than were school boards in Maryland if only because they have more board members for smaller communities. Moreover, the Maine boards were linked to specific towns or wards within their communities because members were elected from specific areas. As a supervisory union, Factory Town was part of the unit with the tightest linkages to particular territories within the area served. Its central office provided administrative services to three towns, each with its own board of education. Farm Town had only one school board for several towns. However, that board had fifteen members who were elected by town with more members from the larger towns. The two at-large members could vote only on matters pertaining to the high school. This voting arrangement guaranteed almost as much sensitivity to sectional interests as in Factory Town. By contrast, River City had a seven member board with three elected at-large and four elected from specific wards, encouraging a more districtwide orientation. All Maryland districts' board members represented the whole county, and Chesapeake's were appointed, not elected, reducing sensitivity to specific interests.

District configurations in Maryland provided relative insulation from the local community while it increased sensitivity to the state. As a result, Maryland districts generally had greater will and capacity to respond to state educational goals than did Maine districts. Variation in district responses to state educational reform policies and their sensitivity to local interests are discussed in the next section.

District Mediation of State and Local Interests

District will to move in the direction specified by state standards is often understood as a problem of how well individual district administrators understand and agree with policy goals. McLaughlin[42] reviews cases where successful implementation can be explained in part by the fit between key decision makers' interests and the intent of the policy. Similarly, Firestone[43] suggests that when the key decision makers in a district have a propensity to act in a certain direction and see the policy as contributing to their own goals, they will implement it aggressively. Rosenblum and Louis[44] found that superintendent support was a key predictor of successful implementation of districtwide innovations, and Spillane's[45] more recent work has highlighted the importance of a variety of district level factors. For example, central office staff have different knowledge and sentiments about state reforms.[46] When combined with the literature reviewed earlier, this work suggests that district will to respond to state policy goals depends on some mix of the nature of those policies (such as stakes or other accountability tools), the size and governance structure of the district, and the values of individual administrators.

While Chesapeake and Frontier districts generally had higher will and capacity (i.e., larger central staff with more subject specialists) than did the Maine districts, agreement with and understanding of the state's standards and performance assessment was uneven. In Frontier, there was a moderate level of will to comply with the state's mandate as a legal requirement. One administrator said, "Together, the state curriculum framework and the MSPAP are the *bible* of what we have to teach" (emphasis in original). One of the superintendent's main goals was to get the district's test scores into the "top twenty-five percent in the state." The superintendent did not wholly endorse the instructional goals behind the MSPAP and preferred the more basic skills view of achievement that is reflected in the state's Functional Tests. Yet he believed there was a strong connection between the perception that the district was effective when students scored well on state tests and funding from the county commissioners. Therefore, he pressured staff to raise scores on all tests and staff worked with teachers to align curricula with state standards and the two assessment programs. Interviews in this district revealed a low level of interest in assessment among parents and board members. The superintendent said this community was most interested in the athletics program.

Similarly, Chesapeake administrators felt strongly compelled to comply with state directives to implement the standards and attend to the MSPAP. The superintendent said that the MSPAP was the "yardstick we are using to measure success," and that "assessment is driving what we do." Clearly, the monthly meetings of superintendents, testing coordinators, and subject specialists between district and state levels was an important factor, helping to build the necessary will to respond to state mandates. Yet there was also a concern by district administrators to help students score well so funding levels and public support would not be jeopardized. Test scores were higher in this district so administrators were not as concerned about revising curricula or teaching practice.

Frontier and Chesapeake administrators made an effort to build teachers' capacity (human and social capital) by organizing staff development centered on conducting and scoring MSPAP-like activities. Teachers met districtwide by subject groups, and sometimes made up their own activities. They used materials from the Maryland Assessment Consortium and a large volume of tasks was available as a resource for teachers. The districts required teachers to conduct the activities a few times during the year. While Chesapeake subject supervisors and teacher leaders delivered most of the inservice, Frontier most often relied on external experts from local universities or the state educational agency. Chesapeake staff had a more sophisticated understanding of the state standards and focused more effort on improving instructional strategies than did Frontier administrators. They organized interdisciplinary activities as well as a districtwide science fair.

By contrast, the Maine districts had generally low will to respond to the state standards and, in particular, state assessment. They also had lower capacity to help teachers learn more about the standards and new instructional strategies. In these small districts, leadership came sometimes from a principal (Farm Town), or a curriculum coordinator (Farm Town and Factory Town), who provided support to teachers seeking professional development on their own and permission to revise curricula or instruction. Administrators in these small districts were most concerned with maintaining adequate funding levels for educational programs and passing bond issues to replace aging facilities.

In Factory Town, there was little concern about state tests or leadership for change. The superintendent did not even open the MEA results until our field visit. The middle school principal said categorically, "I *will* not teach to the test." This district made some curricular accommodations to the test, but preferred to keep things as they were. The superintendent in this supervisory union said his main priority was dealing with aging facilities and responding to the particular interests of his three school boards.

Farm Town's administrators were only moderately concerned with the MEA scores. The school board worried about the high school's low scores but the district had no plan for improving curriculum, instruction, or professional development. The primary leadership for change came from a Title I coordinator who helped teachers in the lower grades learn new instructional strategies in language arts. She also provided information about the MEA and scoring rubrics to other teachers in the district. In this district, teachers were on their own to figure out what the standards meant. A few teachers made significant efforts to increase their knowledge and skills and were encouraged by the district to share their ideas with other teachers in the district.

River City was somewhat more concerned about state standards and reforming instructional practices than the other two Maine districts. The district had just hired a new curriculum coordinator who focused on getting teachers to develop standards or learning outcomes locally, which corresponded with the NCTM standards. She tried to move the district in this direction in anticipation of the state's standards and assessment. This administrator also offered some subject-specific professional development for teachers. Yet teachers in this district and others in Maine commented that district inservice focused on general topics or topics not related to instruction (e.g., CPR or blood borne pathogens) and was not very useful to them. River City parents were more concerned about a recent effort to introduce the middle school philosophy in one school and to return to the practice of tracking students in mathematics and focusing on basic skills than about state test scores.

Clearly, the level of will and capacity to respond to the state reform policies was higher in the Maryland districts than in the Maine districts but was tempered by the individual views and knowledge of district staff and sensitivity to local concerns and priorities. The Maryland districts organized more staff development opportunities for teachers, focusing much of the inservice on state assessment. Yet inservice generally did not go very deep into the mathematical ideas or topics around which the MSPAP-like activities were created. The Maryland districts also provided teachers with more time to plan lessons or to collaborate with peers on developing interdisciplinary activities by allowing time for ten planning periods per week as opposed to only one (Farm Town) or five periods per week in the Maine districts.

Districts and Teachers

To shift from conventional modes of practice to the more challenging paradigm implied by state educational reform policies and national standards, teachers must be both willing and able to revise habitual ways of delivering instruction. Like district will, individual will can also be viewed as a fit between one's own views of teaching and learning and one's understanding of the proposed reform goals. The will to develop or revise individual knowledge and skills may also be interpreted as professional commitment.[47]

Yet the will to change instructional practice presupposes that teachers understand (to some degree) the nature of the change being sought by educational policies. Thus will and capacity can overlap or interact. Much recent attention has been given to clarifying the different kinds of knowledge (human capital) which teachers require to enact the reform goals. A recurring concern is the lack of deep and well-integrated understanding of subject content and pedagogy that teachers would need to implement the reform paradigm.[48]

While demands on teachers are growing, the question is whether districts can help develop the will and capacity of teachers to promote substantial change in practice. Some recent studies suggest that districts can make a useful contribution.[49] More cognitively oriented researchers believe that when teachers are introduced to more specialized knowledge and reflect on how to use new instructional approaches after trying them in the classroom, these teachers revise conceptions about their discipline and student learning and want to use these new approaches. Several studies support this hypothesis.[50]

Conventional inservice or workshop training is usually inadequate to help teachers develop the discipline-based, conceptual understanding that would enable them to implement the curricular and instructional reforms envisioned in the NCTM standards.[51] To significantly influence practice, teachers' learning experiences must challenge their pre-existing views of mathematics and student learning and engage them in the kinds of authentic, nonroutine problem solving that is envisioned for students.[52] Unfortunately, all but the highest capacity districts may have difficulty mobilizing the necessary resources to promote deeper and sustained teacher learning.[53]

Considerable literature suggests a cautious view of the district's influence on teacher practice. This includes an older literature that emphasizes teachers' autonomy from higher levels of formal authority.[54] This research, and more recent work, suggest that teachers are impervious to many of the formal sanctions available to districts and that teachers' beliefs and will may not be amenable to policy influences.[55]

To explore these issues, we now describe variations in teaching practice within and across districts. While state and district policies influenced teachers' choice of content, they had less influence on pedagogy. We suggest that teachers' own beliefs about mathematics and student learning were a more important factor shaping teachers' choice of instructional strategies and goals for mathematics lessons.

VARIATION IN TEACHING PRACTICE

We observed a fair amount of experimentation and changing practice among some teachers in all five districts. In Maryland, this experimentation was influenced by state assessment policy reinforced by district activity. Maryland's high capacity districts promoted curriculum alignment and greater use of MSPAP practice problems. In Maine, revised practice reflected teacher initiative more than state or district direction. While these instances of change were important, they generally did not translate into changes in the basic teaching approach.

For instance, we grouped the districts into three levels of capacity. The two Maryland districts had the highest, Farm Town and Factory Town had the lowest, and River City was in between. When we coded classroom observations on the TIMSS video study dimensions, over three-fifths of the mathematics teachers were observed doing practice activities without application in all three sets of districts. There was also no pattern with regard to telling students how to do procedures versus developing an understanding of them. Most teachers in the highest and lowest capacity districts (ten of eleven in the former and seven of eight in the latter) only told students how to do procedures. The River City teachers were split evenly with three only telling and three developing procedures.

Maryland teachers responded to state and district pressure to prepare students for the MSPAP by adding more test practice activities to their conventional practice. Teachers periodically conducted larger, multi-step problems taken from MSPAP release items or MAC materials. Some teachers conducted these activities at the end of a unit on a given mathematics topic in order to provide opportunities for students to apply factual or procedural knowledge. Other teachers introduced the activity explicitly as test practice and emphasized how students should format their written work to obtain the maximum number of points using the MSPAP scoring rubric. Although MSPAP-like activities often involved more hands-on or group work than conventional lessons, teachers rarely used these activities as a vehicle to move beyond computational procedures and a step-by-step approach. There was more variation in instructional approach in Frontier, due to the use of MSPAP-like activities, than there was in Chesapeake. Still, instruction in both districts was predominantly conventional.

In Maine, some teachers also experimented with larger, more open-ended problems that required students to explain their reasoning and to apply knowledge in new situations. However, these activities were conducted by teachers on their own initiative without formal pressure from district or school administrators. Teachers sometimes used MEA release items but more often found inspiration from professional development they had obtained outside the district or from professional mathematics teacher publications (e.g., NCTM standards and journals). Overall, mathematics instruction was quite conventional in River City and in Factory Town and more diverse in Farm Town. Lessons observed in Farm Town most closely approximated a standards-based approach than lessons in any other district.

The larger problems which Maine and Maryland teachers conducted with students involved mathematics topics and skills emphasized by the state performance assessments, such as geometry, probability and statistics, discrete mathematics, and graphing, and were sometimes interdisciplinary in content. Teachers in both states indicated they were giving more attention to these topics in their mathematics lessons as a result of the state assessments. While there was clearly an effort by teachers to broaden the range of content taught, there was less effort to revise instructional strategies, the nature of students' mathematical work, and goals for student learning.

While more test-related activity was observed in the higher capacity Maryland districts, more proficient use of a standards-based approach to instruction was observed in some Maine lessons. Six teachers, including three from the low capacity Farm Town district, appeared to have made a greater shift in their pedagogical views and instructional approach than the other teachers. These teachers used a wider range of instructional strategies, conducted activities involving more complex problem solving, and focused their lessons on patterns, relationships, or concepts more routinely than did the other teachers. For example, one River City teacher used a Marilyn Burns activity where students worked in teams to use six different methods of finding the area of a circle. Students were asked to reflect on the methods and to invent a new method, leading them to better understand that the area of a circle equals pi r^2. A Farm Town teacher had student teams figure out the dimensions of a fish tank in order to hold a given volume of water. Students had to reason about what algorithms to use to solve the problem.

The most expert teacher we saw was in Farm Town. Ms. Davis, along with her seventh grade team, had reorganized the curriculum around thematic units using an interdisciplinary approach. This team of teachers seldom used textbooks anymore and based their decisions about what topics and skills to teach on the NCTM standards. In a lesson on theoretical and experimental probability, Ms. Davis' students explored the idea of fairness through a dice game and then invented their own dice games, explaining why the games were fair. Ms. Davis consistently urged students to explain their solution methods verbally and in writing, and to explore different approaches to problem solving during her lessons. District and school administrators encouraged Ms. Davis' and her team's effort to learn new instructional approaches and they provided financial support for professional development activities outside the district. However, the impetus to acquire new knowledge and to revise practice came from the teachers' own initiative and was done on their own time.

TEACHER WILL AND CAPACITY

The heavy emphasis on conventional practice found in most lessons reflected teachers' training and beliefs about mathematics teaching. First, there was a fairly strong relationship between teachers' beliefs and teaching approaches. Using interview data, we classified teachers as to whether they believed that mathematics should be taught as a set of rules and procedures and those who thought they should try to develop mathematical concepts. Fifteen of the twenty-five teachers believed in stressing rules and procedures rather than trying to develop concepts, and fourteen of them only had students practice applications. The three teachers who believed that mathematics should emphasize patterns and relationships all did more than one application-oriented lesson. Two of the seven teachers who had mixed beliefs did all practice lessons, two did one application-oriented lesson, and three did two or more application-oriented lessons.

Teachers' views were partly rooted in their preservice training that focused on general education rather than mathematics education. Only two teachers had undergraduate majors in mathematics and few teachers had taken any college level mathematics courses. Further, teachers' inservice activity related to mathematics or assessment was usually limited to one or two days per year and addressed general topics like cooperative learning strategies and rubrics, rather than specific topics and skills within mathematics or the standards. Thus teachers' educational experiences typically gave them only a superficial understanding of mathematics topics and pedagogy.

By contrast, the six teachers who made the greatest shift toward a standards-based approach shared some important characteristics that relate to individual will and capacity. First, all six teachers had a strong personal desire to improve their craft, not to promote higher test scores, but for the personal satisfaction of deepening their instructional knowledge and skills. Second, these teachers sought more intensive, mathematics-focused professional development outside their districts. For instance, they traveled greater distances and attended courses or other activities more often than did the majority of teachers interviewed.

Third, the six teachers were involved in a wider variety of professional activities than most teachers were. Four of the six were working on master's degrees or advanced teaching certificates beyond their master's, and three also worked on district mathematics curriculum committees. These teachers attended state and national NCTM meetings, state-sponsored workshops on mathematics, regional mathematics teacher consortia meetings, and read NCTM publications regularly. They also attended district inservice, but viewed this type of training as too general (non-subject or topic specific) and too brief to be very helpful. They said their out-of-district professional development was the most important reason for changing their practice. While these teachers saw the state standards and performance assessments as consistent with their evolving conceptions of teaching and learning, the policies were not the primary impetus for teachers' efforts to revise practice. Ms. Davis explained, "I do it [teaching the MEA way] not because of the MEA, but because that's the way kids learn math better."

Conclusion

Although the sample of districts studied is limited and the time frame for the work is shorter than ideal, this study offers some hypotheses about the factors that affect districts' will and capacity to implement state educational reforms and about how district and state policies combine to influence teachers' will and capacity in the same area. The cases illustrate why district will is usefully viewed as a matter of fit between state policy and local interests. These district administrators had to operate between state demands and local expectations but a variety of factors tipped the balance in different directions in the two study states.

Several factors encouraged Maryland districts to attend more to state policy. These included the threat of reconstitution, other accountability policies (e.g., the requirement for School Improvement Teams), the climate of cooperation between the state educational agency and districts, governance factors that partially buffered district administrators from local concerns, and networks supported by the state (e.g., the Maryland Assessment Consortium and others) which provided teachers and districts with professional development and materials such as lesson activities.

Yet the increased attention to test-related activity in the higher capacity Maryland districts produced instructional practices that were only partially consistent with state or national mathematics standards. Teachers were conducting isolated, test-like activities that included a greater emphasis on mathematics topics or content that had formerly been ignored. However, teachers continued to conduct lessons in ways that emphasized procedural skills and factual knowledge rather than creating opportunities for students to engage in reasoning, complex problem solving, and connecting important concepts in mathematics. Overall, district and state policies in Maryland were particularly effective in changing the content of middle-school mathematics lessons. With regard to pedagogy, teachers were being introduced to the words but they didn't have the tune—that is, they were beginning to try new things but had not consolidated a new approach to practice.

Some Maine teachers were making similar changes, but when they did so, it was not in response to state policy. First, the Maine districts had very low capacity to provide the direction or new knowledge teachers needed to revise their instructional practices. The inservice that was offered was too superficial to be of much help and teachers were largely on their own to figure out what they should do to help students perform well on the state test. Second, only a handful of teachers were involved in more focused, intensive professional development from sources outside the district. While the state or districts provided some funding for professional development outside the district, there were no other incentives or sanctions that could have motivated more average teachers to seek professional training beyond inservice days.

Beyond changes in materials and assignments, the kinds of changes needed to move from conventional to more standards-based teaching are quite subtle and require a deeper understanding of the subject content and pedagogy.[56] The nature and amount of teacher professional development, even in Maryland's higher capacity districts, has not been enough to lead to the extensive revision of both conceptions of teaching and daily practice. Yet the evidence of experimentation with larger activities modeled on the state performance assessments provides hope that teachers might reflect on and revise practice if they are provided with more intensive and content specific learning opportunities. To accomplish this, both within district and out-of-district learning opportunities need to be upgraded and teachers need greater motivation to develop their professional knowledge and skills.

The problem of scaling up is also illustrated by these cases.[57] As Cuban[58] has pointed out, something like standards-based teaching has been around for decades as a minority view among teachers. For standards advocates, the challenge in designing state and district policy is not just to increase the amount of standards-based teaching. Rather the task is to increase that amount beyond the levels that are likely to occur among the teaching population naturally. While the instances of teacher self-reform we have seen are exciting, we believe that they are still the exception. If so, the question is whether districts and states can muster the will and capacity to support teacher learning on a more intense level to expand standards-based teaching beyond the pockets where it occurs anyway.

NOTES

1. This research reported in this chapter was supported by a grant from the Spencer Foundation. The opinions stated here are solely those of the authors and not those of the Spencer Foundation or Rutgers, The State University of New Jersey. The authors wish to thank David Mayrowetz who helped with the field work and analysis.

2. James Spillane, "School districts matter: Local educational authorities and state instructional policy," *Educational Policy* 10 (1996): pp. 63-87; Susan Fuhrman, William Clune, and Richard Elmore, "Research on education reform: Lessons on the implementation of policy," *Teachers College Record* 90 (1988): pp. 237-257; Paul Berman and Milbrey McLaughlin, *Federal Programs Supporting Educational Change: Factors Affecting Implementation and Continuation* (Santa Monica, CA: RAND, 1977); William Firestone, *Great Expectations for Small Schools: The Limitations of Federal Projects* (New York: Praeger, 1980).

3. Dan Lortie, *Schoolteacher: A Sociological Analysis* (Chicago: University of Chicago Press, 1975); Karl Weick, "Educational organizations as loosely coupled systems," *Administrative Science Quarterly* 21 (1976): pp. 1-19.

4. H. Dickinson Corbett and Bruce Wilson, *Testing, Reform, and Rebellion* (Norwood, NJ: Ablex, 1991); Mary Lee Smith, "Put to the test: The effects of external testing on students," *Educational Researcher* 20 (1991): pp. 8-12.

5. Joan Baron and Dennie Wolf, *Performance based Student Assessment: Challenges and Possibilities* (Chicago: University of Chicago Press, 1996); Robert Rothman, *Measuring Up: Standards, Assessment, and School Reform* (San Francisco: Jossey-Bass, 1995).

6. Richard Elmore and Susan Fuhrman, *The Governance of Curriculum* (Alexandria, VA: Association for Supervision and Curriculum Development, 1994); Michael Knapp, "Between systemic reforms and the mathematics and science classrooms: The dynamics of innovation, implementation, and professional learning," *Review of Educational Research* 67 (1997): pp. 227-266.

7. Marshall Smith and Jennifer O'Day, "Systemic school reform," in Susan Fuhrman and Betty Malen, eds., *The Politics of Curriculum and Testing* (Bristol, PA: Falmer Press, 1991), pp. 233-267; Knapp, "Between systemic reforms and the mathematics and science classrooms."

8. National Council of Teachers of Mathematics, *Curriculum and Evaluation Standards for School Mathematics* (Reston, VA: Author, 1989); National Council of Teachers of Mathematics, *Principles and Standards for School Mathematics* (Reston, VA: Author, 2000).

9. James Stigler and James Hiebert, "Understanding and improving classroom mathematics instruction," *Phi Delta Kappan* 79 (1997): pp. 14-21.

10. Ibid.

11. David Cohen and Deborah Loewenberg Ball, "Policy and practice: An overview," *Educational Evaluation and Policy Analysis* 12 (1990): pp. 347-353.

12. Scott Grant, Penelope Peterson, and A. Shojgreen-Downer, "Learning to teach mathematics in the context of systemic reform," *American Educational Research Journal*

33 (1996): pp. 509-541; Penelope Peterson, Sarah McCarthey, and Richard Elmore, "Learning from school restructuring," *American Educational Research Journal* 33 (1996): pp. 119-153.

13. Robert Yin, *Case Study Research: Design and Methods* (Newbury Park, CA: Sage, 1989).

14. Stigler and Hiebert, "Understanding and improving classroom mathematics instruction."

15. For a more detailed description of the research methods, see William Firestone, David Mayrowetz, and Janet Fairman, "Performance based assessment and instructional change: The effects of testing in Maine and Maryland," *Educational Evaluation and Policy Analysis* 20 (1998): pp. 95-113.

16. Michael Fullan, *The New Meaning of Educational Change* (New York: Teachers College Press, 1991).

17. David Cohen and Carol Barnes, "Pedagogy and policy," in David Cohen, Milbrey McLaughlin, and Joan Talbert, eds., *Teaching for Understanding* (San Francisco: Jossey-Bass, 1993), pp. 207-239.

18. William Firestone, "Using reform: Conceptualizing district initiative," *Educational Evaluation and Policy Analysis* 11 (1989): pp. 151-165.

19. James Spillane and Charles Thompson, "Reconstructing conceptions of local capacity: The local education agency's capacity for ambitious instructional reform," *Educational Evaluation and Policy Analysis* 19 (1997): pp. 185-203.

20. Corbett and Wilson, *Testing, Reform, and Rebellion*.

21. George Madaus, *Critical Issues in Curriculum: Eighty-seventh Yearbook of the National Society for the Study of Education* (Chicago: University of Chicago Press, 1988).

22. Corbett and Wilson, *Testing, Reform, and Rebellion*; Mary Lee Smith, *Reforming Schools by Reforming Assessment: Consequences of the Arizona Student Assessment Program* (Tempe, AZ: Southwest Educational Policy Studies, Arizona State University, 1996).

23. Smith, "Put to the test."

24. William Firestone and James Pennell, "Designing state-sponsored teacher networks: A comparison of two cases," *American Educational Research Journal* 34 (1997): pp. 237-266.

25. Smith, "Put to the test."

26. Catherine Marshall and Frederick Wirt, *Culture and Education Policy in the American States* (New York: Falmer Press, 1989).

27. Corbett and Wilson, *Testing, Reform, and Rebellion*.

28. National Council of Teachers of Mathematics, *Curriculum and Evaluation Standards for School Mathematics*.

29. This description is based on public release documents made available to school districts. Especially in Maryland, where test security is heavily emphasized, the amount of such material is limited so judgments are based on a limited sample of assessment tasks.

30. National Council of Teachers of Mathematics, *Curriculum and Evaluation Standards for School Mathematics*; National Council of Teachers of Mathematics, *Principles and Standards for School Mathematics*.

31. Firestone, Mayrowetz, and Fairman, "Performance based assessment and instructional change: The effects of testing in Maine and Maryland."

32. Ibid.

33. Firestone and Pennell, "Designing state-sponsored teacher networks: A comparison of two cases."

34. Joseph Murphy, *Restructuring Schools: Capturing and Assessing the Phenomena* (New York: Teachers College Press, 1991).

35. As opposed to "Deweyan." See David Tyack, *The One Best System* (Cambridge, MA: Harvard University Press, 1974).

36. Robert Alford, "School district reorganization and community integration," *Harvard Education Review* 30 (1960): pp. 350-371; Alan Peshkin, *Growing Up American: Schooling and the Survival of Community* (Chicago: University of Chicago Press, 1978); Alan Peshkin, *The Imperfect Union: School Consolidation and Community Conflict* (Chicago: University of Chicago Press, 1982).

37. See Jane Hannaway and Kristi Kimball's chapter in this volume.

38. Dennis Judd and Todd Swanstrom, *City Politics: Private Power and Public Policy* (New York: Harper Collins, 1994).

39. James Conant, *The American High School Today* (New York: McGraw-Hill, 1959).

40. See Tyack, *The One Best System*, for a review of these debates.

41. Peshkin, *The Imperfect Union.*

42. Milbrey McLaughlin, "Learning from experience: Lessons from policy implementation," *Educational Evaluation and Policy Analysis* 9 (1987): pp. 171-78.

43. Firestone, "Using reform."

44. Sheila Rosenblum and Karen Seashore Louis, *Stability and Change: Innovation in an Educational Context* (New York: Plenum, 1981).

45. Spillane, "School districts matter."

46. James Spillane, "A cognitive perspective on the role of the local educational agency in implementing instructional policy: Accounting for local variability," *Educational Administration Quarterly* 34 (1998): pp. 31-57.

47. William Firestone, "Continuity and incrementalism after all," in Joseph Murphy, ed., *The Educational Reform Movement of the 1980s: Perspectives and Cases* (Berkeley, CA: McCutchan, 1990), pp. 143-166.

48. Richard Elmore, "Getting to scale with successful educational practices," in Susan Fuhrman and Jennifer O'Day, eds., *Rewards and Reform: Creating Educational Incentives that Work* (San Francisco: Jossey-Bass, 1996), pp. 294-329; Elizabeth Fennema and Megan Franke, "Teachers' knowledge and its impact," in Douglas Grouws, ed., *Handbook of Research on Mathematics Teaching and Learning* (New York: Macmillan, 1992), pp. 147-164; Elizabeth Fennema, Penelope Peterson, and Thomas Carpenter, "Learning with understanding," *Advances in Research on Teaching* 1 (1989): pp. 195-221; Grant, Peterson, and Shojgreen-Downer, "Learning to teach mathematics in the context of systemic reform"; Lee Shulman, "On teaching problem solving and solving the problems of teaching," in Edward Silver, ed., *Teaching and Learning Mathematical Problem Solving: Multiple Research Perspectives* (Hillsdale, NJ: Erlbaum, 1985), pp. 439-450.

49. Fuhrman, Clune, and Elmore, "Research on education reform"; Spillane, "School districts matter."

50. Fennema, Peterson, and Carpenter, "Learning with understanding"; Nancy Knapp and Penelope Peterson, "Teachers' interpretations of 'CGI' after four years: Meanings and practices," *Journal for Research in Mathematics Education* 26 (1995): pp. 40-65; Judith Warren Little, "Norms of collegiality and experimentation: Workplace conditions of school success," *American Educational Research Journal* 19 (1982): pp. 325-340; Deborah Schifter and Catherine Fosnot, *Reconstructing Mathematics Education: Stories of Teachers Meeting the Challenge of Reform* (New York: Teachers College Press, 1993).

51. Paul Cobb, Terry Wood, and Erna Yackel, "Classrooms as learning environments for teachers and researchers," in Robert Davis, Carolyn Maher, and Nel Noddings, eds., *Constructionist Views on the Teaching and Learning of Mathematics: Monograph*

No. 4, Journal for Research in Mathematics Education (Reston, VA: NCTM, 1990): pp. 125-146; David Cohen and Heather Hill, "Instructional policy and classroom performance: The mathematics reform in California," *Teachers College Record* 102 (1998): pp. 294-343; Thomas Corcoran, *Transforming Professional Development for Teachers: A Guide for State Policymakers* (Washington, DC: National Governors' Association, 1995).

52. Cohen and Ball, "Policy and practice"; Cohen and Hill, "Instructional policy and classroom performance"; Schifter and Fosnot, *Reconstructing Mathematics Education.*

53. Knapp, "Between systemic reforms and the mathematics and science classrooms."

54. Lortie, *Schoolteacher: A sociological analysis*; Weick, "Educational organizations as loosely coupled systems."

55. Richard Murnane and David Cohen, "Merit pay and the evaluation problem: Why most merit pay programs fail and a few survive," *Harvard Education Review* 56 (1986): pp. 1-17.

56. Magdalene Lampert, "When the problem is not the question and the solution is not the answer: Mathematical knowing and teaching," *American Educational Research Journal* 27 (1990): pp. 29-63; Grant, Peterson, and Shojgreen-Downer, "Learning to teach mathematics in the context of systemic reform."

57. Elmore, "Getting to scale with successful educational practices."

58. Larry Cuban, *How Teachers Taught: Constancy and Change in American Classrooms, 1890-1980* (New York: Teachers College Press, 1993).

CHAPTER VIII

The Theory and Practice of Using Data to Build Capacity: State and Local Strategies and their Effects[1]

DIANE MASSELL

Introduction

The theory of standards-based reform argues that schools will improve if states provide more explicit guidance about academic goals and outcomes and hold local educators responsible for meeting them. At the same time, states will offer educators greater flexibility to address these goals as they best see fit.[2] Emerging state accountability systems and standards-based testing programs reflect this approach. While they represent an effort to get the goals and incentives for improvement right, the outcome data they produce are seen as an integral part of the improvement process. As Elmore and Rothman[3] note, "The theory of action of the basic standards-based reform model suggests that, armed with data on how students perform against standards, schools will make the instructional changes needed to improve performance."

In fact, data-driven decision making is also seen as an antidote to the susceptibility of public schooling to fads and political pressures. Administrators tend to legitimize education and signal progress by adopting the latest reforms.[4] They appease political interests rather than choose innovations for their proven ability to improve teaching and learning. Indeed, often only minimal efforts are made to ensure that adopted reforms are practiced.[5] Policymakers today argue that basing classroom, school, and district decisions more 'rationally' on problems uncovered by empirical data and selecting programs proven effective by research to raise student achievement will produce more meaningful and positive changes to teaching and learning.[6] For example, the Comprehensive School Reform Design program seeks "to

Diane Massell is a senior research associate at the University of Michigan's School of Education.

provide financial incentives for schools to develop comprehensive school reforms, based on reliable research and effective practices . . ." Outcome data and research have become part of the text of school improvement—curricula, if you will, for educators to read, interpret, and follow on a path to improvement.

But while data-driven decision making has gained centrality in policy rhetoric, has it had any discernible effects on schooling practices? Is it, too, a fad to cloak education in a mantle of scientific legitimacy? Or are data and research becoming a motive force in educational decisions? I begin to answer these questions by looking at whether and how states and districts are promoting the use of data and whether and how data are affecting educators' attitudes and practices. I conclude with a discussion of issues and challenges for policymakers to consider. But first I will review our methodology.

Methodology

The findings here are based on a three-year study of standards-based reform in eight states—California, Colorado, Florida, Kentucky, Maryland, Michigan, Minnesota, and Texas. Beginning in the fall of 1996, our research team collected information on state policies and in subsequent years visited twenty-three school districts selected for their involvement in improvement initiatives and standards-based reform.[7] In 1998, we interviewed principals and school improvement committee chairs in a sample of thirty-three elementary schools in California, Kentucky, Maryland, and Michigan; in 1999, we included twenty-four schools in Colorado, Florida, and Texas study districts. At least two of the three schools in each district participate in the Title I program. This chapter draws heavily on the state-level research and interviews with administrators in a sub-sample of schools in Colorado, Maryland, and Texas. It also utilizes information gathered from surveys of second through fifth grade teachers in seven of our study states in 1999 (all except Minnesota).

The State Role in Promoting Data

States' most important roles in the data arena are quite apparent: generating data and designing incentives for their use via state testing and accountability. However, as Maryland Superintendent of Schools Nancy Grasmick's comments illustrate, states also use other mechanisms:

While Maryland's accountability system was instituted to benchmark progress, accountability, alone, is not sufficient to improve student achievement. For that, you also need committed school improvement teams that have the data to make informed, school-specific curricular and instructional decisions and the authority to carry them out. The assessment and accountability systems, augmented with data- and improvement-driven web sites, were designed to invest school improvement teams with both.[8]

Our eight study states created school improvement planning procedures to encourage data-based decisions, designed Internet systems to make data accessible and user friendly, and offered professional development to improve data analysis and application. They vary in how they design and in how extensively they utilize these mechanisms, with some offering substantially less assistance for reasons that range from low state education agency capacity to the relative newness of their assessment and accountability programs. With this in mind, I will provide a general review of these four major data promotion efforts.

STATE ACCOUNTABILITY AND TESTING

While accountability and testing are not new state policy initiatives, the nature of these programs is changing in ways that intend to alter the way data are used. In the 1980s, concerns about students leaving high school without basic skills led state policymakers to mandate minimum competency tests. Accountability for meeting these outcomes essentially fell to students; failing students were barred from extracurricular activities, promotion to the next grade, or high school graduation. By contrast, the most severe consequences for educators came via the public reporting of results, but typically scores were recorded only for the district and state, not for particular schools.

New models of accountability are different. In their ideal form, they hold *schools* primarily responsible for meeting performance targets on student achievement tests as well as other, non-cognitive measures such as attendance.[9] Designers argue that old accountability approaches implicitly blame students or their families for poor performance and allow educators to shun responsibility. Significantly, all of our study states now produce and publicly report school level results. In addition, school level performance is the subject of an attention getting system of sanctions. Consequences for failing schools can include replacing staff, allowing students to leave, or reducing the school's autonomy. Some states also provide fiscal and other rewards to successful schools or teachers that meet high performance standards.[10] State accountability strategies are bolstered by federal policies, particularly by 1994 Title I program changes which, for example, allow the use of state assessments for evaluation purposes.

Many of the student achievement tests at the center of new accountability systems are also different from the norm- or criterion-referenced, multiple choice and basic skills tests that proliferated in the 1970s and 1980s. Studies show that teachers mimicked the multiple choice formats of basic skills tests, encouraged rote memorization of disconnected facts, narrowed curricula to tested content, and reduced or eliminated challenging thinking skills, particularly in disadvantaged communities.[11] Basic skills tests are seen as poor measures of student ability that yield data of little relevance to the classroom.[12] Norm-referenced testing is challenged for not evaluating students with set standards of academic performance, thereby lowering expectations. But the fact that testing could influence both the form of instruction and curricular topics was not lost, even on critics.

The antidote has been to develop assessments that could turn mimicry into a more positive and compelling affair.[13] Many emerging state tests are keyed to more challenging academic and performance standards. To promote higher order thinking and more engaged teaching, states are supplementing or replacing multiple choice items with performance tasks and (to a lesser extent) student work portfolios.[14] While pressure for comparable results led some jurisdictions to maintain norm-referenced testing, states like Maryland and Kentucky are not including these results in their accountability ratings of schools. Many states reduced their testing to a smaller set of elementary, middle, and high school grades. Such benchmark testing is promoted to alleviate testing burden, recognize that children learn at different paces, and provide more flexibility for local practice.

These new ideals have been embraced by our study states in various degrees and ways. Some kind of school based accountability is common to all and each includes some performance based tasks in their testing programs. Rewards and sanctions differ as does the extent of testing, the rigor of performance standards, and the degree to which tests measure basic skills. But the essential point is that these newer models of state testing generate a different data script to guide educators' practices with a set of accountability incentives that focus particular attention on schools as critical agents of change. The hope is that this new approach will focus teaching on more challenging academic skills and guide administrative practice at the level—the school—that research suggests matters the most in improvement.

SCHOOL IMPROVEMENT PLANNING

Many states, including the eight in our study, require or encourage schools to develop school improvement planning or site-based decision making processes, with the expectation that testing and accountability data will be central to their planning. Colorado, Florida, Kentucky, Maryland, and Texas actually mandate that schools set performance goals in their plans around outcome data although the schools in our study typically do so whether the state requires it or not.

INTERNET TECHNOLOGY

States have taken advantage of computers and the Internet to provide greater access to accountability data. Conventional performance reports in paper formats may or may not be distributed by local administrators to public groups or even to teachers. But electronic formats are instantly accessible to all who have the technology. Further, since anyone can download the data, more independent analyses are occurring. For instance, a leading Kentucky newspaper analyzed school data to produce its own widely read report on public education. The more sophisticated state web sites include a wealth of data and supplemental information to assist decision making. Maryland includes district and school scores over time on each element of the state test, compares how a school does relative to their district and state averages, breaks down student performance on components of their assessments, provides technical background for scoring, offers information on best practices, and more. Texas and Florida are providing computer access to information on a broad array of indicators, such as teacher characteristics and school funding, to assist educators in planning, budgeting, and comparative analyses.

PROFESSIONAL DEVELOPMENT

Finally, states offer professional development to help districts and schools interpret data results. Local administrators frequently mentioned contacting state staff directly for immediate assistance, but states also have other initiatives to enhance local knowledge in this area. One strategy offers data analysis training to a select group of individuals who then become resident experts in their districts or schools. Minnesota, for instance, trains its Graduation Specialists this way. Kentucky embeds data training in other program agendas. Improvement staff who serve lower performing schools receive data analysis training and one teacher from every school in the state learns to interpret reading results through Kentucky's *Reading Leaders* program.

In sum, states' role in data creation, dissemination, and accountability has changed substantially since the late 1970s and 1980s as a result of the theory and practices of standards-based reform as well as technological change. There is a more intense focus on school data and new assessments, with accountability incentives and procedural mechanisms like school improvement planning to encourage the use of data to devise improvement strategies as well as professional development. Data bases are more widely accessible, at least to those with the technology and skills to use it.

The Local Role in Promoting Data

Are data receiving comparable attention from local educators? In her research on the use of Title I evaluations in the late 1970s, Jane David noted a glaring lack of administrative attention to data. Only rarely did administrators do more than circulate written reports about aggregate changes in test scores. Nor did they visit schools to discuss the implications or even disaggregate data for particular schools.[15] In the districts in David's study, administrators treated data primarily as an accountability mechanism, not as a text to guide educational improvement.

In contrast, the majority of administrators in our study districts and schools actively promote and support the use of data, though certainly there is variation in how wholeheartedly they embrace data into their theories of action. Local strategies dovetail with what states are doing, although they expand on these efforts in ways that reflect local needs and resources as well as staff knowledge, commitment, and capacity. Local administrators in our study try to build knowledge and skills about data throughout the district or school, elaborate on school improvement planning, create additional data and materials, and build new incentives to use data.

PROFESSIONAL DEVELOPMENT

Nearly all districts in our study take measures to improve their staff's ability to interpret data. The three most common approaches are distinguished by who receives training and whether they use externally generated data or data developed and collected by local staff.

Dispensing knowledge from the center. A majority of districts in our study train central office or local area office staff, or hire outside experts to provide feedback to schools on information from state and local assessments and other indicators of performance. Assessment staff from a Florida district, for example, hold more than a hundred meetings with individual schools to explain test results. The Research and Evaluation team in a Maryland district meets with small groups of schools to analyze state test results item-by-item and look at the number of students scoring at the different proficiency levels in each content area. They discuss progress over time, what it means to have students achieving at different levels, and how to interpret the outcomes. The district also works individually with schools and produces profiles for them. In large districts, area offices designate individuals to provide these services. Minnesota and Michigan districts in our study often turn to consultants or state education agency staff for special, on-site assistance with data analysis.

Training key school personnel. Some districts also instruct staff within schools to do their own analyses of external data, although they usually provide the training to a select group, such as principals, school improvement team members, or a designated teacher or noninstructional staff member. Many districts are including data analysis training in their work with school improvement team members. One Texas district places instructional guides in each school for the purpose of analyzing data for the staff.

Schoolwide data production model. A few districts and schools in our study encourage teachers and administrators to be more active participants in the process of data production, in part to improve their understanding of data for instruction but also for other purposes, such as to create data that are more relevant to their particular curriculum. In several study districts, teachers and administrators develop and/or participate in the application of common scoring rubrics or engage in action research projects and study groups where they have to use data or review research as part of the process. In one California district, two of the three area superintendents require principals to conduct action research projects and collect data. The principals meet and discuss their research with the area superintendent and their peers and sometimes with their own school staff. Some of the principals mirror these activities with their teachers. In addition, some schools establish study groups.

SCHOOL IMPROVEMENT PLANNING

While states provide some guidance as to what should go into school improvement plans and how they should be developed, it is primarily up to local district and school administrators to decide upon the details of, and confer authority to, these plans. (Kentucky alone is quite prescriptive.) Many, but not all, of our districts and schools take school improvement planning as a serious and important part of the change process, and intend data to be central to their decision making. For instance, a Michigan district recently began focusing on school improvement planning as a lead instrument for change. Each area superintendent assigns staff to help with implementation of the improvement plans, specifically attempting to strengthen connections between conclusions drawn from data and school practices. A Colorado district asks its schools to develop study groups around areas identified as weak by the data, and to develop proposals for the school improvement plan.

ADDITIONAL DATA AND MATERIALS

As the conversation about school improvement becomes informed by state data, teachers and administrators are pressing for more comprehensive information on student achievement. Districts and schools are supplementing state tests to measure continuous progress toward district and/or state standards, provide instructional feedback, offer student level information for parents and teachers, reinforce constructivist teaching through performance assessments, evaluate programs, and more.[16] This is particularly the case when state testing is only in benchmark grades or in a small number of subjects, or when it is a matrix sample that does not provide reliable information about individual student performance. It is somewhat ironic that while many states scaled back the number of tested grades, the appetite for data led locals to fill in where they left off. In some cases, such as in one of our California districts, teachers are demanding more data to help them make better instructional decisions. Locals want more than just information on student achievement. A Kentucky district administers student surveys and parent questionnaires to inform their consolidated planning processes (i.e., improvement planning). One Minnesota district plans to gather information on co-curricular activities, student absenteeism, suspensions and expulsions, student satisfaction, parental participation, and more to inform its strategic planning process. Districts in Maryland and Florida are developing tools to help schools manage the occasionally overwhelming amount of data that are being generated.

ADDITIONAL INCENTIVES FOR DATA USE

Districts and schools are also creating new incentives that help to encourage data use. For instance, some districts go beyond what is required by their state accountability systems to identify low performing or at-risk schools. A Texas district identifies "priority" schools that could be classified as low performing under the state system the following year since the state annually raises its performance requirements. Although most districts tend not to include progress on measured outcomes in their formal teacher or administrator evaluations unless the state requires it,[17] supervisors say they informally consider this information when they recommend dismissals, demotions, or transfers. Some district administrators apply other informal pressures on schools to attend to data, such as by persistently questioning principals about how they plan to address declines in test scores. School principals also are using data to frame conversations about instructional improvement with their teachers. For instance, one Maryland principal requires staff to regularly submit portfolios of student work to her for discussion. Another Maryland district requires portfolios to be part of the teacher evaluation process, again with the hope that it structures professional dialogue around improvement.

Variations in the Practice of Promoting Data

While the strategies described above are used by districts and schools across our sample states, there is clearly a spectrum in how creatively these elements are assembled and how extensively data are promoted. At the low end are people like those in Jane David's study who perceive of data as a begrudging feature of the landscape to which they must conform to satisfy accountability goals. Curriculum is adjusted to align with state tests, and some add-on or remedial programs are put into place. But little more is done and data are not used as a serious feedback mechanism to guide the core of instructional practice or school organization. At the other end of the spectrum are a cluster of "intensive" districts and schools. These intensive sites have absorbed the standards-based data ideology into their own theories of action. The words of one Texas superintendent and a Colorado principal are illustrative:

There has been a major change in the culture of the district. We are now a data-driven district. Data can be our best ally. It has not always been considered that way but it is hard to dispute the data regarding student achievement. The data can be compiled in such a way to create a sense of urgency that I felt was necessary to bring about change.

We sort of have broken the mold in that the idea of status quo doesn't work anymore . . . I was a teacher in this building eight or nine years ago for a year. We were very comfortable . . . we didn't challenge ourselves. We didn't look at things differently. One of the things I can really appreciate about the CSAP [the Colorado State Assessment Program] and the testing and standards is it is forcing us to get out of this mold of complacency, if you will . . . It has begun to translate into some different kinds of things we're doing.

These kinds of administrators see data as having the potential to culti-vate more instructionally oriented professional dialogues and to improve their decision making. The majority of our study sites fall between these two extremes, but it is useful to take a look at an inten-sive one and to ask what seems to contribute to its more expansive embrace of the data theory in standards-based reform.[18]

COLORADO EXAMPLES

One of our Colorado districts is establishing several new manage-rial structures and strategies to boost the use of data to make decisions. These include a district-designed school improvement planning pro-cess, teacher-led action research, administrative monitoring of practice, and program evaluation. Under the school improvement process, for example, schools must create Student Focused Action Teams (SFATs) for areas that data reveal to be problematic. Staff on these teams must conduct research on the problem, collect data, and develop a work plan. The district also requires each school to select at least one in-house data analyst and pays them a stipend. The district's professional development division, in conjunction with a local university, provides these people with three years of data analysis training. Finally, the superintendent offers additional support and uses informal incentives to focus schools' attention on data. For example, although neither the state nor the district formally identifies low-performing schools, the superintendent assigns district staff to schools performing poorly on the state assessment to help with school improvement planning. A principal has also been removed from one of these sites. The district also encouraged one of its Title I schools to apply for school improve-ment status[19] since it was not faring well on the state assessment.

The principal and chair of the school improvement team in another Title I school have enthusiastically embraced the data-oriented philos-ophy. Although new district policy does not mandate full staff in-volvement, this principal requires *all* of his teachers to be involved on one of the SFATs in order to nurture a professional community com-mitted to data and research. In addition, the school moves beyond the analysis of student achievement data and other information collected by local or state officials to research their own problems and develop solutions. For example, one of their school improvement planning goals concerns discipline and academic learning. The SFAT decided to have all third through fifth grade teachers count how many missing homework assignments they had from the beginning of the school year. Since this exercise revealed a sizable amount of missing work, the school created a detention center for students who did not turn in assignments. Continuing in the data collection mode, the team discovered that thirty-three students were doing sixty-five percent of all the detentions and that high proportions of them were identified as special needs. The school also noted which teachers were sending the largest number of students to detention and began working with those teachers to improve their practices. Finally, they developed a mentoring program for those high risk students, after examining the research on how best to help these students. Similarly, rather than rely on more customary word-of-mouth recommendations about training, they began investigating the impact of these activities on actual student achievement.

POSSIBLE EXPLANATIONS FOR INTENSIVE USE

Clearly this school and its district are taking a more expansive and creative approach toward data. What might explain the differences between these kind of intensive sites and those at the lower end of the scale? Given the duality of purpose in state assessment and accountability programs—intended as both pressure to perform and as a general text for scripting improvements—I expected to see a greater emphasis on data in districts and schools located in high stakes state accountability environments. Other studies suggest that higher consequences attached to student test results produce greater pressure and behavioral changes.[20] Since the consequences for poor performance include more radical remedies for school failure in our study states of Florida, Kentucky, Maryland, Texas and, to a lesser extent Michigan, I expected to find more intensive sites there than in the comparatively weaker and/or emerging systems in California, Colorado, and Minnesota.

But intensive data promoters were scattered across all kinds of state and district accountability environments. As the above examples show, some of our best cases are in Colorado. Other intensive sites are in California with some keen promoters emerging in Minnesota and Michigan. High stakes systems also contain many moderate promoters, those who facilitate data use but do not place it at the center of their theories of action or invest substantial resources. For example, one of our Texas districts only recently began to take an interest in seriously using data to inform their practice and improve on the state testing and accountability system. A Maryland district provided very little data training or analysis.

Why do some see data as a critical part of instituting change and building capacity, and others not? Our cases suggest that what seems to matter most is a combination of factors that includes the *pressures of an accountability system, but also the expectation that its consequences will have some direct impact* on the organization. For example, the Texas district just noted could ignore data in part because its schools had always scored reasonably well on the state accountability index. But district leaders began to realize that districts with less potential were achieving "recognized" status in the state accountability ratings while they were just earning "acceptable" ratings. A competitive desire to improve their status, along with a stimulus from district growth, yielded new and higher expectations. The intensive Colorado school was a Title I school which must meet stronger accountability requirements than the average school in the state. Our study school was being pressured to improve in certain areas.

Another important factor is *whether local district or school leaders think the outcomes and performance goals represented by the data are important and, to some degree, achievable.* If educators think the outcomes are irrelevant to their students, and/or the goals unattainable, they seem less likely to invest energy and resources in creative strategies to improve on these measures (unless strongly forced to by state or other external agents). For example, one of the fairly low performing schools in our study does not have the kind of systematic and comprehensive approach to data that is characteristic of more intensive sites. At least in part this is because the principal views the state test as substantively inappropriate for her urban students,[21] and as keyed to performance standards that the very lowest achievers are unlikely to meet. Consequently, to acquire better results they focus their energies on improving students closest to meeting satisfactory scores rather than invest in deeper instructional or managerial changes. Finally, and perhaps most importantly, is *whether district or school building administrators embrace the philosophy of data-based decision making as a key, motive force for improvement.* Another school in that same city participates in a curriculum reform program that provides continuous, ongoing feedback on student achievement to teachers, with training and interventions designed to address problems revealed by data. This principal embraces the package built around the data as a critical path to improving student learning and ultimately meeting the more challenging standards of the state assessment. Administrators' interpretation of reform channels action in ways that critically affect policymakers' intent.[22]

Effects of State and Local Efforts

What effect are these efforts having? Here I examine two primary areas of impact: (1) the attitudes of local educators about the utility of data as a script for guiding practice, and (2) the application of data in local decision making.

ATTITUDINAL CHANGES

Perhaps the most striking effect of the new emphasis on data is the change in administrators' and teachers' attitudes about its value to practice. Many of the veteran educators in our study perceive substantial changes in their views. A Texas principal said:

I can remember being in the classroom as a teacher and not ever looking at TAAS [Texas Assessment of Academic Skills] data when it was called TEAMS or whatever. And nobody talked about it. All we got was scores back. We didn't do as good as we should, but okay, let's get to what we do all the time. I think the good thing about all the publicity with TAAS is that it has made us take a good look at that data. What does it say, what does it mean, what do we need to do differently, better, more of? When I meet with my teachers at the end of the grading periods, I want them to come in, bring the data, see how their kids are doing in reference to TAAS as well as reading levels. I was so impressed because my teachers knew so much about where their kids were. And kids and parents know a lot about where they are academically. And those results have to guide what we do so that we can continue to improve, do better, work harder.

One principal from Kentucky added:

I don't know if the whole accountability piece with rewards and sanctions is still the deal. It was at the beginning. Now it's a matter of pride. Before, we didn't want the scores to slip; now it's self-examination. Without the state assessment, I don't think that would have come into play.

They have absorbed the standards-based reform ideology that data can be critical stimuli to change and key to building capacity. Our interviews also suggest that there tends to be stronger support for and satisfaction with the kinds of standards-based assessments being used today. While educators often viewed minimum competency basic skills tests as having negative effects on curriculum and instruction or as unfair and of little relevance to practice, the overriding sentiment of administrators in our study seems to be that the new, more challenging tests are broadly supportive of good instruction. Our findings are compatible with the results of other studies of new assessments in

Kentucky and Maryland as well as North Carolina and Vermont.[23] Positive views coexist with criticisms of the tests. In two of our Maryland sites, for example, many of our respondents thought the elementary assessments were too difficult or not appropriate for all students, had lingering technical problems, and did not provide sufficient information or feedback on a schedule that would allow them to adequately address their deficiencies. Some administrators in Kentucky, Texas, and elsewhere thought that performance data had become *too* important, crowding out other educational goals. Our Texas educators were especially concerned that their more conventional test and, at this point,[24] relatively modest performance standards were not challenging enough. These qualms may explain why teachers in our seven-state survey view their state assessments and standards as among the most important influences on their curriculum content and instructional methods (after student needs, and closely followed by district standards and assessments), but also believe they are not completely accurate measures of their students' ability (see Tables 1 and 2). But, again, our interviews suggest a strong belief that most new assessments are pushing curriculum and instruction in the right direction. Finally, new accountability practices are seen as stimulating a search for new ideas, and respondents in several sites noted that they have encouraged them to pursue more professional development.

TABLE 1

To What Extent do the Following Influence the Content and Methods of Your Reading Instruction?

	Student Needs	State Standards	State Assessments	District Standards	District Curriculum Guide	District Assessments	State Curriculum Guide	Student Interest
Sample Mean	2.82	2.68	2.68	2.67	2.59	2.50	2.42	2.25
Total N	416	418	415	416	418	415	413	419
Rank	1	2	3	4	5	6	7	8

	My Knowledge	My Beliefs	Principal	Inservice	Textbook	Teacher Preparation	Other Teachers	Journals	Parents
Sample Mean	2.18	2.18	2.15	2.08	1.92	1.86	1.83	1.33	1.29
Total N	418	419	413	419	416	417	418	415	416
Rank	9	10	11	12	13	14	15	16	17

Scale:
0 = No Influence
1 = Minor
2 = Moderate
3 = Major Influence

TABLE 2

FORMAL ASSESSMENTS GIVEN BY THE DISTRICT OR STATE ACCURATELY
MEASURE MY STUDENTS' ACHIEVEMENT

RESPONSE	STRONGLY DISAGREE 1	2	3	4	5	STRONGLY AGREE 6	TOTAL CASES	TOTAL SAMPLE MEAN
Percent	18	23	22	26	9	2	100	2.9
(N)	(77)	(95)	(92)	(109)	(40)	(9)	(422)	

Scale:
1 = Strongly Disagree
6 = Strongly Agree

USES OF DATA: A MIX OF OLD AND NEW

In districts and schools in our study, data are being applied in many expected and novel ways. Matching curriculum subjects and topics to tested content has long been a common response to assessment[25] and our study districts and schools are no different. They create compatible standards, frameworks, and other documents to guide school curricula and adopt textbooks aligned to state standards and tests. Many of our schools establish common planning time for grade level teaching teams to coordinate their curricula with each other and with assessments.

Such traditional responses to testing as alignment are not surprising in a climate where, despite policymakers' intentions to the contrary, fragmentation and uncertainty continues to be the norm. A disconnect often persists between state and local standards and assessments or across state policies themselves. In Michigan and Texas, for example, state assessments and standards were not well aligned during the period our research was conducted. Colorado educators want greater clarity from the state on aligning their practices to broad state standards. Since the state is just phasing in its assessments, they lack the kind of data or guidance materials (such as test specifications or released items) that educators want. One Colorado school improvement team member said:

I'm not against standards-based education. What I'm against is everybody yelling standards, standards, standards. But . . . standards are so broad I don't know what you want me to teach. You're saying, tell kids ahead of time what they need to know. Well, I'm looking at geometry. You're not telling me what these fourth graders need to know.

Finally, the many assessments adopted by local districts and schools to supplement data provided by states creates additional fragmentation.

In this climate, alignment becomes an understandable preoccupation and first step.

But local educators are also using data in some more unusual ways. One of the more interesting examples is their use of data to communicate and network with other schools and districts. Some district policymakers encourage or require low performing schools to interact with higher performing ones. A Kentucky district, for example, pairs its more successful principals with those in low performing schools to model different strategies. But with or without explicit policy, we found that many districts and schools were seeking others with similar demographics but better success on outcome indicators. When one of our Maryland districts received the news that its eighth grade scores were flat, they located districts with higher performance on the state's reading and writing exams to study their improvement strategies. Such communication challenges educators' characteristic isolation.

More important, this communication, and the prevalence of comparative data in general, appears to be altering some educators' attitudes about the ability of different groups to achieve on challenging assessments. An underlying premise of standards-based reform is that *all* children can learn to high standards,[26] a view not widely shared by teachers and administrators. Indeed, a long line of research argues that students from economically disadvantaged homes, single parent families, parents with less educational attainment, and minority groups achieve at lower levels, and that schools have only marginal effects on these outcomes. While the effective schools literature of the 1970s and 1980s began to contest this argument, its findings are based on school success as measured by basic skills tests. Can schools make a difference in helping all students achieve more challenging standards? The comparative school level information provided by current accountability designs is affirming this assumption and it is doing so in contexts that are meaningful to local educators—in their neighboring schools and districts. Research suggests that teachers trust other teachers about program effects more than published studies[27] which tend to refer to unnamed sites. The networks based on comparative local data thus have the potential to shatter old assumptions about who can and cannot achieve. In a commonly expressed sentiment, a principal in Maryland said:

State performance standards for students have helped cause leaders to address directly, head on, the excuse making for education. You know, parents aren't involved, they don't care. It doesn't matter. It's up to us to make a difference

for them. I think, in that respect, it has given everyone a kick in the pants . . .
teachers' excuses don't cut it . . . It has emphasized, re-emphasized, that it is
teachers as people who make the difference.

The policies and rhetoric of our administrative respondents also
suggest that they are paying more attention to research to decide
whether to adopt or maintain particular innovations. One of our Texas
districts, for example, adopted standards for curriculum selection that,
among other things, requires it to be based on research. A Kentucky
district sees one of its primary roles as providing schools with research
on learning and best practices. And a California district cultivates a
culture of inquiry among its staff by strongly supporting action research and study groups, distributing research to all teachers, and creating professional libraries at all schools.

In another uncommon move, several of our study sites use data to
tightly guide certain professional development activities. This stands
in contrast to the more typical needs surveys where teachers and
administrators identify what professional development they would like
to receive. For example, a Texas district requires teachers to receive
training in areas where their students performed poorly. A Florida district examines and compares test scores over time, identifies needs for
schools, and then helps principals set up training programs. Our
intensive Colorado school is using data to more stringently evaluate
the effects of teachers' professional development on student achievement. This kind of outcomes-based evaluation of professional development is especially rare.[28] Less unusual, but appearing more frequently across the sample, districts use aggregate test performance
data to point out areas of weakness where more professional development is warranted. For example, poor performance on the reading
portion of the state MSPAP exam led one of our Maryland districts to
introduce mandatory phonics training.

Schools and districts also are introducing changes and shifting resources to address other data-identified problems, such as low student
attendance (a component of several of our study states' accountability
indices). Some of our Maryland schools hire attendance monitors, and
districts made improving attendance a focus of administrative oversight. One principal acknowledged that having performance targets for
attendance included in accountability ratings, rather than just vague
statements, more strongly motivated action to improve in this area.

In sum, districts and schools are applying data to make decisions in a
mix of old and new ways. But it is clear that many respondents perceive

a real change in the way they think about data to make decisions and often attribute it to the pressure of assessments and accountability even in relatively low-stakes systems.

Challenges for Policymakers and Practitioners

Standards-based reform's strategy of using data to build capacity is having some very tangible effects on district and school practices and educators' attitudes. But a number of challenges remain, as well as assumptions that require further investigation.

COMPREHENSIVENESS OF PROFESSIONAL DEVELOPMENT

While districts are taking steps to improve knowledge and skills about data interpretation and use, much of this training targets building administrators or a select group of teachers such as those on school improvement teams. The majority of classroom teachers are simply receiving direction from others about how to proceed, or are expected to tease out the implications of the data for teaching on their own. Even the principal in our intensive Colorado school said:

We have handed back last year's CSAP results to teachers and said, 'Here's how your kids did.' And when a teacher looks at their class and sees only two of their class were proficient or fourteen were proficient, that's information for that teacher. So there's an accountability simply there that says that we're giving teachers that information. What I believe is the teachers will be responsive.

But other administrators see a compelling need to make the feedback loop between data and practice more explicit. They recognize that traditional teacher education programs do not show teachers how to use data to direct comprehensive improvements or make daily adjustments to their classroom curriculum and instruction. In one of our Kentucky districts, for example, administrators felt that teachers had no understanding of the diagnostic uses of testing or other school data. Teachers thought that data gathering and analysis tasks interfered with the "real" work of schooling, and saw curriculum alignment with the tests as the most important thing they should do. Perhaps a tendency to gravitate toward alignment as a primary strategy for improving test scores explains why teachers in our survey strongly believe they have the requisite knowledge and skills to improve students' performance on formal assessments (see Table 3). But longer-term improvements will likely require deeper instructional changes, and a tighter and more creative connection between data and classroom practice.

TABLE 3

I HAVE THE KNOWLEDGE AND SKILLS I NEED TO RAISE MY STUDENTS'
ACHIEVEMENT ON FORMAL ASSESSMENTS

RESPONSE	STRONGLY DISAGREE 1	2	3	4	5	STRONGLY AGREE 6	TOTAL CASES	TOTAL SAMPLE MEAN
Percent	.4	1.6	9	20	39	30	100	4.9
(N)	(2)	(7)	(37)	(85)	(167)	(128)	(426)	

Scale:
1 = Strongly Disagree
6 = Strongly Agree

COMPLEXITY OF THE DATA

Deriving the implications of the data is no simple task in the complex environment that exists for schools. Late returns of state assessments often stymie local ability to make effective changes before students or teachers move to new venues. The assessments generated by states and supplemented by districts, schools, teachers, and others create an often overwhelming amount of information to which teachers and administrators are expected to respond. While many argue that no one indicator accurately measures students' knowledge and tout the notion of "multiple measures" to evaluate performance, using these various data creates a major intellectual challenge. The various tests are frequently not aligned and often offer competing views of student achievement. To help resolve the problem, some states and districts are seeking to correlate tests. For example, local educators in Maryland were concerned that the standards-based Maryland State Performance Assessment Program was not well aligned with the norm-referenced CTBS-5 which is also required by the state. They asked publishers to compare the two, which turned out to have a correlation of sixty-six percent. One of our study districts used these results to make sure that its own local assessments measured similar content and did not push schools in other directions. But information on test correlation is just one step that needs to be taken to help local educators make appropriate decisions based on multiple streams of data.

TAILORING DATA INTERPRETATIONS TO SPECIFIC SCHOOL NEEDS

Efforts to network schools with similar demographic populations but differential student achievement rest on a notion that imitating the practices of more successful organizations will produce similar results. But many factors can influence whether importing the models and strategies of a more successful school will have the same outcomes.

The knowledge and skills of the teachers, organizational culture, professional norms, teacher and student mobility, and other factors come into play. Understanding and helping educators work with these differences is essential if importing practices is to be productive.

THE EFFECTS OF DATA ON FOCUS

Using data to drive decisions can lead to rapid-fire shifts in focus. Respondents in one Colorado school talked about their confusing, and quite painful, struggle to interpret and use data. This confusion led them to jump from one strategy and one subject to another each year as they tried to fix problems the data seemed to uncover. A Texas district purchased the University of Chicago School Mathematics Program (UCSMP) based on a study showing strong correlation with state and more challenging national standards. But although they warned their community that scores on the Texas state assessment would likely decline at first (as is often the case when new practices are introduced), people who opposed UCSMP on other grounds used the decrease as a justification for abandoning it.

Critics would say such shifts are too quick to produce any meaningful improvement in a school's curriculum and instruction. Others would argue that these searches are doing just what is needed: shaking up a complacent educational bureaucracy to pursue alternative strategies for improving achievement. The answer probably lies somewhere between these two extreme positions: finding data-driven solutions that balance the need for continuity in order to allow changes to take root and mature with a feedback mechanism that allows for adjustments or removal if, after a time, success is not forthcoming.

Conclusion

In the final analysis, one must continue to explore the underlying premise that data will inject a kind of super-rationality into local decision making. The evidence of problems does not automatically express what one must do about them. At the individual level, a 'rational' solution is affected by the ability of teachers and school administrators to implement the new strategy. Other organizational needs may also affect choices about solutions. If one solution comes with funding and another, more appropriate reform does not, a school may feel compelled to adopt the first. If one solution is held in high esteem by professional colleagues and/or the public, administrators may select it to acquire legitimacy. And it is unlikely that data will eliminate the play of interest group politics, the effects of organizational power structures, and other such factors. But it is also important to recognize that the data and research orientation stimulated in part by standards-based reform has the potential to shine a new and positive light on old problems.

NOTES

1. This research reported in this chapter was supported by grants from the United States Department of Education's Office of Educational Research and Improvement, the Pew Charitable Trusts, and the Annie Casey Foundation.

2. Marshall Smith and Jennifer O'Day, "Systemic school reform," in Susan Fuhrman and Betty Malen, eds., *The Politics of Curriculum and Testing* (Bristol, PA: Falmer Press, 1991), pp. 233-267.

3. Richard Elmore and Robert Rothman, eds., *Testing, Teaching, and Learning: A Guide for States and School Districts* (Washington, DC: National Academy Press, 1999).

4. Packaged innovations create the appearance that education is progressive and thus create public confidence in what tends to be the very uncertain technology of teaching and learning.

5. John Meyer and Brian Rowan, "Institutionalized organizations: Formal structure as myth and ceremony," *American Journal of Sociology* 83 (1977): pp. 341-363; John Meyer, W. Richard Scott, and Terrence Deal, "Institutional and technical sources of organizational structure: Explaining the structure of educational organizations," in John Meyer and W. Richard Scott, eds., *Organizational Environments: Ritual and Rationality* (Beverly Hills, CA: Sage Publishers, 1983).

6. National Governors' Association, *Time for Results* (Washington, DC: Center for Policy Research and Analysis, 1986); Richard Wallace, Jr., "Data driven educational leadership," *Evaluation Practice* 3 (1986): pp. 24-36.

7. We were only able to visit two districts in California, but three each in the other seven states.

8. Nancy Grasmick, "Looking back at a decade of reform: The Maryland implementation, assessment, and accountability—The keys to improving student achievement," *Closing the Gap: A Report on the Wingspread Conference, Beyond the Standards Horse—Implementation, Assessment, and Accountability, The Keys to Improving Student Accountability* (Racine, WI: The Johnson Foundation, 2000).

9. Richard Elmore, Charles Abelmann, and Susan Fuhrman, "The new accountability in state education reform: From process to performance," in Helen Ladd, ed., *Holding Schools Accountable: Performance Based Reform in Education* (Washington, DC: The Brookings Institution, 1996), pp. 65-98; see Goertz's chapter in this volume.

10. See Goertz's chapter in this volume.

11. Donald Dorr-Bremme and Joan Herman, *Assessing for Student Achievement: A Profile of Classroom Practices* (Los Angeles: Center for the Study of Evaluation, University of California-Los Angeles, 1986); George Madaus, "The influence of testing on the curriculum," in Laurel Tanner, ed., *Critical Issues in Curriculum* (Chicago: University of Chicago Press, 1988); H. Dickinson Corbett and Bruce Wilson, "Raising the stakes in statewide mandatory minimum competency testing," in William Boyd and Charles Kerchner, eds., *The 1987 Politics of Education Association Yearbook* (New York: Falmer Press, 1988), pp. 27-39; Joan Herman and Shari Golan, *Effects of Standardized Testing on Teachers and Learning: Another Look* (Los Angeles: National Center for Research on Evaluation, Standards, and Student Testing, University of California-Los Angeles, 1991).

12. David Goslin, *Teachers and Testing* (New York: Russell Sage Foundation, 1967); Leslie Salmon-Cox, "Teachers and standardized achievement tests: What's really happening?" *Phi Delta Kappan* 62 (1981): pp. 730-736; Jane David, *Local Uses of Title I Evaluations* (Washington, DC: Office of the Assistant Secretary for Planning and Evaluation, Department of Health, Education, and Welfare, 1978); Dorr-Bremme and Herman, *Assessing for Student Achievement*.

13. Lauren Resnick and Daniel Resnick, "Assessing the thinking curriculum: New tools for educational reform," in Bernard Gifford and Mary Catherine O'Connor, eds., *Changing Assessments: Alternative Views of Aptitude, Achievement, and Instruction* (Boston: Kluwer Academic Publishers, 1992).

14. Linda Bond, David Braskamp, and Edward Roeber, *Status Report of the Assessment Programs in the United States* (Oakbrook, IL: North Central Regional Educational Laboratory and the Council of Chief State School Officers, 1996).

15. David, *Local Uses of Title I Evaluations*.

16. Margaret Goertz, Diane Massell, and Tammi Chun, *District response to state accountability systems* (Paper presented at the annual meeting of the Association for Public Policy Analysis and Management, New York, NY, 1998).

17. Florida and Texas in this sample.

18. Because of the limited sample size, I can only advance plausible explanations.

19. Districts in Colorado are responsible for determining whether a school is to be identified for Title I school improvement.

20. Madaus, "The influence of testing on the curriculum"; Thomas Romberg, Anne Zarinnia, and Steven Williams, *The Influence of Mandated Testing on Mathematics Instruction: Grade 8 Teachers' Perceptions* (Madison, WI: University of Wisconsin, National Center for Research in Mathematical Science Education, 1989) as cited in Herman and Golan, *Effects of Standardized Testing on Teachers and Learning*.

21. She recalled an item that asked them about gazing at stars and commented, "My students can't see stars at night in the city."

22. James Spillane, "School districts matter: Local educational authorities and state instructional policy," *Educational Policy* 10 (1996): pp. 63-87.

23. Daniel Koretz, Karen Mitchell, Sheila Barron, and Sarah Keith, *Final Report: Perceived Effects of the Maryland School Performance Assessment Program* (Los Angeles: University of California, National Center for Research on Evaluation, Standards and Student Testing, 1996); Daniel Koretz, Brian Stecher, Stephen Klein, Daniel McCaffrey, and Edward Deibert, *Can Portfolios Assess Student Performance and Influence Instruction? The 1991-92 Vermont Experience* (Los Angeles: University of California, National Center for Research on Evaluation, Standards and Student Testing, 1993); Lorraine McDonnell and Craig Choisser, *Testing and Teaching: Local Implementation of New State Assessments* (Los Angeles: University of California, National Center for Research on Evaluation, Standards and Student Testing, 1997).

24. Texas' standards of performance increase annually. During the period of our study, less than half of the total students and each student subgroup had to pass each subject to be rated academically acceptable. Less than a six percent dropout rate and attendance of at least ninety-four percent also had to be achieved.

25. Corbett and Wilson, "Raising the stakes in statewide mandatory minimum competency testing"; Herman and Golan, *Effects of Standardized Testing on Teachers and Learning*.

26. Smith and O'Day, "Systemic school reform."

27. Catherine Belcher and Susan Fuhrman, *Measuring comprehensive reform model effectiveness: Schools, student learning, and responsibility* (Paper presented at the annual meeting of the American Educational Research Association, New Orleans, LA, 2000).

28. Thomas Guskey, *Evaluating Professional Development* (Thousand Oaks, CA: Corwin Press, 2000).

Section Four
SCHOOL IMPLEMENTATION
AND INSTRUCTIONAL EFFECTS

CHAPTER IX

Patterns of Response in Four High Schools
Under State Accountability Policies
in Vermont and New York[1]

ELIZABETH DeBRAY, GAIL PARSON,
AND KATRINA WOODWORTH[2]

This chapter examines the responses of four high schools to new accountability policies in New York and Vermont.[3] In each state we selected a school that was "better-positioned" with respect to the policy and a school that we considered a "target" of the policy.[4] The differences in these two state policies were dramatic; therefore, we anticipated that we would find important variation in school response between the schools in New York and Vermont. We found instead that the state policies interacted with existing school structures and norms to produce divergent responses by school *type*. The two better-positioned schools went beyond compliance with policy requirements, launching coherent responses that exceeded the mandate, finding ways to use the policy to effectively enhance and drive their own missions. In contrast, the two target schools also complied with the policies' technical requirements, but did not have the internal structures needed to translate the mandate into the kind of coherent action that could more effectively lead to the improvement of instruction and student achievement.

Elizabeth DeBray and Gail Parson are doctoral candidates in Administration, Planning, and Social Policy at Harvard University's Graduate School of Education. They both also serve as research assistants with the Consortium for Policy Research in Education. Katrina Woodworth is an education policy analyst at SRI International.

170

This chapter illustrates the differences in the stories of the four schools, one of each type in each state. Through an analysis of these schools, we explicate how and why the state policies landed so differently, with special focus on the degree of alignment between the states' accountability policies and the schools' internal accountability systems, and specific school level activities in response to the policies.

There are several design differences between the two states' policies. While both centered on state testing systems, New York's policy attached high stakes for students via the Regents high school exit examination. Until 1996, high school students in New York State earned either a "local diploma," after passing five Regents Competency Tests (RCTs), or a Regents diploma, which meant passing eight higher level subject matter exams. In 1996, the Board of Regents announced that over the ensuing eight years, the competency tests would be phased out; all students would be required to pass five higher level Regents exams to graduate (in English, mathematics, global studies, United States history, and science). This meant that the graduating class of 2000 would be held accountable for passing the English examination, and the class of 2001 for passing both English and mathematics examinations. In contrast, there were no stakes attached to Vermont's New Standards Reference Exam (NSRE) except the printing of results in local newspapers. Neither state had clearly defined stakes for adults or a specified role for districts.

Vermont school accountability was part of a much broader policy, Act 60, which was passed by the Vermont legislature in 1998. Act 60 was a comprehensive finance equalization plan which included statewide testing, a process of school level "action planning," and technical assistance for low-performing schools. Action planning was designed as a self-assessment *process* for capacity building at the organizational level, whereas New York policy focused only on measurable *outcomes* (i.e., individual students' passing scores). Action Plans were to include identified areas of improvement (in part, utilizing data from the NSRE) and specific goals. Schools were to submit plans to the district and state. Vermont offered no concrete performance targets that schools should aim for in their Action Plans.

Vermont's inclusion of action planning stood in contrast to New York's focus on "Regents tests for all," which was intended to be a lever for demanding high performance standards for all students and, as a result, for decreasing the statewide performance gap. Unlike in Vermont, New York State policymakers did not offer any specific guidance about *how* high schools should adjust to this significant policy shift.

The details of implementation and organizational incentives were left entirely up to schools and districts. In both states, we studied the early implementation of these policies: the testing system was being phased in for juniors in New York, and the first cycle of testing and action planning was being carried out in Vermont.

In our examination of the schools' responses to the state policies, we focus first on the alignment between internal, school level conceptions of accountability and the external, state level accountability policies. In conducting these analyses, we relied on the working theory of school-site accountability developed by Abelmann, Elmore, and colleagues in an earlier phase of this study of accountability. This theory posits that a school constructs a system of accountability out of the "relationships among three factors: individual conceptions of *responsibility*, shared *expectations* among school participants and stakeholders, and *internal and external accountability* mechanisms."[5] The theory assumes that there may be inconsistencies or complementarities in these relationships, and argues that internal accountability systems are likely to be stronger where there is alignment among these factors. Abelmann, Elmore, and colleagues developed this working theory based on the assumption that, "The long-term fate of educational reform, as it is presently conceived, lies largely in th[e] tension between uniform requirements of external accountability systems and the particularities of real schools."[6]

With this in mind, in addition to expecting variation by state, we expected that school level responses to the external accountability systems would depend on how well these policies aligned with the schools' existing internal accountability systems. We found this to be the case in both states.

In the sections that follow, we examine these four schools, looking first at the better-positioned school, followed by the target school, in each of the study states.

Rivera High School, New York

Serving approximately 1,500 students, Rivera is a "screened" high school, that is, the school can be selective in choosing academically oriented freshmen. The student population is predominantly Hispanic (sixty-three percent) and African American (thirty percent). Thirty percent of students receive free or reduced-price lunch. Historically, all students took Regents courses, and most sat for exams in mathematics, science, and English. Among graduates of the class of 1999, thirty-five percent received Regents diplomas by passing all eight required exams. Therefore, Rivera was well positioned to accept the state's challenge of getting all students to take and pass Regents exams because this had been its prior function.

INTERNAL CONCEPTIONS OF ACCOUNTABILITY

Rivera educators were clear about their goal: to prepare students for college. As one English teacher said, "I'm not here to prepare them for their career. I'm here to prepare them for college . . . I want to teach them how to write analytically. And I think the Regents is a good assessment of it." The principal clearly stated that preparing students to pass the Regents had long been a schoolwide reality:

There's very . . . little flexibility in what we need to teach, if you care about your kids passing that test . . . [it's] the reality of this school, and now it's really a reality for everybody. I mean, it's been a reality for us for . . . many years, because we were always very . . . concerned about our data, and about the kids doing well here.

In this sense, Rivera is the school that best illustrates external accountability having been a factor in shaping the teachers' expectations in the years before the "Regents for all" policy took effect. Rivera's positioning with respect to the new policy reflects the fact that its prior function shaped an internal accountability system that is aligned with the new external system.

The state testing mandate was readily embraced as the driving force behind the school's efforts, and was accepted as the measure against which Rivera educators judged their success. The principal spoke clearly about increasingly holding teachers accountable for student performance on the Regents. Although she did not have the authority to hire and fire, she used more informal means to hold teachers accountable for results:[7]

We're all going to be looking at your results, and you're going to be held accountable . . . Can I fire teachers? No. Can I make them feel uncomfortable when they're not performing? Yes.

This translated into an internal accountability system that included publicizing individual teachers' Regents results. An English teacher explained:

Q: What are teachers actually held accountable for here?

A: Regents results certainly count. Those are public.

Q: And are they individually tied to teachers?

A: Oh, yeah.

Q: This group of students didn't do well and they all had Miss X?

A: Absolutely. Everybody knows that. And not only in our own subject area, but there's like a school report card that comes out, and it's broken down by subject and then by individual class.

At Rivera, scores did not vanish into the organization, but were used.

Another mathematics teacher talked about feeling personally responsible for these results in two ways:

The principal and the [department chair] for mathematics look at the pass rates on the Regents exams as kind of a guideline of what's going on. And people whose pass rates are low are going to be scrutinized to see what they're doing and what they can do differently. So I have an incentive to . . . get my students to do well on the exams . . . These kids come in expecting to learn things and get ready for college. And I would feel remiss if I weren't supplying the best possible instruction for them.

What she believed she personally owed her students was supported by the school's internal accountability system. Teachers' feelings of personal responsibility formed a set of shared expectations that were reinforced internally by collaborative work and an active and focused administration. Teachers told us about analyzing test results within departments, as well as with the principal, who conferred with individual classroom teachers about their performance. All these elements played a strong role in establishing internal accountability:

The administration in this school is very . . . very focused. They're very actively involved in the staff and the staff's performance . . . What I mean by focus is that . . . we are all working toward the same goal . . . Everybody's pushing toward high achievement, in terms of state standardized exams . . . The first week that I taught in the school, the principal had already made an appointment, scheduled an appointment to sit in on one of my classes, just to be sure that I am following the standards of [Rivera], which is tremendous. I felt that that showed that even the principal was actively involved in every single one of his staff's performance, and how they're carrying through their objectives.

Clearly, the school had a strong internal accountability system that was aligned with the state's accountability system.

THE RESPONSE TO THE POLICY

We found a schoolwide consensus that Rivera was experiencing new pressures to improve its performance. Specifically, the responses involved using data to inform instruction, as described above, engaging in ongoing professional development, and adding instructional time before and after school, particularly for students most at risk of not passing the Regents.

Opportunities for professional development were varied. Most professional development was school based, including formal faculty and department meetings as well as study groups formed by teachers to discuss specific topics of interest. The principal described the array: mandated meetings twice a month, staff development days, subject area department conferences, and a forum she created, teacher study groups.

Department meetings covered a range of topics. The mathematics department met in different configurations depending on the subject they were addressing. For example, members of the department met in sub-groups based on the courses they taught in order to share curriculum and assessment. Across departments, the topics of rubrics and standards were integral to these conversations.

To achieve the aggregate goal of the "Regents for all" policy, teachers and administrators were paying increased attention to those students most likely to fail. Mathematics tutorial was available before school for those students most at risk of not passing the Sequential I exam (which every student eventually had to pass for graduation). The school offered courses in English, mathematics, and American history after school for Regents preparation, and there was a study skills course after school for ninth graders. The school had sought external funding from a foundation to support much of this after school work, demonstrating their ability to increase capacity through external partners.

SUMMARY

Rivera educators anticipated the challenge of getting all of its students to meet the state's standards by building on their existing capacity. New York's policy shift provided a galvanizing moment for staff to consider a variety of academic interventions for students. It is a goal that most believe they will meet. Robinson High School, our next case, was situated very differently from Rivera relative to the new state accountability system.

Robinson High School, New York

Robinson is a large, comprehensive urban high school, serving 3,300 students in grades nine through twelve. Of those, fifty-eight percent are African American and thirty-seven percent are Hispanic.

Roughly seventy percent receive free lunch. The school is required by the district to enroll students with a broad range of academic skills (as measured by standardized tests administered in middle schools). While official dropout statistics at Robinson hover around five percent, there is a significant disparity between the number of ninth graders (over 1,000) compared to twelfth graders (under 400).

INTERNAL CONCEPTIONS OF ACCOUNTABILITY

Robinson did not have a history of preparing students to earn Regents' diplomas; in recent years, roughly five percent of graduating seniors earned them. Instead, Robinson's prior function included the myriad goals of a comprehensive high school (i.e., general education, college prep, school-to-career) as well as preparing students for minimum competency exams (the RCT) which had been the state's bar for graduation until 1996. In this context, most characterized the new policy as a significant challenge in terms of both teachers' previous practices and students' skill levels.

Several teachers talked about the magnitude of this change by explaining how differently positioned this school was from those in other parts of the state. Many of the teachers' comments reflected pessimism about their students' readiness for Regents testing. One said, "Our schools are not functioning and haven't been for a really long time. I'm sorry to see the students be penalized for that in the name of raising the standards." As another teacher indicated, educators often felt powerless to affect their students' chances: "I think it's ridiculous to expect kids who have been basically allowed to get to high school with inferior skills, to improve in their high school years." While these comments reflected teachers' senses of efficacy with respect to the policy and their concerns about the stakes falling on students, many teachers agreed with the idea of raising standards. As one said, "Passing the Regents is something that's long overdue. It's not something that the kids cannot achieve . . . If we lift the standards and say, 'Let's aim for something else,' they will rise to the occasion."

Given the contrast between Robinson's prior function and the goal of the new policy, it is not surprising that we found little evidence of formal, internal accountability mechanisms that aligned with the new policy. In fact, teachers talked about the absence of any mechanisms (internal or external) aimed at holding them accountable for student performance:

I'm not going to be accountable, nobody is. If they look at my class list and see that ninety-nine percent of my students fail, is anything going to happen to me? No.

One teacher acknowledged that if she were held accountable for the performance of her students, "I would lose my job overnight."

Because teachers' feelings of personal responsibility were not shaped by a clearly defined prior function or by formal accountability mechanisms, there was no coherent schoolwide system of accountability. Instead, educators at Robinson essentially operated in isolation. In the terms of Abelmann, Elmore, and colleagues' theory of school-site accountability, this school is a place where individual responsibility dominates and accountability is "atomized." In this kind of environment, "the school's conception of accountability collapses, by default, into individual teachers' conceptions of responsibility."[8]

RESPONSE TO THE POLICY

The school and the departments followed a pattern of compliance with external requirements (i.e., the elimination of an RCT track). However, the school's response to the policy along three dimensions (teacher professional development, using student achievement data to set goals and monitor progress, and adding time and remedial instruction for students) was limited or non-existent. The absence of any school or department level response led to a range of individual level responses and a district intervention.

The lack of schoolwide response. Carrying on their tradition of operating in isolation, Robinson teachers did not participate in departmental professional development or engage in instructionally focused conversations that would help them prepare students for the exam. Among teachers who saw this lack of professional development as problematic, at least one argued that support for this work should come from the state:

What I really need from the state . . . is some resources and training . . . I feel ill-equipped . . . I feel as though I'm learning on the fly . . . It's not that we're unwilling to develop our own stuff, but a little more help would be welcome.

The absence of professional development aimed at helping teachers make instructional changes in alignment with the "Regents for all" policy extended to the use of data. In 1998-99, we did not hear about any use of data in preparing for the exams. Based on comments, such as the following made by the former mathematics chair, it appeared that school based administrators lacked the capacity or resources to make use of the data, and again they called for support from the state:

Last year, [the state] did give us results . . . [But] it should have been done with support, training, supplemental material, extra resources, consultants, everything. If they thought this was really important, it should have been done with the teachers, not told to the teachers.

When we collected data in the fall of 1999, the results of the previous spring's Regents were in, but were not being used. In fact, English teachers gave us varying accounts of the overall percentage of students who passed. One teacher explained how teachers could learn about students' performance on the Regents: "I think if you asked and you inquired and you needed to know some information, yeah, sure, you can get the information." When we asked, many teachers said they did not know if the students in their classes had passed or not, or if the students they had taught the previous year had been successful.

In 1998-99, the most significant response to the policy came in the form of added time for instruction (i.e., before-school tutoring, additional courses). However, in the fall of 1999, teachers reported significant problems with "programming"—getting students into the right classes. These problems undermined efforts to organize students in preparation for the Regents. For example, many students were not placed in the appropriate mathematics classes by mid-semester. In English, a class that was established for seniors who had failed the Regents was filled with sophomores, juniors, and seniors (including some who may have already passed the English Regents).

Individual responses and a district intervention. Without a coherent school or departmental response to the policy, there was a range of teacher responses based upon their personal senses of responsibility and efficacy. We illustrate this range using English teachers' responses to questions about the implications of the "Regents for all" policy. One tenth grade teacher, who indicated that she was not changing her teaching to align with the new Regents, explained why she threw away any state standards guides given to her:

If we had much better students, then we might wish to focus on the details of, "Oh, we need to polish up this skill or that skill." But we're dealing with kids who are mostly drowning. When you're drowning, you don't discuss which life belt is better, you just throw out the nearest life belt.

In contrast, a member of the department who was convinced of the merits of the new test had attended several state-sponsored sessions on the test. Her response to the policy reflected her personal commitment to ensuring its success:

I am truly convinced of the merits of this exam, and it's a very exciting time to change and to have the courage at the Empire State to say, "This is no longer a good exam," and to go forward and change.

Most teachers at Robinson fell somewhere in between these two.

While the district seemed to provide little support for a more coherent school level response (i.e., in the form of information, professional development, or assistance with whole school change), there was a serious district intervention during our second year of data collection. In the aftermath of very low pass rates on the June 1999 mathematics Regents (estimated by teachers at four to five percent), the principal and mathematics chair were both replaced. During the 1999-2000 school year, the new principal focused mostly on building staff morale and developing high-profile relationships with the community. The new mathematics chair, who was very specific about her plans ("I'm very narrow-minded . . . My interest right now is to raise the results"), began to use data as a "reality check," straighten out programming problems, and initiate team-based work as a forum for course planning and sequencing.

SUMMARY

Robinson's response to the new state accountability system illustrates what happens when an external policy lands in a school where student skill levels are significantly below the policy goal, and there is little organizational capacity, incentives, or support for coherent response to the policy. The lack of capacity to respond reflects the school's prior function, the lack of shared expectations among teachers with respect to their work, and the absence of any internal accountability mechanisms aligned with the external policy goals. It remains to be seen whether the district intervention will help to build school level capacity for reform and establish a coherent internal system of accountability.

Glen Lake High School, Vermont

Glen Lake, the only high school in a district on the outskirts of a small city, serves approximately 840 students. The student population is homogeneous, almost entirely White. Approximately thirteen percent of students are eligible for free or reduced-price lunch. Glen Lake is a school that has long emphasized attainment. Prior to the arrival of the New Standards Reference Exam (NSRE), Glen Lake was consistently among the top two high schools in the state on its standardized test scores. Seventy-five percent of 1999 graduates matriculated to college. Although it has historically been a high performer in the state, the new performance based system has caused the school to look carefully at the performance of all of its students. The school's administration and academic departments have not merely accepted the challenge of improvement, but carried it forward in a concrete way.

INTERNAL CONCEPTIONS OF ACCOUNTABILITY

Glen Lake staff talked about traditions in the building: community support for funding (the teachers are among the highest paid in the state), and a large number of veteran teachers who are both independent practitioners and experts in their subjects. In this environment, teachers held mutual expectations about being the best at what they do. Individual teachers felt responsible to parents to deliver a traditional, pre-college education, so there was high alignment between collective expectations and the staff's personal responsibility. These collective expectations were used to embrace external demands, such as the NSRE and action planning.

These collective expectations also helped to create a strong, albeit informal, internal accountability system. For example, at Glen Lake, participating in external initiatives was an expectation. According to the chair of the mathematics department, who had been in that position for thirty-three years:

We're involved in everything in this school. We just buy into everything that comes down the pike. We try to meet every state standard. We try to meet the needs of all the parents . . . We're just that kind of a school. We're not a school that very often says no. That kind of explains us.

In this context, we found surprisingly little resistance to curricular change. Being a teacher at Glen Lake seemed to be a stronger influence on collective expectations than teachers' individual practice, expertise, or preferences. Since "being out in front" and "involved" in external demands is part of the school's culture, teachers were willing to make adjustments to further collective school priorities.

The school's internal expectations provided the incentive to align with the external requirements, more than any pressure from the state or district. Action planning was a school level activity, subject so far to virtually no external stakes. The school board did not choose to review or approve the state-mandated Action Plan at all in the last cycle, and the state's only feedback was to ensure Glen Lake conformed precisely to a state rubric. And that, said the chair of the School Development Team (responsible for action planning), suited Glen Lake just fine:

We're doing this because we think it's valuable for us. And we're going to keep doing it, even if the state backs off . . . We're conforming to the state series of boxes, but we have something we want to get out of it . . . I know there are other schools that are just filling the boxes just to get past this . . .

As exemplified here, the culture of the building, the tradition of success, and the pressures of Act 60 converged, and the teachers and administrators were eager to respond to the external changes when they easily might have coasted on their pre-existing successes without extreme pressure from the community to change.

THE RESPONSE TO THE POLICY

For teachers, who were accustomed to the school being perceived as a state academic leader, the spring 1998 NSRE test results were startling. Only thirty-one percent of tenth graders "achieved the standard" or "achieved the standard with honors" in the area of "reading for analysis and interpretation." In mathematics, twenty-six percent of students taking the exam "achieved the standard" or achieved "with honors" in the area of problem solving.

In response, Glen Lake embraced the state-mandated action planning. Act 60 did not specify how action planning should be done, simply that every school must have an Action Plan on file with the district at the end of every school year. Glen Lake's decision to require every department to set data-driven goals was initially viewed as too ambitious by the state, but the principal maintained that this was how the school wanted to do it. In part, Glen Lake took the process seriously because of budget cuts. Under Act 60, the school district lost $2.2 million through "recapture," or giving back to the state. In May 1999, the school board voted down a measure to replace $600,000 of that loss. A community that had offered its unwavering support for funding increases would no longer do so. With school board members under pressure to keep the budget down, the staff recognized that documenting performance was inevitable.

Before action planning was mandated, Glen Lake had an "Indicators of Success" committee, whose function was to begin to look at data and quantifiable goals for the departments. The principal was able to smoothly transform this group into the action planning team, comprised of various department chairs, the principal, and other volunteers.

No department, including such areas as guidance and music, was exempt from action planning. We found that the school's academic departments embraced the process. The action planning team's role was to help departments define problems based on data, and set annual goals; these plans then became the school's Action Plan that was submitted to the district. The team leader compared the process to the "scientific method."

In both the English and mathematics departments, we found evidence of strong alignment across three levels of goal-setting: the school level Action Plans, the departmental plan, and individual teachers' goals for the classroom. We also found that the establishment of student achievement goals with respect to the state test led to changes in curriculum and pedagogy in both the mathematics and English departments. As described below, each department set goals, teachers changed practices, and students performed better on the test.

The mathematics department's goal was that the number of Glen Lake students who "achieved the standard" would increase by at least twenty percent on the next NSRE problem solving section. The department easily met the goal. The 1999 results achieved a sixty percent increase in this area over the 1998 results. To achieve this result, mathematics teachers consistently told us that they were emphasizing "open-ended" questions more than they had in the past. Another adjustment to align practice with the exam was the approach to teaching algebra. The NSRE in mathematics is given at the end of sophomore year, and tests algebra and some geometry concepts. The department, facing the challenge of how to help all students become adequately proficient in algebra, this year created a "Level Two" algebra sequence serving between a quarter and a third of the entering class. In Level Two, instruction was drawn out over the freshman and sophomore years. In regular algebra, instruction was heavily focused on textbook exercises that involve graphing calculators and explanations of how answers were derived—signs of alignment with New Standards.

In Glen Lake's English department, staffed with independent practitioners who had worked there for twenty years or more, the curriculum had been notable for its emphasis on traditional literature, with a focus on novels. But the New Standards English exam results raised concern that only about the top twenty-five percent of students were flourishing with this approach. The department, with the goal of exposing students to the variety of literary styles and genres that they would be asked to analyze on the state assessment, built a new ninth grade curriculum around a literary anthology with a broader selection.

While the anthology did not completely replace the teaching of novels in freshman year, teachers paid greater attention to what was required by the exams.

In 1998-99, the English Department's goal was that fifty percent or more of tenth grade students would "achieve" or "achieve with honors" the reading skills on the New Standards exam. The chair hired a reading specialist as part of its Action Plan to assist students who were having the greatest difficulty, and she offered a variety of types of reading assistance across the curriculum. This investment paid off: the number of students reading for basic understanding increased by fifteen percent and the number reading for analysis and interpretation increased by twenty-nine percent.

SUMMARY

Like Rivera, Glen Lake's compliance with the policy complemented their mission, or the school found ways to make it do so. They made changes in their curriculum to prepare students for state exams, and made the action planning an exercise that was useful for the school. Thus it was a case of a school's internal accountability mechanisms (i.e., using data to make instructional decisions) being reinforced by an external policy (action planning), and becoming even more highly aligned. At the same time, the assessment results caused the school to look carefully at which students were achieving, and make changes in teaching and curriculum in an effort to reach more of them. Much less internal-external alignment was evident in the other Vermont school in our study.

Garrison High School, Vermont

Garrison High School serves a small Vermont town of 6,500, with significant populations of migrants and refugees (twelve percent) and low-cost housing areas. The school has 220 students, sixty-four percent of whom receive free or reduced-price lunch. Per pupil expenditure at Garrison was $4,500 in spring 1999, as compared to the Vermont average of $5,600. While ninety-seven percent of students graduate from Garrison, only thirty percent generally go to four-year colleges.

INTERNAL CONCEPTIONS OF ACCOUNTABILITY

When Vermont's Act 60 and standards-based reform policies arrived, Garrison was struggling with serious communication, discipline, and attendance problems. Administrators were preoccupied with crisis management and operations issues, resulting in a laissez faire approach to instruction, and a long history of only minimal demands placed on staff and students. Many members of the small, veteran staff had not been formally evaluated in years. They were too few in number to have functional departments, often a productive unit of accountability in larger schools.

Garrison's NSRE scores for 1997-98 were low. Only two percent of students met the standard in mathematical concepts and problem solving. Similarly, only nine percent of students met the standard for reading analysis and interpretation. In response, Garrison sought and received technical assistance, and complied with Vermont's Act 60 and standards-based reform policies. In the following year, 1998-99, some scores rose. But with the exception of writing conventions, all the tested areas in mathematics and English remained far below state averages. The state then raised the bar, and its lowest "requiring assistance" category expanded from four to thirty-nine schools; Garrison was one of them.

Weak alignment of external and internal accountability. With its required testing, action planning, and standards-based curriculum, the state policy seemed to offer a springboard for schools to generate shared goals around which to align individual responsibility and internal accountability mechanisms. But as Abelmann, Elmore, and colleagues point out, external accountability systems like Vermont's policy "operate at the margins of powerful factors inside the school."[9]

"Powerful factors" were at work inside Garrison. It had an atomized culture and no coherent system of internal accountability. Individual teachers' feelings of personal responsibility, idiosyncratic and widely varied, were not aligned in ways that created common expectations, nor were they shaped by informal or formal accountability mechanisms such as administrative evaluations.

And the leadership team itself was atomized. The principal and the curriculum coordinator each espoused belief in the importance of improved instructional practice focused on standards, but operated on separate tracks, with no consistent or unified expectations toward holding teachers accountable for student achievement. This schism exacerbated the lack of alignment between the external accountability policy and the school's inner workings. The curriculum coordinator had the requisite knowledge but no authority, while the principal's ability to recognize good practice was not bulwarked by a willingness to confront teachers in core areas who were not teaching to standards. By December of the second year, no teachers in the core tested areas, with some of the lowest scores in the state, had been evaluated.

The years of non-existent or weak evaluation mechanisms had taken their toll. Teachers felt little accountability to formal authority or to the community:

Q: *Who do you feel accountable to?*

A: I don't know . . . I don't feel anything from the outside . . . even when the test scores come out, there are kids that are getting this information, and so you're constantly trying to do better . . . And I think if the administrators didn't think I was doing okay, then I would feel like there was—maybe because they think I'm doing okay, that that's an accountability that just is sort of seamless and I don't think about it. Same thing with the parents.

Q: *No news is good news?*

A: Sort of . . . there are communities in this area where . . . the parents are just constantly in your face. "You got to do this, this, and that." That doesn't happen here, so you don't think of them as being your customer either. You think about getting these kids good jobs and good schools.

This sense of "no news is good news" reflected how weak the internal accountability system was at Garrison. With little consistent communication and evaluation, external demands for accountability could not take hold.

Individual responsibility in a culture of low expectations. The curriculum coordinator spoke often of teachers' low expectations for, and beliefs about, students. Teachers could not or would not make the connection to the need to change and improve their own practice, particularly in the absence of any real pressure to do so. Students were not expected to go to college here, said several teachers, "and, [parents] are not pushing their kids to do better either . . . that's the reality of it."

In a school with these generally low expectations, and an incoherent organizational response, any external initiative will devolve to individual responsibility. This became very clear as we spoke to teachers about their responses to the various initiatives the new policy had generated; specifically, the encouragement of curriculum alignment with state standards and standards-based teaching. As one mathematics teacher explained, the curriculum coordinator led attempts to align standards with the curriculum, but there had been no assessment of what teachers were actually doing in their classrooms.

In the core area of English, two veteran teachers (both with over twenty-five years in the school) acknowledged that they had been exposed to reform ideas about teaching and aligning curriculum to standards.

They each said there was no real English curriculum, and they were aware of the school's low scores, but they weren't particularly disposed to fundamentally changing their practice, nor did they feel compelled or accountable for doing so. As one said:

I really don't see a commitment to changing the typical courses in the typical high school merely to meet the standards . . . I don't sit down everyday and say, "What standard am I teaching today?" Which maybe I should be. But I don't.

Teachers felt that working with standards or changing their practice was a matter of individual discretion. While there were individual teachers with thoughtful and/or improving practice, this work was self-initiated and inconsistent across the school.

THE RESPONSE TO THE POLICY

At Garrison, professional development and the push for instructional improvement stopped at the classroom door where it became an individual teacher's choice. Vermont's required action planning process had the same stunted quality. An official Action Plan was generated, but the plan reflected the nature of the school: disjointed with no internal accountability mechanisms that could actually begin to change the collective norms of the atomized culture.

The principal looked to the Action Plan as an opportunity to dovetail schoolwide initiatives, but the final product was a patchwork of visions and goals with weak accountability mechanisms. The principal said the process began with a staff-wide "satisfaction survey," followed by work with a standing committee of representatives from the high and middle schools. An outside consultant, she informed us, wrote the final product. The teachers did not have any ownership of this plan because, the curriculum coordinator said, "It was just done by a committee somewhere." Not surprisingly, teachers we interviewed referred very little to the Action Plan.

The final Action Plan focused on discipline, curriculum alignment with standards, and the improvement of mathematics problem solving skills, in response to low NSRE scores in that area. (New mathematics texts were purchased with Act 60 money.) The abysmal scores in writing and reading were not addressed as an official focus, except as embedded in the goal of having a "coordinated, challenging" standards-based curriculum. There were no formal accountability measures in the plan. In short, the action planning process was a missed opportunity to create a cohesive response to problems in the school.

Professional development had little coherence as well. It was either personally motivated and individually sought out in isolation, or offered schoolwide, but it alternately featured different programs. In a school as atomized as Garrison, with little internal accountability and few collective expectations, professional development, even the mandated implementation of state curriculum standards, did not "take hold" in any consistent way across the staff.

SUMMARY

Garrison's story is one of a school whose disjointed leadership, atomized culture, and lack of coherent internal accountability mechanisms rendered it almost impervious to the intentions of Vermont policy. It did not respond to recognized needs or identified problems other than how it always had: in a compartmentalized, fragmented way, with leadership working at cross-purposes and understandings, all in a context of low student expectations.

In a state famous for its fierce commitment to local control around educational matters, the individual educator at Garrison was able to take local control to its logical extreme. Instructional improvement, aligning curriculum with standards, accountability for raising test scores—these were just options, choices—and student achievement was a sad testament to the choices many educators had made.

Conclusion

In New York and Vermont, both policies held the goal of equalizing performance over time, and addressing the problem of low-performing schools and students. Both states' theories of action[10] assume that "performance information from the accountability system will drive change in schools and districts. The theory of action is that the accountability system will provide feedback on school performance that will then be used in school improvement planning."[11] The key limitation of this theory, however, is existing local capacity for an alignment of internal and external accountability. As Massell explained, "Performance data often are not transparent and readily understandable [and] educators often do not have the requisite knowledge and skills to translate them."[12] The mechanisms of this theory of action vary and look different once they are *in use* at the school level. For example, public reporting, which assumes that if local stakeholders are uncomfortable enough with low performance they will provide the necessary local level pressure to bring about improvement, was the most salient feature of Vermont's accountability system at the school level. In New York, the new tests with high stakes for students were the most prominent feature of the state's accountability system from the school perspective, suggesting a simplified theory of action—that is, that policymakers posit that giving a single set of tests statewide, and placing stakes on students, will cause schools to improve.

Despite these differences in state accountability policies and mechanisms, we found that the variation between types of schools in response to the policies far exceeded the variation attributable to state policy design. However, before we describe this variation, we want to remind the reader that these findings are limited in at least two important ways. First, the fact that the accountability policies in Vermont or New York at the time of our study did not involve explicit rewards or sanctions for adults raises a question about whether our findings about school response would hold in states that do. For example, in another state in our study, Kentucky, the state's incentives are designed to foster school improvement relative to its prior performance levels, and the entire organization is rewarded or sanctioned based on this performance. Our findings about school type and response may differ greatly under such policy conditions, and we intend to extend this analysis about school type and state policy design in a future paper. Second, our findings about the similarities of response by school type are not generalizable to the broader population of high schools. In other words, we do not want to suggest that every low-performing school fails to use data well in planning, nor do we conclude that all better-positioned schools respond actively to accountability policies. Schools' responses to policies are dependent on a wide range of contingencies. Here, we note the similarities that were present in this small sample across similar types of schools operating under two very different sets of state incentives that shared the goal of spurring improvement in low-performing schools. We highlight these different patterns of response by school type.

HIGH-PERFORMING SCHOOLS

The policy, whether New York's or Vermont's, reinforced the schools' identity, prior mission of attainment, and mechanisms of using data. The policies at work in these schools put a spotlight on helping low-performing students, which staff accepted as a worthwhile, significant challenge. Addressing the learning needs of these students with a coherent plan reinforced their sense of efficacy. Both Rivera and Glen Lake began to learn how to set short-term performance goals for making improvements in student achievement, especially by sharing performance data within the department and setting corresponding instructional goals. In both of these schools, the policy developed a momentum of its own that "fit" the schools' goals. As the head of action planning at Glen Lake put it, "We're doing this because we think it's valuable for us. And we're going to keep doing it, even if the state backs off."

LOW-PERFORMING SCHOOLS

We identified a pattern of "compliance without capacity" in the lower-performing schools. Compliance was *pro forma*, with minimal meaningful or productive engagement on the part of the staff. In these schools, other "survival" needs often eclipsed new, external demands. At Robinson, for instance, teachers reported that poor course scheduling and sequencing for students was a barrier to tackling any further challenges. At Garrison, serious discipline and attendance problems were a daily reality. While both schools managed to comply with the policy, they failed to use it as a vehicle for instructional improvement. This failure to respond coherently was due, in large part, to the absence of collaborative structures and routines. Both Garrison and Robinson were responding to policies that did not specify short-term performance targets or achievement goals. In New York, Robinson was faced with the challenge of having to climb a very steep curve of getting all students to meet the standard, which overwhelmed them. At Garrison, the state had not specified any incremental achievement targets, so they selected "areas for improvement," but were not under any pressure to quantify by how much they would improve.

The needs of the low-performing schools in our small sample suggest several "blind spots" of these two state policies, as we see them. These can be thought of as ways that the state policies were underspecified with regard to improving student performance in all schools.

The theory. Policies are landing in high schools that have their own particular internal accountability structures. If the elements of internal structure and external accountability systems are not aligned, then the policies may not pierce the instructional core and foster improvement. For instance, at Garrison, neither the presence of a common assessment nor the requirement of a planning process was able to overcome the inertia of the atomized internal structure of the school.

Use of data. Because of this lack of internal structure, schools may not have internal mechanisms for how to use the data in planning, or even understand its consequences for the school. As Massell noted above, it is an assumption that simply because a school receives results from a state assessment, it will know how to respond to it, and will possess the knowledge, skills, and resources to respond. This also is a lot to expect from schools concerned with "survival," as we observed earlier.

Incentives. Using data may in turn generate an incentive problem: results may reinforce eductors' beliefs about student abilities to learn, or their own efficacy to turn the problem around, which can perpetuate a cycle of even lower expectations. Examples of this scenario in our schools are abundant. In New York, the theory assumes that giving the Regents with stakes for students in and of itself will be an incentive for improvement. We wonder, when performance scores are as abysmal as they were in basic Regents mathematics at Robinson last year, whether this may move from serving as an incentive, to instead, serving as reinforcement of blame and helplessness. At that school, a new mathematics chair is arriving in the wake of a ninety-five percent failure rate on the basic mathematics Regents last spring. The policy offers her nothing in terms of support, incentives, or models for addressing instructional change. She arrived in a school absent collaboration or a functional internal accountability structure, and faced a policy that neither acknowledged nor supported her in dealing with that.

Short-term, school level goals for continuous improvement. While the state policies envision improved long-term outcomes for schools, neither addressed how a low-performing school would set *short-term* performance goals. If Vermont's goal, for example, is for low-performing schools to tackle continuous improvement, it may have to mandate some reasonable performance target, or monitor schools in their selection of reasonable goals. Should Garrison, a school with only thirty-three percent scoring "acceptable" in reading interpretation and analysis, be permitted to submit an Action Plan that does not address literacy?

In addition to these policy shortcomings, we have two closing observations about each state policy in particular.

In New York, the policy assumes that students will be motivated to re-take failed exams repeatedly, and that teachers will be motivated to engage in endless remediation. Teachers are the reform's implicitly relied-upon partners. Their motivation and effort are assumed in the state's additive equation about how it will work to keep students in high school for as long as it takes them to pass. The teachers are simply present, and presumably (since no state policies have provided otherwise) will be willing to commit extra time to teach the same content repeatedly in any way they know. Rhetoric at the state level has emphasized that students will have numerous chances to keep trying to attain a diploma if they fail; if they will not give up, they will have more than one chance to re-take an exam. Robinson's situation calls these assumptions into question. Will teachers there be called to repeatedly deliver remedial instruction to students who did not meet the state standard the year before? What are their incentives?

In Vermont, the policy assumes that giving all schools latitude to develop and execute an Action Plan that "makes sense" for their community will be fruitful, that local control will become part of the planning process that drives improvement. Act 60 assumes that test scores are an incentive, and that requiring action planning will result in productive, collaborative identification of priorities and goal-setting. Garrison's experience demonstrates how problematic these assumptions are. The administration drew up an Action Plan that failed to address a major area of weakness: literacy. The planning process involved minimal buy-in of teachers, with no apparent community activism or stakeholders scrutinizing achievement results. In a deeply atomized school, the teachers felt they had a choice of whether or not to participate in any kind of improvement, let alone change their practice. The state was able to document schools' achievement deficits, but did not help to set concrete, realistic goals to strive for in the short run.

The common patterns of response we identified in these high schools indicate that state policymakers need to re-think policy instruments for the lowest-performing schools. Further, high schools' internal accountability structures are complex terrain, and how schools navigate external policy requirements is quite dependent on it. The response of the schools in this small sample points to the potential for the policies to increase the achievement gap within each state, exacerbating differences in school performance.

NOTES

1. This work is part of a larger, five-year study of the Consortium for Policy Research in Education (CPRE), supported by a grant (No. OERI-R308A60003) from the National Institute on Educational Governance, Finance, Policymaking, and Management; Office of Educational Research and Improvement; United States Department of Education. The principal investigators are Richard Elmore and Leslie Santee Siskin of Harvard University, and Martin Carnoy of Stanford University. The views expressed in this chapter are those of its authors and are not necessarily shared by the United States Department of Education, CPRE, or its institutional members.

2. The three authors contributed equally to the writing of this chapter.

3. The data collected for this chapter was part of the second phase of field work, in which a research team conducted interviews in twelve different high schools in four states: Kentucky, New York, Texas, and Vermont (the sample consists of three high schools per state). In this chapter, we analyzed English and mathematics teacher interviews, including

department chairs, and drew on notes from classroom observations conducted in those departments. We chose English and mathematics because they were tested subjects, and could be compared across states. For each school, we also analyzed administrator interviews and interviews with selected teachers in special roles. This field work was conducted over the course of several consecutive site visits in the 1998-99 and 1999-2000 school years.

4. The design for the larger CPRE study called for selecting schools that were differently positioned with respect to the reform. The terms "target" and "better positioned" were applied to schools in reference to their position. A "target" school was not seen as successfully preparing its students (according to prior measures), but was also not identified as a candidate for state intervention; a "better positioned" school's prior performance was deemed adequate with regard to student performance on existing assessments. The rationale for selecting differently positioned schools in each of the four states was to explore the effect of uniform policies in schools with different histories. For a more detailed discussion of the project design, see Leslie Siskin and Richard Lemons, *Internal and external accountability and the challenge of the high school* (Paper presented at the annual meeting of the American Educational Research Association, New Orleans, April 2000).

5. Charles Abelmann and Richard Elmore, with Johanna Even, Susan Kenyon, and Joanne Marshall, *When Accountability Knocks, Will Anyone Answer?* (Philadelphia: Consortium of Policy Research in Education, University of Pennsylvania, 1999), p. 3.

6. Ibid., p. 1.

7. The feminine pronoun is used throughout this chapter to ensure confidentiality.

8. Abelmann, Elmore, Even, Kenyon, and Marshall, *When Accountability Knocks, Will Anyone Answer?*, pp. 39-40.

9. Ibid., p. 38.

10. Donald Schon, *The Reflective Practitioner: How Professionals Think in Action* (New York: Basic Books, 1983).

11. Diane Massell, *State Strategies for Building Capacity in Education: Progress and Continuing Challenges* (Philadelphia: Consortium for Policy Research in Education, University of Pennsylvania, 1998), p. 32.

12. Ibid., p. 33.

CHAPTER X

Hedging Bets:
Standards-based Reform in Classrooms[1]

SUZANNE M. WILSON AND ROBERT E. FLODEN

Introduction

Historians will no doubt note the predominance of standards as they recount the late 20th century history of education. Throughout the 1980s and 1990s there was a virtual standards tidal wave. Some were issued by professional organizations as efforts to build consensus in vision and obligation.[2] Others were issued by states as the foundation for system-wide alignment of policy levers, including assessments, textbook adoption, teacher education, and professional development. Standards for students led to standards for teachers, curriculum, evaluation and assessment, and opportunities to learn. Standards, some believed, held great promise:

[Standards] are critical to the nation in three primary ways: to promote educational equity, to preserve democracy and enhance the civic culture, and to improve economic competitiveness. Further, national education standards would help provide an increasingly diverse and mobile population with shared values and knowledge.[3]

Interest in standards emerged alongside the call for systemic reform.[4] The combination of these attractive and complementary education reform perspectives led to "standards-based reform" (SBR):

Standards-based reform developed out of the common sense notion that student effort and level of achievement are directly affected by the expectations that have been set. Thus standards-based reform calls for the setting of standards in academic subject areas as an important means of improving student achievement. Once agreed upon, standards are expected to affect performance by focusing the efforts of students, teachers, and schools, and by providing a yardstick to monitor progress.[5]

Suzanne M. Wilson is an Associate Professor of Teacher Education, and Robert E. Floden is a Professor of Teacher Education, Measurement and Quantitative Methods, and Educational Psychology, in the College of Education at Michigan State University.

In the late 1990s, SBR picked up momentum. Most states proclaimed that they were engaged in such work, hundreds of districts implemented their version of SBR, and dozens of consulting agencies advertised their services in helping districts develop, teach to, and assess standards.

As standards picked up steam, discussions became more heated. Would standards constrain or liberate? Would they raise the floor or impose a ceiling? Would they enhance equal educational opportunity or exacerbate extant inequalities? For some, standards seemed heartless, the antithesis of what one would want in an education.[6] Assuming that one-size-fits-all students is problematic, for standards can lead to a tyranny of sameness.[7] Porter enumerated the concerns:

> Those who believe that national standards in education, accompanied with student performance assessments, are not an appropriate strategy for education reform, fear that standards will trivialize education and de-skill teaching by being too prescriptive. They fear that the one-size-fits-all approach of national standard setting will create an inflexible delivery system that will be incapable of coping with differences between poor schools and rich schools, able students and weak students, well-prepared teachers and teachers teaching out-of-subject.[8]

For every hope, there was a potential problem. The debate's major themes are detailed in Table 1.

TABLE 1

THE HOPES AND CONCERNS OF STANDARDS-BASED REFORM

HOPES	CONCERNS
Create teaching and learning better suited to a rapidly changing society	Give too little emphasis to some learning outcomes (e.g., the "basics")
Accountability mechanisms in SBR will produce desirable changes in teaching and learning	Improved test scores will come from attention to specifics of test formats rather than from desired student learning
Improve communication through stipulating goals	Trivialize education
Provide an image of teaching to inspire good teaching	De-skill teaching through over-prescription
Promote equity	Minority students and students from low-income families will fail through no fault of their own
Preserve democracy, enhance civic culture	Silence those whose knowledge and skill did not comprise the standards' core
Provide shared knowledge	Elevate the one group's values over others
Set high standards for all students	Standards will become the new minimum

While both interest in and concerns about standards have been high, we know little about their impact. As Porter noted, "Virtually all of the arguments, both for and against standards, are based on beliefs and hypotheses rather than on direct empirical evidence" (p. 427).

It is within this context of initial enthusiasm for and subsequent heated debate about standards that we offer a preliminary analysis of schools' experiences. In a three-year study conducted by the Consortium for Policy Research in Education, researchers tracked curriculum and assessment reforms in twenty-three school districts in eight states.[9] We interviewed teachers, principals, and district staff as they responded to local, state, and national pressures to reform teaching and learning. In four states (Maryland, Kentucky, Michigan, and California) we did more intense data collection, interviewing, and observing teachers in three elementary schools in each of three districts. In the study's third year, we surveyed teachers. This chapter draws on preliminary analyses of those data.

The Disparate Meanings of Standards-based Reform

The slogans of standards and SBR spread widely in the 1990s, but the meaning varied across contexts for several reasons. First, the widespread support of standards was due, in part, to the multiple meanings of "standards." For some, a standard was a principle around which professional and public discourse could occur. Rather than a mandate, this kind of standard enables discussion about educational goals and practices. For others, "standard" evoked the image of a bar—a criterion to hold everyone accountable to. One image is of a vertical standard, a pole around which a community can gather and rally. The other is horizontal, a bar one must be able to leap over.[10] Further, as standards gained popularity, the meaning became vaguer, its analytic power watered down.[11]

Similarly, SBR meant varied things across states and school districts. In some states, standards had been in place for years, supplemented with assessments and curricula; in other states, standards were implicit in state assessments, rather than existing as separate policies. For some districts, SBR involved hiring consultants to help educators adopt a ready-made system. In other districts, teachers pored over state and national resources as they authored their own standards.

To ascertain SBR's impact, one must first describe what SBR means. Thus we begin our analysis with the question: What varieties of SBR do teachers encounter in schools? We then ask a second question: What is the impact of those reforms?

Simply put, we found remarkable consistency. The reforms neither fulfilled all hopes nor justified all concerns. Most common were modest improvements, with some feared drawbacks. We begin by describing the experiences of four schools that illuminate issues in the larger sample. We then examine three central issues in debates concerning SBR: improved teaching and learning, accountability, and improved communication.

Four Illuminating Examples

PEACOCK

Peacock Elementary is located in a large southern California district, one of the fastest growing in the state. The school has enjoyed a reputation for high achievement, and its principal prides herself on being on the cutting edge of reform. Five years before state-mandated class size reduction, Peacock staff were busily reorganizing resources to have smaller classes. Years before the state and district mandated a "balanced" literacy curriculum, Peacock teachers discovered "Zoo Phonics," and used it to increase phonics instruction. Teachers also created their own scoring rubric for English/language arts (ELA), social studies, and mathematics. Peacock was named a California Distinguished School and, during this study, the school submitted its application to the National Blue Ribbon competition.

Peacock's school district has invested considerable resources in SBR. Central office staff coordinated the development of K-12 standards across the curriculum, well before California convened the commission to establish standards and aligned, challenging assessments. A full array of assessments, aligned with those standards, were also developed by the district, ranging from "mathematics fact tests" to running records to open-ended problems.

Over the course of our study, district decision making became increasingly centralized. In the past, schools like Peacock had latitude to develop local assessments and scoring rubrics. Recently, however, teachers found themselves receiving more messages from the central office about what assessments must be given, when, and how. Near the end of our study, all low-achieving schools had their decision making severely constrained.

As Peacock's principal, Ms. Roberts, sees it, her teachers "like to please." However, the increased centralization of mandates concerning standards, curriculum, and assessment have begun "irritating" them:

"We'd already done a lot of this and it is not like we're being punished, but we were doing just fine without getting directives from the district."

With the increased centralization comes less room to move. Ms. Roberts reports that the district's march toward assessing all subjects at all grade levels across multiple domains means that "creative teaching" is compromised because teachers are "forever assessing":

We have a math facts test and the SAT-9's nine sessions. We have the writing assessment. We have the open-ended mathematics assessment. Then this year, grades K, 1, 2, and 5 have an end-of-the-year final math testing by the district. The kindergarten and first grade have literacy screens.

While the principal reports that the district is generous with its support while also increasing its demands, she believes that one size does not fit all. The state, from her perspective, has been consistently issuing new mandates: "All teachers need this, all schools need that . . ." But her school district began many reforms long before the state. In fact, it created its own content standards and benchmarks, and its own aligned assessments (performance assessments and standardized tests). It terminated social promotion at third, fifth, and eighth grades; it initiated a summer school in the early grades and class size reduction. Within that context, Ms. Roberts and her staff enjoyed considerable leeway. Teachers developed their own scoring rubrics, selected additional curricula to supplement the district's, and created targeted professional development events.

Ms. Roberts' problem is that, as the district has tried to make some of the "best practices" (most often generated by teachers and principals in schools like Peacock) more uniform, her freedom has been constrained. The teachers we observed and interviewed concur. Susan Wood is a highly regarded teacher whose classroom is brimming with student work, writing journals, and mathematics journals. Descriptions of the district's standards line the walls, alongside colorful posters, lists of classroom rules, number lines, vocabulary lists, and student essays. Exhibits of student answers to problem solving tasks spill into the hallway and cover the walls around her classroom door. The students are busy all day, sometimes working as a large group with Wood at the overhead, sometimes working on individual or small group projects.

The classroom is an advertisement for many innovative pedagogies. Wood uses writers' workshop and materials from Marilyn Burns.

Colorful crates of student portfolios are stacked side-by-side. According to the principal, Susan is a dream teacher: her students consistently score well on assessments, she prides herself in keeping up-to-date. She's been a mentor teacher and teacher leader in district-sponsored workshops. Wood embraces change instead of rejecting it.

But the march of increasingly more standardized practices from the central office is crowding Susan's already crowded curricular plate. Now, in addition to her own elaborate assessment system, Susan must also find time for the district's running records, open-ended mathematics tasks, mathematics fact tests, and writing assessments. The scoring rubric that she and her colleagues worked so hard on recently was replaced with a districtwide rubric.

All of this puts Ms. Roberts, Ms. Wood, and their colleagues in an awkward position, for they neither reject accountability nor the challenge to meet high standards. But the room the staff has enjoyed for making their own professional decisions shrinks with every new mandate, as does their sense of ownership and autonomy. Not wanting to complain, they nonetheless feel constrained.

For Peacock, SBR initially meant the development of standards and aligned assessment and instruction. Gradually, however, state standards and assessments began to jostle with the local ones. Moreover, state mandates were in flux. Despite these confusing and conflicting messages, teachers adopted many reform practices—writing journals and problem solving—while maintaining balance with more traditional content. The school has changed, without taking change to extremes. Assessments have supported change, but the move toward standardization is beginning to pinch.

GRAY

In Gray Elementary School, SBR prominently features Maryland's assessment system (MSPAP), but other aspects of the system seem out of sync. Teachers give varying reports about how much attention they pay to MSPAP, but it has led them all to adopt some new practices, such as increased emphasis on writing in both ELA and mathematics. Curriculum materials emphasize a different mix of instructional content. With this conflicting mix of explicit and implicit content standards, teachers reported that they had to sift the good from bad. The result is instruction that balances reform content with mathematics computation and phonics-based literacy.

Mrs. Chandler is prototypical. Given a new textbook which she reported, "took a while to get used to," Chandler combined that textbook with other, more familiar practices. She continued to use "the old math structured lesson, I think it's from Madeline Hunter," as well as open-ended problems and performance assessments that arrived after a county materials selection. Similarly, although there has been much talk about returning to phonics in the school, another teacher, Mrs. Gail, believes that "a combination approach is the best idea, mixing in phonics with the newer strategies for teaching reading and writing."

"Teachers have good judgment about what's important and what the kids need," Chandler explained, and she uses her judgment daily to decide whether to emphasize skills ("In division, I've spent eighty to ninety percent on proficiency") or problem solving. While she does not ignore the push for standards, she thinks of them as a resource, not a script:

The National Council of Teachers of Mathematics (NCTM) doesn't dictate what I teach . . . The county doesn't come in here and tell me how to do it either. They expect what I teach to be in line with what they want me teaching, but everyone has their own style.

Mrs. Welland, her colleague, echoed the sentiment: "To be honest, policy doesn't affect me. I don't even know what the major reform policies are." For Chandler, standards "haven't changed the curriculum, it's just phrasing it differently." The largest hurdle has involved aligning tests with curricula:

What's tough is when they set the standards and say your kids have to pass the test but the curriculum doesn't match the test. Now my curriculum matches the MSPAP, but it's taken five to six years.

Despite Chandler's claim that her teaching is not driven by new mandates, in observations, we found evidence that the pending assessments shaped classroom practice. For example, Chandler focused students on "getting the right answers." Students were directed to explain their answers in writing (an expectation on MSPAP). They were reminded to be specific (e.g., not just that they moved a decimal, but in what direction and how many places). Chandler also referred students to the components they would need in responses to match MSPAP's scoring rubric.

We saw a similar phenomenon in Mrs. Gail's class when she distributed a worksheet concerning MSPAP writing prompts. Of the teachers interviewed in Gray, Mrs. Gail was the only one who explicitly mentioned MSPAP. As a teacher in a "tested grade," Mrs. Gail claims that her teaching is "absolutely guided" by district requirements:

The basic philosophy is that if something is not covered in the outcomes, the teacher doesn't spend a lot of time on it. Mostly, this is a positive change, but there are some things missing, including some fun "holiday things," that fall by the wayside.

To help her remember what the students need to be prepared, Gail uses a "cheat sheet"—a list of Maryland's learning outcomes and the district required elements of a mathematics lesson—to help in her planning.

Mrs. Gail's comments resonated with the school's principal, "MSPAP drives the educational train . . . it's the locomotive. If they tell you that MSPAP is not the driving force behind what we do, they are insulting your intelligence." He continued:

MSPAP created a sword of Damocles for elementary schools. Every year the report comes out and your school is there. I am required to report to parents within thirty days. It has put the spotlight on academic achievement.

Another teacher, Ms. Hale, agrees:

MSPAP totally influences teaching. For better or worse, kids are assessed and news is published . . . I think assessments are great and changing education for the better . . . It is much more challenging now.

MSPAP appears to match both the hopes and concerns. Teachers adapted their practice to focus on the assessment, yet their adaptations varied. Some teachers inserted test-taking skills ("include these steps in your test response," "remember these dimensions of the scoring rubric"). Other teachers, like Hale, were excited about the opportunities MSPAP offered—challenging students to think critically and write coherently.

With curriculum materials somewhat out of line with the assessment, messages from SBR are mixed. The Gray teachers see SBR as yet another mandate to respond to. They do so, from their perspective, critically, combining previous practices with new ones.

WILLIAMS

Accountability systems have also gotten educators' attention in Michigan. Teachers at Williams School reviewed the test to improve alignment and gave students extra practice on test content, vocabulary, and formats. But the story of change at Williams is also grounded in communication among teachers. Some communication, such as discussions concerning alignment, did not get beyond listing the names of objectives and slotting them to a grade. Although these discussions were a step away from complete isolation, they probably did little to deepen teachers' understandings of standards. But teachers had also taken part in more intense talk about what they were teaching as part of a districtwide movement to adopt an ELA workshop approach. Those discussions began before the state moved to adopt new ELA standards, but the discussions were furthered by the district's participation in a state Goals 2000 project.

Williams is one of three elementary schools in a rural Michigan town. When we visited classrooms, instruction appeared balanced. Memorization of mathematics facts and terms was mixed with requests for student explanations and pattern identification. Grammar and spelling were taught in conjunction with workshop approaches emphasizing composition, revision, and interpretation. Teachers combined the workshop approach with material on phonics, grammar, and usage, sometimes included as "mini-lessons" during a workshop period and typically the focus of DOL (Daily Oral Language) activities used to begin the day. During DOL, the class would, for example, identify errors in sentences written on the board. Teachers believed that their ELA instruction had changed substantially recently, now following the general workshop model in which students learned writing processes and read trade books, rather than basals.

Teachers see the state test, the Michigan Educational Assessment Program (MEAP), as a major influence, with discussions sometimes focused narrowly on the test's alignment with the curriculum:

It's an awful thing to say but I think a lot of schools are MEAP driven . . . I mean we meet almost three or four times a year on different aspects of the MEAP: How can we improve our total scores in this area? How can we improve our children's scores in another? How can we change our instruction?

Analysis of mathematics test results, for example, revealed a mismatch between when topics were covered and when they were tested, prompting reordering of the curriculum. Teachers noted that some MEAP terminology was unfamiliar to students, so teachers worked specifically on mathematics vocabulary:

We just put together a whole packet of vocabulary for math for every grade . . . We have kindergarten, first [grade students who] need to know these words

. . . So when you . . . start a new unit, you look at this and it says, "Okay, MEAP uses these words, be sure to emphasize [them]."

But teachers also reported the effects of talking among themselves at professional development events and in everyday conversations. Particularly important was a charismatic college professor who initiated talk about what children might accomplish in language arts. Seven years before we visited Williams, a shift in ELA instruction began in the district's elementary schools. Starting with a few teachers, inspired by books and by the dynamic professor, teachers began to adopt a workshop approach. They increased emphasis on writing, taking students through the processes of brainstorming, drafting, revising, and responding to peers' drafts. In reading workshop, teachers shifted from basal readers to trade books, so that in the last curriculum adoption the district did not purchase basals. Gradually, these discussions got a broader reach when the district agreed to be part of a Goals 2000 project (in which the aforementioned professor was involved) established to revise the state's ELA standards.

Because of these changes, the district was one of four demonstration sites for the proposed state ELA standards. In the eyes of Williams' teachers, the new standards—and the corresponding changes in assessment—fit with what they were already doing. As a demonstration site, discussions about what children should be learning and how teachers would help them broadened (to include more teachers) and deepened, as teachers moved beyond the structure of the workshop to consider what students were learning.

All the Williams teachers we spoke to wholeheartedly embraced the change in ELA instruction, which incorporated phonics and grammar, as well as giving students opportunities for expression and analysis. Williams exemplifies two ways in which SBR affects teachers' conversations, both engaging them in serious talk about the goals of learning and encouraging them to spend time on bureaucratic, but important, tasks of mapping tested topics to grade levels.

MARLOWE

Marlowe is in a blue collar suburban/rural Kentucky district. The school enrolls about 500 students, sixty percent of whom receive free or reduced lunch. About ninety percent of students are white, with the remainder African American. The atmosphere is business-like, bristling with the feeling that the staff is exceptional and operations efficient.

Here, as in other Kentucky schools, SBR looks different than it does in other states because the district role was much reduced. Largely, SBR in Kentucky refers to interactions between state and school. While the district tries to facilitate, it does not establish standards, select materials, or set the professional development agenda.

As in the other schools we visited, teachers aimed for balance, infusing reform ideas into instruction, while maintaining traditional elements. Writing instruction, for example, uses a process approach, with steps in the process (e.g., brainstorming, editing) displayed prominently. Yet teachers have not abandoned the writing basics. Grammar and spelling are the focus of Oral Daily Language exercises. Students examine sentences and identify spelling and punctuation errors. Marlowe teachers wish to avoid the extremes of writing instruction, with their sole emphases either on communication or isolated skills.

In reading, students mostly read trade books. Discussions of readings ask students to articulate inferences based on texts, to use webs and concept maps to represent connections among story elements. Teachers sometimes use basals to help students master particular skills. One teacher had students read a basal selection that was focused on distinguishing fact from opinion.

In mathematics, the content likewise mixes old and new. Some problems require computations and practice, but can be solved by two or three different sequences of calculation. Other problems introduce concepts like the number of pairs that can be made by choosing different pairs of items from two sets.

Here again, teachers see assessment as a major catalyst for change. Some teachers report that they teach what is on the state tests. Students' writing, for example, includes pieces in the genres required for the state's writing portfolio assessment. Teachers score these portfolios, and the state scores a subset of them as a check on the quality of local scoring.

Other teachers also list the state framework as a guiding factor. When asked whether framework was influential, one teacher said, "Of course. In fact, we're required to put those goals on our actual lesson plans." But when asked about the state test, the same teacher said, "That really doesn't affect me, but I try to keep my kids prepared so they don't freak out when they get to that point."

As some feared, the state assessment also leads to classroom time spent practicing testing formats. At the time of our second visit, the state was revising the assessment. The details of the change were not yet available, but rumor had it that multiple-choice items would be included.

Consequently, teachers began to teach strategies for taking such exams: when to guess, how to eliminate options, and so forth.

Here, as in other schools, SBR led to more professional discussion. As they examine state assessment results, Marlowe teachers try to understand why students are missing items schoolwide. Teachers also talk across grades, with those in higher grades discussing what entering students are like. These discussions, which may have predated SBR or may have been prompted by the new assessments, lead to talk about topics like curricular balance.

Across our larger sample, we found evidence that advocates' hopes and critics' concerns about SBR were realized, albeit modestly, on both fronts. Teachers incorporated writing, reading for meaning, and having students discuss their solutions to mathematics problems. This additional emphasis meant less time spent on traditional topics like phonics and computation, but these topics never disappeared.

Across these schools, teachers see assessment as an important influence. As hoped, SBR has promoted intended instructional changes. Teachers sometimes also spend time teaching testing formats, which may (or may not) promote student learning. SBR has led to more teacher talk, sometimes to substantive discussions of teaching and learning. But some talk also focuses on details of testing and curriculum that have some value but might not constitute serious educational discussion.

Hopes and Concerns Realized

Although the experiences of these schools do not fully account for the breadth in our sample, they are representative of the view of SBR when one documents what happens in schools. We now return to three issues that take center stage in debates concerning SBR (see Table 2).

TABLE 2

HOPES AND CONCERNS REVISITED

HOPES	CONCERNS
Create teaching and learning better suited to a rapidly changing society	Give too little emphasis to some learning outcomes (e.g., the computation, knowledge of phonics)
Accountability will produce desirable changes	Improved test scores will come from attention to specifics of test formats rather than from desired student learning
Improve communication through stipulating goals	Trivialize education

TEACHING AND LEARNING

Critics worried that standards would lead to an over- or under-emphasis on some learning outcomes. We saw little evidence of either. Teaching remains predictably traditional, with most teachers aiming to balance attention to basics with opportunities to problem solve. Teaching and learning were neither being re-invented nor more narrowly focused.

Let us consider this claim more closely. We had several ways to assess teaching. In four states, we visited classrooms—two visits a year apart. We observed ELA and mathematics instruction noting what was taught in what organizational structures (whole group discussion, cooperative groups, and individualized instruction). We also noted where the locus of authority was: Was the teacher the source of knowledge? The textbook? Students? We asked about discourse: Was it student- or teacher-dominated?

In addition, we interviewed teachers about their typical instruction. We asked them about the materials they used, effects of recent reforms, and professional development opportunities. We asked them what they thought of curricular debates in ELA and mathematics.

Together, field notes and interviews provide multiple indicators of classroom practices. Given our reading of the reforms, one would expect that the trend in reform-oriented classrooms would be toward a discourse that included more student talk. One would also expect that authority would be located outside of the teacher and textbook, and that teachers and students alike would search for warrants for claims and would question unsubstantiated assertions. Teachers would take on multiple roles: guide, facilitator, coach, and the more traditional role of teller.[12]

When asked what they thought of the debate about phonics versus whole language, every teacher in every school across all four states said that they believed both were important. Teachers who taught lower grades spoke of the need for more emphasis on phonics for early readers; teachers who taught upper grades reported using phonics instruction more selectively, targeting poor readers. Every teacher embraced *both* whole language and phonics:

I have a mixture of methods to teaching ELA. I use phonics. I tried for a little while teaching without phonics and the children did not seem to read as strongly and as quickly as they do with phonics, so I use phonics. I use whole language—not as much as phonics—but I have used it. I read to [them] and they read from trade books . . . I like all the methods . . . I like some of them more than the others, but the children learn from all of them. (Hilgard, KY)

A few teachers discussed their problems with textbook authors who boarded the "whole language" bandwagon:

Phonics is very important. When we started this literature-based program, the consultant came in and said, "Don't worry about phonics. They'll all learn to read." They didn't and people said, "Back off, these children are not learning to read. They can't sound out words." Our best readers were picking up vocabulary like any normal child would be doing. But the weaker children couldn't remember the sight vocabulary and they weren't able to sound it out . . . So I definitely and strongly believe that phonics has to be there. (Palley, KY)

When we visited classrooms, we saw trade books and basals (more of the former, less of the latter). We saw phonics, spelling quizzes, journal writing, and writers' workshops. Teachers were always in charge and the locus of authority. Instruction looked traditional, but teachers had woven reform-oriented practices into their instruction. Trade books were popular, and used hungrily in schools that could afford class sets. For poorer schools, children were encouraged to borrow trade books from the library or bring them from home.

Mathematics was similar. When asked, every teacher explained that students needed to master basic facts and skills, as well as have plentiful opportunities to solve problems. No one endorsed a narrow conception of mathematics teaching—say, a steady diet of memorization—but every teacher explained that basic skills were essential. Without mastery of basics, students could do little else. Teachers at the lower grades reported emphasizing the basics over problem solving, teachers in upper elementary reported more variation, depending on how solid students' basic knowledge was.

Again, the familiar and new were combined. We did not meet teachers who did not use manipulatives, but this was not necessarily a sign of progressive instruction. Many teachers reported that they used the manipulatives to help students understand new algorithms.

Teachers commented wearily about the history of extremes, focusing too much on rote memorization, only to overcorrect with too much problem solving:

We went through a phase where everything was memorization. And then we went through a phase where it was totally the opposite . . . I do not memorize very well and I'm not going to penalize my children for not being able to memorize facts. The more they use them, the more they'll learn them. But at the same time, children who have their facts memorized do so much better with grouping and re-grouping because they don't have to sit there and . . . touch their fingers to their chin to count fifteen minus eight or draw little sticks. And children who do have to draw little sticks get so lost in drawing lit-tle sticks that they lose the problem. (Palley, MD)

In the larger study, we administered a survey to all second through fifth grade teachers in the schools we studied. We asked teachers about instruction, their opportunities to learn, and accountability. Information from this broader sample[13] suggests that teachers typically balance reform and traditional elements. We asked, "How often do most students in your class take part in . . . ?" for a series of instruc-tional activities. Teachers indicated frequency of use by marking each activity as "never," "a few times a year," "once or twice a month," "once or twice a week," or "almost every day."

For mathematics, results illustrate instructional balance in virtually all districts. For example, two activities associated with mathematics reform are "writing about how to solve a problem" and "using manipu-lative materials." Two activities associated with more traditional mathe-matics are "practice or taking tests on computational skills" and "mem-orization of facts or procedures."

On the survey, teachers report that they are now using the two reform activities, but also continue to use the traditional activities. Manipulatives are prevalent, with at least half the teachers in every district using them at least once or twice a week. Writing about how to solve mathematics problems has also been adapted, albeit less fre-quently, with the median response either a few times a year or once or twice a month. Computation practice and memorization remain com-monplace, with the median response in almost every district being that these practices are used once or twice a week. (See Table 3.)

TABLE 3

FREQUENCY OF MATHEMATICS INSTRUCTIONAL PRACTICES*

	NEVER	A FEW TIMES A YEAR	ONCE OR TWICE A MONTH	ONCE OR TWICE A WEEK	ALMOST EVERY DAY
Write how to solve	0	3	3	5	0
Use manipulatives	0	0	1	7	3
Practice computation	0	0	0	11	0
Memorize	0	0	1	10	0

* Each cell indicates the number of districts with respective median. When the median fell exactly between two categories, it was recorded in the lower category.

For ELA, reports were similar. Some reform practices were present, but teachers continued with practices some analysts feared would be abandoned in the wake of SBR. We look again at two reform and traditional practices. Among the reform practices were "respond in a journal to something they read" and "revised something the student has written." Among traditional practices were "practice word attack" and "practice writing basics, such as spelling, grammar, and punctuation."

All four practices are part of instruction. In every district, the majority of teachers used each practice more than once a month; in almost all districts more than once a week (see Table 4). The response about revision, together with related survey responses, suggests that most teachers now teach process writing. Having students respond to texts is part of an emphasis on personal meaning. But these components have not pushed out spelling, word attack skills, and other traditional content.

TABLE 4*

FREQUENCY OF LANGUAGE ARTS INSTRUCTIONAL PRACTICES

	NEVER	A FEW TIMES A YEAR	ONCE OR TWICE A MONTH	ONCE OR TWICE A WEEK	ALMOST EVERY DAY
Respond in a journal	0	0	2	8	1
Revise student writing	0	0	1	10	0
Practice word attack	0	0	1	7	3
Practice writing basics	0	0	1	10	0

* Each cell indicates the number of districts with respective median. When the median fell exactly between two categories, it was recorded in the lower category.

Teaching remains largely traditional, with some additions. Teachers tinkered, adding selected innovative strategies like writers' workshop or manipulatives, weaving those practices into a recognizable, relatively stable practice. Teachers remained the primary authority alongside textbooks. Students learned vocabulary and spelling, they kept journals, and read trade books. They practiced mathematics facts, and solved problems which were sometimes authentically open-ended and challenging, but more often less so. Teaching was neither radically different nor overly narrow. The blend was of old and new—a "balance" that tilted more toward the traditional (memorization, phonics, basic skills instruction) in the lower grades, with slightly more variation in higher grades.[14]

ACCOUNTABILITY

Some reformers hoped that aligned, consistent assessments would help improve teaching and learning; critics worried that the tests would become the curriculum. To understand accountability's effects, we looked for effects of assessment. Did teachers mention tests to students? Did curricula reflect concerns for state tests? We asked teachers whether and how accountability policies affected their teaching.

Again, we saw little evidence of extremes. Every teacher reported that tests affected instruction. Yet when we observed instruction, tests were neither predominant nor entirely absent. Specific state policies also had considerable effect. In Maryland, where the state test included performance assessments, teachers wove performance assessment into instruction, students practiced responses to writing prompts, and teachers coached children on scoring rubrics.

Maryland teachers were aware of public debates about "teaching to the test." While some rejected the claim outright, others saw it as a non-issue for the test pushed in positive directions:

You hear so many people say we're teaching to the test when actually we've changed our whole mode of instruction to . . . better teach the kids. We do a lot of higher order thinking skills and not so much drill . . . They've put the hands-on aspects of learning into the performance task . . . I don't think there's anything wrong with that . . . That's good instruction. We're trying to teach children strategies and . . . higher order thinking skills. How can that be wrong? (McJay)

Although many teachers were not as enthusiastic as McJay, most thought that the assessments had a positive effect overall. They reported that linking instruction to Maryland's outcomes had helped teachers focus and that expectations for all students were considerably higher; all in all, a good thing:

I think today we are teaching math . . . a whole lot better than we have ever taught before, because the expectations for the kids are a lot higher . . . It has forced us to take a look at how we were teaching and to go off in different directions . . . It's been good and I've kind of enjoyed seeing the change. (Glen)

In California, which did not have a state level high-accountability system at the beginning of our study but then adopted the SAT-9, teachers had different experiences. In Peacock's district—with its comprehensive, homegrown assessment system—teachers integrated running records and open-ended problems into curricula, hoping to prepare students for district assessments. Generally, teachers regarded these assessments positively, feeling that they supported a balanced, coherent view of instruction.

Nonetheless, teachers felt overwhelmed by the growing number of assessments, especially time-consuming performance assessments. Then the state mandated the SAT-9 and promised to rank each school's performance on a website. Our study ended before we could document the effects on district policies and practices of California's administration of the SAT-9 and web publication of school rankings. We do know that the superintendent of Peacock's district declared that his district would have a "laser-like" focus on raising SAT-9 scores. Meanwhile, central office staff began to lessen the burden of the homegrown assessments, and prescribe a stricter diet of phonics in low-performing schools.

In Kentucky, teachers often denied that assessment had much impact on instruction, although most reported that school staff worked with test results, disaggregating data on fifth graders' performance to target areas for improvement schoolwide. However, the teachers did see the reforms as having had high impact on their teaching, and every teacher spoke of the powerful influence of portfolios:

Teachers are expected to have their students write every day. We're expected to use open-response questions on a regular basis . . . It's just changed almost every aspect of what's going on in the classroom.

Across and within states, we observed considerable variation in the impact of accountability. Some teachers turned innovative features of assessment—for example, holistic scoring rubrics—into steps to be mastered. In much the same way that traditional mathematics story problems can become algorithms thinly veiled in narratives, some scoring rubrics—meant to push teaching toward more conceptual ends—became algorithms for test-taking. Bureaucracies often turn the complex into the procedural, and we saw this occasionally. More often, we saw assessments woven into traditional instruction in much the way that innovative practices were.

While many teachers reported that they were now being "driven" by assessments, few were critical of them. While some Michigan teachers worried about the MEAP-tail wagging the curricular dog, no one questioned the MEAP's legitimacy. The case was similar in Maryland, where educators agreed with the assessment's content, but worried about its predominance in educational discourse. Kentucky teachers valued the portfolios, and California teachers did not disagree with district assessments.

The survey asked teachers to indicate the extent to which a variety of factors influenced instruction. They responded separately for mathematics and ELA, but the response patterns were similar (see Table 5).

State assessments, state standards, district standards, and student needs were perceived as the most influential factors. State and district curriculum guides and district assessments were also seen as major influences; other factors were rated as moderate or minor influences.

The strong influence of state assessments is consistent with what we saw and heard. But the strong influence of student needs is also a part of that pattern. While instruction is affected by SBR, especially by the assessment systems, teachers also take account of what they see as students' particular needs.

TABLE 5*

MEAN TEACHER RATING OF INFLUENCE ON INSTRUCTION

SOURCE	MATHEMATICS	ELA
Student needs	2.85	2.86
State standards	2.73	2.75
District standards	2.71	2.68
State assessment	2.68	2.74
District curriculum guide	2.64	2.62
District assessment	2.53	2.51
State curriculum guide	2.44	2.45
My knowledge about particular topics	2.17	2.19
Student interests	2.16	2.26
My beliefs about what topics are important	2.16	2.20
My principal	2.15	2.20
Inservice training	2.01	2.10
Textbook/Instructional materials	1.97	1.90
Initial teacher preparation	1.87	1.89
Other teachers	1.84	1.88
Parents	1.31	1.32
Professional journals	1.27	1.31

* (0 = none; 1 = minor; 2 = moderate; 3 = major).

This bifocal vision—with one eye on policy and one eye on the student—echoes the findings of other researchers and may explain teachers' consistent and insistent push toward some balance of old and new. Teachers did not whimsically mix the traditional and innovative. Instead, they went back to materials and strategies that worked in the past. They embraced anything new that promised to help with traditional problems—stimulating student interest, helping children overcome problems with understanding—and they held on to what they knew students needed to master mathematics and ELA—the "basics."

COMMUNICATION

Critics of standards-based reform were concerned that a focus on narrow standards would trivialize education. Reform advocates argued that the visibility of standards would create more occasions for teachers to talk. Such conversations, essential to the creation of learning communities, are another of the current "best hopes" for reform. Reformers argue that schools should move away from the individualist model, toward more collegial relationships among teachers.[15] With an emphasis on substantive discussions has come recognition that committee work can become professional development, and that professional development can encourage professional dialogue. If all went well, standards would create occasions for such dialogue.[16]

The concerns accompanying standards-as-a-stimulus-for-discussion were that the standards would narrow educational goals and that fixing those goals from outside the school would shift teachers' attention from understanding standards to finding efficient ways to boost test scores.

In the schools we visited, standards have indeed led to teacher discussions and, when asked about the most powerful educational opportunity available to them, many teachers reported that conversations with peers were the most productive and meaningful professional development they encountered. We saw and heard about two kinds of discussions.

First, we heard about conversations concerning the match between enacted curricula and state standards. Across all four states, we heard about schoolwide or grade level meetings in which teachers and principals carefully examined standards or outcomes, often "mapping" them onto the K-6 curriculum. When teachers in one Maryland school decided that their new literature-based textbook did not include enough phonics and spelling, they decided to use older texts to fill this gap. In another school, teachers adopted a spelling book after similar discussions. Such dialogue is unusual, for traditionally teachers simply taught the textbooks they were handed, without discussing curricular principles upon which textbooks were selected.

A second kind of conversation involved using test results to pinpoint topics where students are doing worse than expected. In Peacock, for example, the district area superintendent expected the principal to use student achievement data when discussing the school's progress, interrogating the principal about which teachers' students are achieving (or not) and which students are being targeted for extra assistance. The principal, in turn, used the same questions with teachers. Teachers in all four states spoke about using data to locate curricular weaknesses:

It wasn't real happy here when we found out our scores weren't good for this year. We didn't like that feeling. I said, "Maybe reading had something to do with it . . . Maybe the fact that these kids had only whole language, and not any phonics. Maybe that was part of it." But then they went down in mathematics, too. We have a grade group meeting next week when we're going to think about where we're going and what we can do. (Thurn, MD)

We all look at what the third, fourth, and fifth grade students do and even second grade when they are tested randomly and . . . we look at those scores and see what we are lacking. What the weaknesses are and strengths . . . We work to bring the areas that are weak up. (Mandel, KY)

The discussions had elements of both the hopes and fears in varying proportions. Before SBR, it was a truism that teachers seldom talked to each other about instruction. Teachers at one grade might complain that students coming to them had not learned enough, but those conversations were brief and one-sided. Standardized test scores were returned to schools, but seldom used. Relatively speaking, *any* teacher discussion would be a notable increase in communication, and across all schools we visited, we saw more professional dialogue, although there was considerable variation in how professionally substantive the discussion was.

The Impact of Standards-based Reform

Recall our initial questions: What varieties of SBR are teachers encountering in schools? What (if any) is the impact of those reforms on teaching and schooling?

We are struck by the variety of interpretations of standards-based reform. For some teachers, the reform is hardly noticeable, flowing into a long stream of other reforms, or so our informants suggest. For others, SBR has provided a clarity and language for thinking about their practice. For a few, it has felt constraining, well-intentioned efforts to raise the quality of all teaching but stifling for teachers who have a history of raising professional expectations on their own. For others, most notably in Maryland, teachers experienced a reform of assessments but without the larger systemic reform that was conceptualized as part of SBR.

Noteworthy regarding our first question—the meaning of SBR— was one other point: SBR was interpreted differently *within* schools. Part of this variation was attributable to testing schedules, for some teachers felt closer to the accountability, teaching at a "tested" level. Variation was also attributable to other factors, for instance, a teacher's

cynicism about reform, or how proactive she was about her own professional growth. These results echo those of earlier studies.[17]

"Balance" has become reform's new slogan. We do not have a normative position about what balance means. To teachers it meant many
things, most notably a commitment to mixing old with new, and using
one's professional judgment. While everyone wanted to follow district
and state mandates, educators worried about blindly following directives. As one state department official said: "What keeps us from
absolute sea-sickness is that locals don't jump as quickly onto some
new reform bandwagon." This has become increasingly so in this age
of heated political debate. Superintendents, many report, are looking
for ways "not to get burned" and increasingly see the state as part of
the problem rather than the solution. One superintendent explained,
"Now they're telling us that what they told us ten years ago is completely wrong. But why—if they were completely wrong ten years
ago—should I believe that they are now right?"[18]

When we consider SBR's impact (in various manifestations), we
find ourselves both hopeful and jaded. For some teachers, the clarity
of standards and aligned accountability systems proved a catalyst for
creating a more coherent practice. Teachers had rationales for what
they taught and when, and a clear sense of direction and obligation.
But most teaching remained more familiar than new, more ordinary
than challenging. As historians of educational reform and teaching
have made abundantly clear, traditional teaching is a sturdy practice
that has weathered many reforms without significant change.[19] Ohanian argues:

Most teachers hedge their bets. Few teach only the facts; fewer still devote
100 percent of classroom time to students constructing their own knowledge.
Few teachers choose to plant only one kind of flower; few risk committing
themselves to a distinct, exclusionary philosophy. Few teachers maintain a
pure world view of what a classroom should be; most put each finger and toe
in as many pedagogical universes as they can stretch to. And so tubs of pattern
blocks sit side-by-side with skill drill worksheets. To straddle the pedagogical
fence—to drill students on math facts and at the same time expect them to
think and discover and create for themselves—may be to plant parsnips and
orchids side by side. But perhaps a good definition of what it means to be a
teacher is to hold two, maybe even fourteen, contrary notions in one's belief
system at the same time.[20]

When we visited classrooms, we saw parsnips and orchids, manipulatives and worksheets, basals and trade books, side-by-side. While

some of the rhetoric would have us believe that SBR has the potential for transforming teaching and learning, we'd be naïve to hold such hope. Most educators we encountered take their obligations both to external policy system and students seriously. Their vision was bifocal. They did not simply go through the motions of enacting SBR. Instead, they went along with the new standards, administered the appropriate assessments, and worked hard to make sure that all students had the chance to do well. While accepting new mandates, however, no one threw the baby out with the bathwater. Rather, the new was woven in with the old. The experienced teachers among our informants trusted their professional judgment and kept an eye on students' needs as they also thought carefully about responding to the new press for standards and accountability.

NOTES

1. Funding for this work was provided by the United States Department of Education's National Institute on Educational Governance, Finance, Policymaking, and Management (Grant #OERI-R308A60003); the Annie E. Casey Foundation; and the Pew Charitable Trusts. Opinions expressed in this chapter are those of its authors, and do not necessarily reflect the views of the National Institute on Educational Governance, Finance, Policymaking, and Management; the Office of Educational Research and Improvement; the United States Department of Education; the Pew Charitable Trusts; the Annie E. Casey Foundation; or the institutional partners of CPRE. The chapter benefited from the extremely helpful feedback of Margaret Goertz, and from conference responses of Tom Glennan and William Firestone.

2. National Board for Professional Teaching Standards, *What Teachers Should Know and Be Able to Do* (Detroit, MI: National Board for Professional Teaching Standards, 1989); National Council of Teachers of Mathematics, *Curriculum and Evaluation Standards for School Mathematics* (Reston VA: National Council of Teachers of Mathematics, 1989).

3. National Council on Education Standards and Testing, *Raising Standards for American Education* (Washington, DC: Government Printing Office, 1992), p. 3.

4. Marshall Smith and Jennifer O'Day, "Systemic School Reform" in *The Politics of Curriculum and Testing*, ed. Susan Fuhrman and Betty Malen (New York: Falmer Press, 1991), pp. 233-267.

5. Milbrey McLaughlin, Lorrie Shepard, and Jennifer O'Day, *Improving Education through Standards-Based Reform* (Stanford, CA: The National Academy of Education, Stanford University, 1995), p. 1.

6. Sara Lawrence Lightfoot, "National Standards and Local Portraits," *Teachers College Record* 91 (1989): pp. 14-17.

7. Nel Noddings, *Challenge to Care in Schools: An Alternative Approach to Education* (New York: Teachers College Press, 1992).

8. Andrew Porter, "National Standards and School Improvement in the 1990s: Issues and Promise," *American Journal of Education* 102 (1994): p. 430.

9. The research was a collaborative effort. Margaret Goertz from the University of Pennsylvania, Diane Massell at the University of Michigan, and Robert Floden and Suzanne M. Wilson at Michigan State University jointly led the project. Data collection in other states was led by Tammi Chun, Catherine Clark, Carolyn Harrington, Janie Clark Lindle, and Joe Petrosko.

10. Deborah Loewenberg Ball, *Implementing the NCTM Standards: Hopes and Hurdles* (East Lansing, MI: National Center for Research on Teacher Learning, 1992); Gary Sykes and Peter Plastrik, *Standard-Setting as Educational Reform* (East Lansing, MI: Michigan State University, 1992).

11. Maris Vinovskis, "An Analysis of the Concept and Uses of Systemic Educational Reform," *American Educational Research Journal* 33 (1996): pp. 53-85.

12. See David Cohen and Heather Hill, *Learning Policy* (New Haven, CT: Yale University Press) for a similar analysis.

13. Here we use results from districts with a survey return rate of sixty percent or higher. The response rate is for eleven districts across six states. (Response rates in the two California districts were less than sixty percent and no surveys were administered in Minnesota.) Districts were selected on the basis of poverty level and reputation for making strong attempts to improve elementary instruction. The districts are suggestive about the views of high-poverty districts attempting to improve instruction, but may not match results in other parts of their states.

14. Our results resonate with those of Cohen and Hill, *Learning Policy*.

15. Ann Lieberman, "Practices that Support Teacher Development: Transforming Conceptions of Professional Learning" *Phi Delta Kappan* 76(8) (1995): pp. 591-596; Milbrey McLaughlin and Joan Talbert, *Professional Communities and the Work of High School Teaching* (Chicago: University of Chicago Press, in press).

16. See, for example, David Cohen and Heather Hill, "Instructional Policy and Classroom Performance: The Mathematics Reform in California," *Teachers College Record* 102 (2000): pp. 294-343; James Spillane and Charles Thompson, "Reconstructing Conceptions of Local Capacity: The Local Education Agency's Capacity for Ambitious Instructional Reform," *Educational Evaluation and Policy Analysis* 19 (1997): pp. 185-203.

17. See William Firestone, Sheila Rosenblum, Beth Bader, and Diane Massell, *Education Reform from 1983 to 1990: State Action and District Responses* (New Brunswick, NJ: Center for Policy Research in Education, 1991).

18. Chrispeels found similar results. Janet Chrispeels, "Educational Policy Implementation in a Shifting Political Climate," *American Educational Research Journal* 34 (1997): pp. 453-481.

19. Larry Cuban, *How Teachers Taught: Constancy and Change in American Classrooms, 1890-1980* (New York: Longman, 1984); David Tyack and Larry Cuban, *Tinkering Toward Utopia: A Century of Public School Reform* (Cambridge, MA: Harvard University Press, 1995); David Cohen, "Teaching Practice: Plus Ça Change" in *Contributing to Educational Practice: Perspectives on Research and Practice*, ed. Philip Jackson (Berkeley: McCutchan, 1988), pp. 27-84.

20. Susan Ohanian, *Garbage Pizza, Patchwork Quilts, and Math Magic: Stories about Teachers Who Love to Teach and Children Who Love to Learn* (New York: W. H. Freeman and Company, 1992), p. 94.

CHAPTER XI

Challenging Instruction for "All Students": Policy, Practitioners, and Practice[1]

JAMES P. SPILLANE

The ultimate goal of mathematics education in South Carolina schools is the development of broad-based mathematical power for all students.[2]

'All students' you can't actually do that . . . You can't say, 'All humans will be nuclear engineers.' Some of us have the ability to become nuclear engineers; some of us are content putting the gas in the car. So some of these people who put these demands on us . . . have never been principals, never worked with children, never had a course on child development. And I don't know where they're coming from with these requirements. What they're saying is not a realistic thing.[3]

The notion of *all students* has become a prominent theme in recent instructional reforms. Professional associations as well as federal agencies and state governments propose a fundamental refocusing of what counts as worthwhile knowledge in classrooms, arguing that *all* students' encounters with school subjects should not be confined to memorizing basic facts, skills, and procedures. They argue that schoolwork should also involve understanding the central concepts, ideas, and ways of knowing literature, mathematics, science, and other subjects. These proposals would require substantial change in the content and pedagogy of the K-12 curriculum if every American child, especially those who have been marginalized historically, has an opportunity to master more rigorous academic content. The quotations that open this chapter suggest that local educators may not see things in quite the same way as school reformers.

In the study reported here, I investigated the local implementation of state policy initiatives that propose more intellectually rigorous academic content for all students. After situating my work in the state instructional policy environment in South Carolina, I describe my theoretical

James P. Spillane is an Assistant Professor in the School of Education and Social Policy and a Faculty Fellow at the Institute for Policy Research at Northwestern University.

perspective and research methodology. I then explore local educators' responses to state policy proposals in relation to their teaching of students who have traditionally not succeeded in school. I analyze local educators' beliefs about, and knowledge of, *disadvantaged* students, learning, teaching, and classroom management, and consider ways in which this web of beliefs and knowledge was influential in the decisions these local educators made about implementing state policy. In light of this analysis, I consider the challenges involved in implementing policies that propose *all* students should do more intellectually challenging work.

The intent of this work is to contribute to a modest, but growing, literature that explores the policy implementation process from local enactors' practices and perspectives.[4] My purpose is to contribute to this literature by analyzing the implementation process in schools that enroll predominantly poor students and students of color. My central argument is as follows: To understand local educators' implementation of policies that challenge conventional wisdom about educating poor students, it is necessary to consider enactors' knowledge and convictions about students *in relation* to their beliefs about teaching, learning, and classroom management.

Situating the Study: The State Policy Context

South Carolina's reform strategy, like those of many other state and national reforms, is to propose a challenging pedagogy and more intellectually rigorous content for everyone. The state's mathematics framework defines *all students* as:

Students who have been denied access in any way to educational opportunities as well as those who have not, students of all ethnic origins, students who are female as well as those who are male, and students who have not been successful in school and in mathematics as well as those who have been successful.[5]

The Early Childhood Development and Academic Assistance Act of 1993 (Act 135) requires districts and schools to develop new instructional plans to educate students with academic difficulties and/or at-risk students. These reforms specifically target academically at-risk students for engagement with more intellectually challenging academic content.

It is not clear, however, whether reformers expected all students to study and gain mastery of the same demanding content. For example,

Act 135 states that "all children will be prepared for the fourth grade and all students will graduate from high school with their peers." A similar sentiment appears in the state's mathematics framework: "All students in South Carolina must experience a common core of relevant mathematics." One interpretation of these statements is that all students in South Carolina should study the same demanding mathematics curriculum. Indeed, parts of the mathematics framework are explicit on this matter, suggesting that "every student in South Carolina must learn the mathematics necessary to experience a successful life." And according to the framework, the mathematics needed "to experience a successful life" is roughly analogous to the National Council of Teachers of Mathematics' (NCTM) standards.

But while proposing a curriculum designed to "provide a common body of significant mathematics" that is "accessible to all students," South Carolina's framework also notes that this curriculum:

Can be modified in a variety of ways to meet the needs, interests, and backgrounds of individual students or groups of students to permit them to progress as far into mathematics as their achievement allows.[6]

Of course, modifications of this sort seem essential to the pursuit of equity: Equity is not a synonym for equality. Still, the prospect of modifications suggests that what reformers intend by a more ambitious curriculum for all students does not necessarily mean that every student will study a subject at the same level of ambitiousness.

Recent reform proposals also provide sparse guidance for teachers about what might be entailed in reconstructing their teaching to actively engage all their students in learning more intellectually rigorous content. For instance, the mathematics framework states that "students must learn mathematics through an active, constructive approach that emphasizes understanding mathematics." This statement raises questions such as what might be involved in creating an active and constructive learning environment for learners who have traditionally been marginalized by the school system? Although the frameworks provide some sample instructional activities and classroom scenarios, they raise as many questions as they answer.

These issues are not unique to South Carolina. The ideas about instruction advanced in the recent state and national reforms are underdetermined.[7] Notions of equity also are underdetermined in these reforms.[8] My analysis of South Carolina's state policy documents, for example, suggests that at least three interpretations of the *all students* ideal are plausible. One interpretation is that all students would master the same demanding content, at the same rate, and with the same instruction. A second interpretation is that all students would have access to the same demanding curriculum and similar instruction but their mastery of the content might vary. A third interpretation is that reformers would simply jack-up the outcomes all students are expected to reach but leave local school systems to decide on curriculum and instruction.

There are plausible explanations for the underdetermined nature of these policy proposals. To begin with, there is no consensus on what might constitute more effective and intellectually rigorous instruction for poor students and students of color.[9] A second reason is that ambiguity is frequently necessary in order for policies to gain the necessary political support for adoption.[10] Unpacking the notion of *all students* might undermine support for the policy.

There are at least two tensions that underlie any attempt to manage these issues. First, recent reforms that promote challenging instruction for all students are in the direction of the democratic goal of schooling and might, if they were taken to their logical conclusion, undermine the social efficiency and social mobility goals of schooling as reflected in the sorting function of schools.[11] Second, while reformers must offer local educators some guidance and incentives to get them to adopt a more intellectually rigorous pedagogy, they are also trying to ensure that those who are closest to students—local educators—develop the instructional strategies that meet their learners' needs. Left unresolved and underdetermined in state policy, these equity and instructional issues are delegated to the local level where administrators and teachers have to make something of them.

Framing the Work: Policy Enactment and Access to Knowledge

Some scholars argue that street level bureaucrats make the only policies that really matter; that is, those that shape the services which clients receive.[12] Teachers and school administrators ultimately decide whether policymakers' aspirations are reflected in students' learning experiences. To cope with limited resources including time, expertise, and materials, as well as with uncertainty about the goals and means of instruction, teachers develop routines that frequently fail to address the needs of particular students.[13] Further, teachers usually practice alone with little peer or managerial supervision. These conditions support the status quo in teaching and undermine the implementation of reforms that aim to fundamentally change it. Further, while the cultural resources of students from middle and upper income families match those of the school, the cultural resources of poor students and students of color (e.g., language, social norms) typically do not.[14] Thus middle class and upper middle class students have a competitive advantage over poor students and students of color because they enter school with cultural capital that facilitate their progress.

These perspectives, however, support a somewhat deterministic view of life in social institutions. The street level bureaucrat perspective suggests that teachers' behavior is determined by the social and organizational conditions of their work. Individual agency is downplayed. Similarly in Bourdieu's cultural capital model, not only does the school remain something of a "black box" but also the agency of practitioners, parents, and students is ignored.[15] Recent scholarship pays more attention to human agency. Research on teacher change and policy implementation suggests that local educators' beliefs about, and knowledge of, subject matter, teaching, and learning are influential on whether and how they revise their practice in response to policy.[16] Similarly, teachers and students are not passive participants in the social reproduction of inequality in schools. Poor students and students of color often engage in passive or active resistance in school.[17] Teachers often believe that children of poverty are incapable of handling instruction beyond basic skills[18] and need highly controlled classrooms to learn these skills.[19] Teachers' assumptions may be rooted in cultural mismatches between teachers and students that lead to teachers misinterpreting the cognitive skills and abilities which students bring to school.[20] Teachers' beliefs influence the learning opportunities they mobilize for students with teachers tending to assign poor students less demanding academic work.[21] Hence, the decisions local educators make about whether and how to enact state policies that encourage more intellectually rigorous instruction for all students are likely to be influenced by their beliefs and knowledge.

In underscoring individual agency, I do not mean to suggest that social and organizational arrangements are not influential in local educators' work. They clearly are, but they do not determine what individuals do, at least not entirely. Social theorists have increasingly tried to attend to both social structure and individual agency, bringing individual constructions of social structure increasingly to the fore, and arguing that social structure is both constituted and constitutive.[22] Social and organizational arrangements influence teachers' work, but how they influence that work depends in part on what teachers make of them.

Methodology

Data was collected in South Carolina between 1992 and 1996 as part of a three state study of the implementation of state instructional policy. For this chapter, I used data from four elementary schools, two of which are located in the same large, urban school district and two of which are situated in two rural districts. The student population in one urban school was almost entirely African American, and almost all were eligible for free or reduced lunch. At the other urban school, sixty percent of the students qualified for free or reduced lunch and approximately fifty-four percent were African American. One rural school enrolled almost all African American students, all of whom qualified for free or reduced lunch while fifty-four percent of students at the other rural school were African American, and approximately sixty-five percent qualified for free or reduced lunch.

State policymakers, central office administrators, school principals, and teachers were interviewed; interviews were recorded and tran-scribed, and ranged from sixty to ninety minutes. These interviews focused on a common set of concerns and issues including how educa-tors viewed the practice proposed by reformers, what they saw to be the key instruments of reform, and their involvement in reform activity. I interviewed eighteen of the thirty-two informants more than once. Interview questions were altered systematically as researchers became more familiar with the circumstances surrounding participants' efforts to deal with reform issues or as new policy issues arose. In response to the passage of Act 135 in 1993, for example, researchers developed a new interview protocol to explore the local response to this state legis-lation. Further, researchers used themes that emerged from ongoing data analysis of state policy documents and interviews to guide subse-quent data collection. The data collected through interviews were sup-plemented with document analysis including school improvement plans and district office policy documents. Researchers also observed class-room instruction using an observation protocol that focused on cate-gories that included the nature of instructional tasks and discourse, grouping arrangements, use of texts, and student engagement with instruction. Observers used audio recordings of classroom discourse to supplement the field notes.

The collection and analysis of data were integrated.[23] Analyzing in-terview, document, and observational data early in the study, research-ers noticed issues that they pursued in later interviews. This interac-tion between data analysis and data collection allowed researchers to test working hypotheses that began to emerge from the data analysis.

By continually considering the interaction of data analyses with data collection, researchers clarified and strengthened their understanding of educators' ideas through searching for confirming and disconfirming evidence. For the purpose of this chapter, I used four coding categories—local educators' conceptions of disadvantaged students, local educators' convictions about and knowledge of teaching and learning, local educators' responses to reformers' press for a more intellectually rigorous pedagogy for all students, and practitioners' efforts to revise their practice.

More Ambitious Pedagogy for All: A Local Perspective

Local reform documents resembled state policy statements with the *all students* theme figuring prominently in the improvement plans of the four schools. The improvement plan of one rural school, for example, stated that "all individuals are capable of success" and "cultural diversity enriches society." Similar sentiments were reflected in one urban school's plan—"all people are capable of learning" and "all people deserve to be treated with fairness and respect." Although statements advocating equity and respect for diversity were plentiful in local written documents, a common theme in local educators' talk was that all students cannot be expected to learn the same content, at the same rate, and to achieve at the same level. An urban teacher argued that "not everyone will achieve, but everyone should have the opportunity to achieve as much as they can, as far as their potential is concerned." A rural administrator expressed a similar opinion:

I think all children can learn. Now, I believe that they all can learn at different abilities. I know that from myself. I would love to be able to know nuclear physics right now, but, I mean . . . the Lord didn't give me what it takes to just put that all in there [points to his head].

A rural school principal remarked:

I do the best I can, I can't save the world. The ones that I can help, I do . . . there will always be some who are not going to come 'up to par.' And I'd just try to prepare them the best I can up to their God-given, natural ability.

These practitioners' comments were representative of those expressed by most interviewees.[24]

The tone of these comments suggests that local practitioners were not convinced that all students had the "God-given, natural abilities" to engage in the rigorous academic work advanced by state policymakers.

Local educators' comments echoed popular societal views that some children will do better than others academically because of "innate ability." But circumstances differ radically in other countries and societies where ability is not seen as a given but something that is malleable, something that hard work by educators and students can develop. For example, one recent study concluded that teachers, students, and parents in China and Japan place much more emphasis on student effort rather than innate ability in students' academic success.[25] In contrast, Americans place much more emphasis on innate ability.

IF NOT FOR "ALL," FOR WHOM IS AMBITIOUS INSTRUCTION NOT A REALISTIC GOAL?

Local educators used terms like *at-risk* and *disadvantaged* to identify students for whom they believed that the more intellectually rigorous instruction was inappropriate. They expressed a sense that these disadvantaged students came to school lacking essential cognitive and social skills as well as lacking motivation and interest in learning, and therefore the higher level learning standards were inappropriate for them. Local educators invariably linked these student characteristics to family background or home environment. They believed that the characteristics that put students at risk of failing in school were a product of their home upbringing. Local educators' talk about the relationship of students' deficiencies to family background at times, though not always, appeared to be a proxy for either social class or race. For instance, a rural school administrator said that White, middle class, and upper middle class students do better in school because their parents give them experiences that prepare them for school. He cited as an example, "They grocery shop with them—the things that we are trying to do now [in school] already have been done by these types of parents." Another administrator said the deficiencies were a product of different cultures, that is, race:

The mother and the children will congregate; the Black males will congregate. And whatever happens when this occurs is detrimental to the Black child. He doesn't have a role model, for one; he feels separate, certainly; and that comes into the school as disrespect [for authority].

Although this perspective was not a dominant one, it did surface frequently in one rural district. To understand these practitioners' rejection of state policymakers' proposals, however, it is necessary to consider their conceptions of disadvantaged students together with their knowledge and beliefs about teaching, learning, and classroom management.

CATCHING UP THE "DISADVANTAGED" BY FIXATING ON BASIC SKILLS

A prevalent pattern in local educators' talk was that many of their students were disadvantaged because they lacked certain verbal skills and experiences that were valued in school, and getting these students up-to-speed on these basic skills was essential if they were to benefit from schooling. Believing disadvantaged students needed to master the basics before they could advance to the more intellectually rigorous instruction advocated in state policy, most local educators argued state reform proposals were inappropriate for their students.

Local educators spoke about differences between the "good" verbal skills needed and learned in school and the "not-so-good" verbal skills at-risk students pick up at home. A rural second grade teacher explained:

A lot of times their vocabulary is very limited from . . . what they're hearing at home, and basically being sat in front of the TV, and that's it, you know, no conversation at home and a lot of time spent watching TV and not reading.

An urban teacher in the same school thought that her conversations with students were, for many students, the only ones they had with adults. Practitioners' concerns about language skills were often intermixed with concerns about the limited experiences that students had outside school. An urban second grade teacher explained, "They [students] have less experience, you know, some of the children you can ask 'have you ever seen a rhinoceros' and a lot of them will say 'no.'" In practitioners' views, because at-risk students did not learn certain language skills outside of school meant that these students were less able to capitalize on in-school learning opportunities.

Teachers and administrators blamed these deficiencies on their students' home environment, referring to things such as lack of reading material in the home. One principal said:

[I]f you go into their [students'] homes, you wouldn't find a magazine and you wouldn't find a newspaper. These children get out of school come May 31st. Very few of them are going to use, especially in the lower grades, the skills they learn. They won't have an occasion to read unless they read a billboard or something . . . We have a small library. It opens once a week, but the ones that it caters to are middle-class kids.

Others saw it as resulting from patterns of adult-child interactions. A rural educator explained:

We're dealing with cultures where children are something that you have there, but they're not to get in your way. They're to be told what to do, but they're not to talk back . . . we have children that come in . . . [and] their vocabulary skills are just nil.

In this administrator's view, these home norms did not prepare students for the classroom.

Local educators' conception of disadvantaged students as deficient in basic language skills, coupled with their understanding of the learning process, meant that teaching disadvantaged students basic skills consumed their instruction. Believing that mastery of the basics was a prerequisite for learning the more intellectually rigorous material and processes advocated in state policy, local educators argued that these reform proposals were inappropriate for their disadvantaged students, at least until these students had mastery of the basics. A second grade teacher, Ms. Brady, was representative. She contrasted her experiences teaching in an urban school with her current class in a rural school:

I did teach . . . in a private school and I felt like I was a facilitator . . . So we did a lot more critical thinking-type activities because they already knew the basics. I didn't have to go back and backtrack to try to get them to where they needed to be. Whereas here [current classroom] I feel like I'm constantly trying to play catch up . . . I repeat myself a lot more here. I do a lot more vocabulary because their vocabulary is more limited.

Ms. Brady believed that understanding of complex concepts and higher order thinking was possible only after students have mastered basic skills.

Teachers' comments in interviews supported a behaviorist view of learning.[26] From the behaviorist perspective, learning proceeds in a hierarchical and linear fashion from basic skills, which form the building blocks or component sub-skills for higher order skills and thinking, to more complex concepts and processes.[27] Cognitive psychologists, however, argue for an alternative model in which learning, even of the basics, involves active mental construction and thinking by students.[28] Learning is more organic, rather than hierarchical and linear, and engagement with more complex ideas and thinking is not dependent exclusively on mastery of the basics.

Ms. Brady's beliefs were reflected in her teaching. Students in this class spent most of their instructional time doing worksheets or board work on basic skills. During one observation, students began the day by trying to alphabetize eight words written on the board (store, corn, morning, thorn, your, born, four, game). They also had to answer six addition and multiplication problems (37+25, 91+9, 38+24, 173+219,

7×5, 5×6). Students worked on these exercises on their own, with some help from the teacher. Although students worked diligently on the assignment, most could not correctly alphabetize the words and they seemed unclear about what it meant to alphabetize. The arithmetic problems appeared equally difficult for students. For the problem 37+25, many subtracted five from seven. Some forgot to "carry" the ten. The individualized work was followed with a whole class review of the exercises. This work took up the entire morning and the teacher informed the observer that she had planned to read a storybook and to talk about main ideas in the story but time did not permit it.

Ms. Brady reported that she often planned to do higher level work but rarely was able to because basic skills took up the time. When asked about the state reforms, she noted:

No, it's not realistic given our student population. No, it's not . . . the more critical thinking type activities and things that they are calling for especially in the [South Carolina] mathematics framework, some of the activities types of things they want us to do are not realistic because we're constantly playing catch up. I mean it's good in theory . . .

This second grade teacher was the rule rather than the exception. Seeing their students chiefly in terms of deficiencies in fundamental knowledge and skills, most teachers filled their instructional time catching up on basic skills. Some teachers, like Ms. Brady, said they agreed with reformers' ideas about conceptual understanding and higher order thinking. But understanding learning from a behaviorist perspective, they never got beyond basic skills.

THE SALIENCE OF STRUCTURE AND THE PROGRESS OF AMBITIOUS INSTRUCTION FOR ALL

Another pattern that figured prominently in local educators' talk concerned disadvantaged students' inappropriate classroom behavior and their lack of motivation and interest in learning. Concerned about classroom behavior and students' lack of interest in learning, local educators focused on creating highly controlled and structured classrooms and many were convinced that enacting more intellectually challenging instruction would undermine order.

Local educators argued that the students they considered disadvantaged did not know how to behave in school. An urban fifth grade teacher argued similarly, "Our children are much less disciplined and that's because of the environment that they come from, most of their parents are either not at home or don't care." Another teacher elaborated on the sort of behavior that she believed placed students at a disadvantage in the classroom: "Talking to each other and yelling all the time . . . when you meet the parents, you understand why [laughs] they do. Maybe there are a bunch of people in the house and they have to yell to be heard." From the perspective of these educators, students were disadvantaged because the behaviors they learned at home were not valued in school.

A related theme concerned student motivation and interest. An urban teacher noted, "It just doesn't seem like they're [disadvantaged students] interested in it [school work]." An urban principal commented:

We have children in this school that we're trying to convince of the value of hard work that are from third and fourth generation welfare families. Yeah, it's hard. They are disadvantaged . . . It makes me angry that we have to do this stuff, to be real honest about it. I have difficulty dealing with parents who I see so clearly should be doing certain things for their own children which they are not doing.

An urban fifth grade teacher argued "That's one thing that keeps the children from being motivated . . . if there is no accountability at home, it's very hard to set up accountability at school . . ." For most local educators, a shared characteristic of students they labeled disadvantaged was a lack of parental support which contributed to their lack of motivation and interest in learning.

These educators were convinced that to address the motivation and behavioral problems of disadvantaged students they had to maintain tight control of classroom activities. Structure was equated with highly regimented classrooms where teachers took complete control and student-to-student interactions were minimized. These concerns were especially important when it came to the implementation of an ambitious pedagogy for all students because local educators were convinced that a traditional didactic pedagogy was more compatible with maintaining classroom order while the instructional changes advocated by reformers were incompatible with this goal.

Ms. Carlton, a fifth grade teacher in one of the urban schools, was representative. Students' behavior was a dominant theme in her comments about teaching. She remarked that, "At home they [students] don't have any structure, they can do whatever they want to do. That's why I believe a lot of children in the school just do what they want to,

they get up and out of their seats or they talk all day." She believed
that if her students, a majority of whom she saw as disadvantaged,
were going to learn she had to maintain a tight rein on them. She took
complete control of all classroom activities, insisted that students sat
quietly at their desks, and that they spoke only when she asked them
questions. Observations of her classroom attest to the importance of
structure in Ms. Carlton's teaching and confirm that reformers' ideas
about a more ambitious pedagogy have not penetrated her practice.
Students spent most of their instructional time doing worksheets or
board work and rarely interacted with each other about the academic
material.

For this fifth grade teacher, the reforms she understood the state
to be promoting—group work and thematic instruction—were not
conducive to the structured classroom environment she struggled to
maintain daily and that she believed was essential for her disadvantaged students. As she explained, this pedagogy was simply not feasible
in her classroom:

They [students] definitely need more structure . . . I've tried to do the thematic units . . . but I think that the students get more out of hand when
they're not very structured. When you work out of the textbook and they have
something directly in front of them and they're constantly working, they're
much more disciplined than if you are doing group activities or even individual activities where there's a lot of movement.

To maintain control, highly determined tasks that had clear steps for
completion, and which students could complete on their own, were
crucial. As she put it, "I find when I do activities that are more creative, where they're more actively involved . . . they think they're playing and they don't think that they're learning. It seems to cause a lot
of chaos in the classroom." Hence, she rejected reformers' proposals
for a more demanding pedagogy for all students.

The public and many professionals appear skeptical about the
appropriateness of more intellectually rigorous content and pedagogy
for poor students. Still, recent studies suggest that poor students and
students of color can master more demanding intellectual content (i.e.,
key disciplinary concepts and ideas) while simultaneously learning
basic skills.[29] A recent study of 140 classrooms suggests that academically demanding work may be especially relevant to, and advantageous
for, poor students' academic success.[30] Further, a recent study, involving ninety-four teachers in forty schools, concludes that the NCTM

teaching approach did not hinder students' performance on traditional tests.[31] While higher ability students benefit more from the approach, the performance of poor students and students of color on traditional tests were not hindered by the teaching approach.[32] Though not conclusive, this research certainly questions the conventional wisdom about educating poor students.

POLICY ENACTMENT AND LOCAL EDUCATORS' WEBS OF BELIEFS

To understand these local educators' responses to calls for more intellectually rigorous instruction for all students, it is necessary to consider their convictions about disadvantaged students *in relation* to their beliefs about teaching and learning. This interlocking web of beliefs is key in understanding what enactors do and don't do by way of implementing state policy.

The pervasiveness of a "deficit" perspective on poor students among these educators was striking. While public policy has helped popularize this deficit perspective,[33] some scholars have critiqued this view, observing that it blames students and their families and shifts the debate about education reform away from improving schools.[34] Adopting a social constructivist rather than an epidemiological perspective, these scholars claim that students are disadvantaged because the school culture, which is modeled chiefly on a dominant middle class culture, does not match their language and learning processes. In this view, students' disadvantaged position is not simply a product of social background but is constructed in the interaction of school and home cultures. Poor students and students of color do have resources for learning but these resources are rarely valued by public institutions like schools, or at least not valued as highly as those of other social classes and cultures.[35] Most local educators in this study believed that the students whom they perceived as disadvantaged had scant, if any, resources that might have helped them learn in school; they saw these students chiefly in terms of their deficiencies. Their convictions about disadvantaged students were supported by their behaviorist views of learning. As most teachers viewed learning as a linear and hierarchical process in which knowledge of the basics was a prerequisite to any engagement with more advanced concepts, it is not surprising that they would define those students who lacked these basics as disadvantaged. Their beliefs and knowledge about poor students, learning, and teaching were mutually supporting.

While poor and minority students do bring resources to school that often go unidentified and unacknowledged by teachers, it is also the case that these students frequently lack conventional basic knowledge and skills that they need if they are to have access to opportunity in contemporary society.[36] Delpit argues that as new instructional approaches find their way into classrooms, many of which are understood by practitioners as focusing on instructional processes rather than content, there is a fear that the content needs of those students who cannot acquire conventional knowledge outside the school will not be addressed. Students need to acquire this knowledge if they are to have access to power and opportunity. While teachers much recognize that poor students and students of color need access to this knowledge, they also must recognize these students' strengths as resources for learning.[37]

An Alternative Local Perspective

The responses of a principal and three teachers in the two urban schools to the state policies contrasted with general patterns described above. To explore these alternative views, I offer vignettes of two of these teachers. Although these teachers' conceptions of disadvantaged students were similar to other educators, their responses to instructional reforms that challenged the conventional wisdom about educating poor students were very different. Both constructed instructional practices that were in the direction of state policy proposals. While these teachers were firmly convinced that their new approaches to instruction were an improvement, they did not minimize the difficulties involved in undertaking these changes. Further, these teachers' efforts to construct their practice were subject matter specific. Ms. Banks focused chiefly on reconstructing her mathematics practice while Ms. Sosa concentrated on revising her reading practice.

A VIGNETTE OF FIFTH GRADE MATHEMATICS

A veteran teacher, Ms. Banks was, as she put it, "big on mathematics." She taught a fifth grade extension class at Forest Elementary and believed that her disadvantaged students lacked basic mathematics skills and were not well behaved or motivated to learn. She remarked, "Our children are much less disciplined because of the environment that they come from . . . they haven't learned the discipline to sit in a school and pay attention and learn." Yet her mathematics instruction contrasted sharply with rote drill in basic skills, and there was much about her practice that resonated with state reforms. Over the past eight years, she reported that her teaching has focused increasingly on understanding mathematical concepts rather than exclusively on skills and procedures. "I kind of like to identify things that are more conceptual," she explained, "that aren't operations." Banks devoted entire units to key mathematical concepts including algebra and number systems.

One unit involved students working in groups to design their own number systems. Banks was excited about the number systems her students developed and their engagement with the mathematics. Students' success with the unit contributed to her conviction that disadvantaged students can learn conceptual material in mathematics. She remarked:

I'm a believer! Don't underestimate what these children can learn. And it is not a necessity that they know how to add or subtract, multiply and divide to do this. They can understand concepts, so there is no point in stopping and drilling the life out of these children for five years.

Ms. Banks developed the unit around mathematical concepts including "place value" and "zero," and she got students to experiment with number systems that had different bases. She noted:

Kids came up with their own symbols, came up with their own rules, came up with their own bases, and actually gave a demonstration of how to count in their numeration system. They understood place value and the zero place value holder.

For Banks, her disadvantaged students' engagement with and success in grasping these concepts, and their ability to think about the concepts, was a primary impetus for her continued efforts to revise her instruction.

Ms. Banks did not ignore students' mastery of mathematical skills. When she taught skills and procedures, her chief concern was getting students to understand the processes. She remarked, "I love even taking the operation of division or multiplication, and showing children what they're doing instead of just saying to them, 'you multiply this number by this number.'" For Ms. Banks, a mastery of the basics was not a prerequisite for understanding mathematical concepts. As she explained it, "Everybody thinks that you can't understand this [place value] until you understand that [basic skills and operations] and they're wrong. This [place value] was done with children who could not add and subtract but they understood this." She held lofty goals for her students, ninety percent of whom she considered disadvantaged. She remarked, "I think children need to learn that numbers are not something you have to be afraid of. Numbers are something you can do something with. You have control . . ."

Banks believed that engaging students who she saw as disadvantaged with mathematical ideas and concepts was necessary because it helped them develop a purpose for learning. She explained, "What you have to add to those children [disadvantaged] is to give them a purpose, a reason [for] why they're learning. A lot of children come with that from the home; this group does not." She was convinced that intellectually rigorous and engaging instruction was the way to address student interest and motivation:

It's the kids that are sleeping. It's the kids that are not motivated. It's the kids that are causing trouble. And I know half of that would disappear if we could provide the motivation, but it's a vicious circle . . . I don't believe we are gonna change these children until we change our instruction 'cause we can't change their homes so we got to change what we do here.

She believed that traditional forms of instruction and motivation did not work well for disadvantaged students: "A report card for the most part here does nothing but depress children and turn them off. So we have to motivate in a completely different manner."

Ms. Banks has devoted much time learning about mathematics instruction, participating in workshops sponsored by AIMS and Math: A Way of Thinking as well as an ongoing collaboration with a mathematics educator, Dr. Apple, at a local university. Speaking about her work with Dr. Apple, she remarked, "I went to the curriculum leadership institute and learned about a unit on the number system . . . Dr. Apple got me interested in whether I could change the ability of the children I work with to understand mathematics." Banks acknowledged the influence of these learning opportunities and was convinced that her colleagues would only change if they had similar experiences. With her new knowledge, she began to revise her teaching and seeing her students' success in grasping difficult mathematical concepts, she continued to change.

A VIGNETTE OF SECOND GRADE LITERACY

Rita Sosa had taught at MacDonald Elementary for sixteen years where, according to Sosa and other staff, students typically live with one parent or other relatives on some form of government assistance, many remained at the school for less than two years, and most read below grade level. She believed that most of her second graders came to school deficient in the verbal and behavioral skills as well as the motivation essential for success in school. Comparing the students she taught to middle class students, she remarked, "They [middle class students] are just more verbal and they have more experiences, [and] they have a lot more attention." Sosa reported that she had taught reading and writing traditionally for most of her career, dividing students into ability reading groups, using basal readers and their accompanying workbooks, and focusing chiefly on the rote acquisition of phonics and sight word skills.

Ms. Sosa reported that her own love of reading and her growing awareness of her students' lack of interest in books were a primary impetus for change. She commented,

I felt like in the past, when I taught reading straight out of the basal and I would say, "Okay boys and girls, it's time for reading." They would say, "Oh no!" You know, big groan. And I thought, I'm teaching these children to hate it. I mean, they associate the word reading with doing worksheets and drilling on phonics . . . Well, I just think that I felt frustrated. I'm a reader. I love to read and I felt like I was not fostering that love through my reading instruction.

She reported becoming increasingly aware that instruction in basic skills was inadequate because without understanding that reading was a way of making sense of the world, students had little desire or ability to learn skills and use them. Taking a course on teaching reading skills through literature and using Regie Routman's book *Invitations* as a text, she began to teach differently:

I thought the course sounded interesting because I liked to teach reading and I liked children's literature. So, I thought, oh well, at least I will learn about some new books . . . and I had heard something about whole language and I knew something had to change. I just couldn't do it [teach reading as she had been] anymore. Once I took the course I got interested and started reading other things . . . As a result of the class, I'm reading Regie Routman's book, *Invitations*, so I'm going to start implementing some of the things she suggests . . .

In one year, Sosa abandoned the basal reader and began to teach reading using children's story books. She took additional courses, read other books about using literature to teach reading, and took a course on Writer's Workshop. Trying out different ideas she learned about, Ms. Sosa developed a practice in which students learned reading and writing skills but in ways that did not delay or foreclose engaging students in conceptual understanding of text. For Sosa, reading was not a set of hierarchical skills that need to be learned in order to reach the culminating activity of reading, but a process that involved motivation, skills, and comprehension, all intertwined and interdependent. Her new approach to reading instruction involved a combination of whole class, small group, pair, and individual activities, and included time each week for listening to students read individually and for work on particular reading skills. She reported, and observations confirmed, that her approach to reading instruction engaged students with central literary concepts including literary genres and character development.

Ms. Sosa claims that she found the changes in her approach to reading instruction useful because all of her students became interested in reading and became better readers. She saw students who came into her class as non-readers learn to read and eagerly pick up books. She explained, "Immediately, I noticed a difference in students. I told them when they came in that the emphasis would be on reading and writing in this class . . . and during parents' night . . . all of my kids came into the room and . . . picked out books . . . just spontaneous." Seeing her students' attitudes toward, and confidence with, reading change, encouraged Ms. Sosa's efforts to reconstruct her practice. When asked about the appropriateness of her approach to reading instruction for her students, she commented:

I realized that most of my students don't have people in their lives who like to read or who do read . . . So, if I don't show them that reading is wonderful, who's going to? They can know all the phonics in the world, but if they don't learn in school that reading is something people do, the phonics aren't going to help.

Ms. Sosa saw reading skills as essential but not sufficient for her students. Engaging students in talking about the books they read, she came to appreciate the valuable resources her students brought to school that helped them make sense of text. Although she saw her students lacking some essential reading skills, she no longer viewed them as lacking experiences which were resources they could use to make sense of the texts they read.

Discussion and Conclusion

When it comes to providing all students with opportunities to engage with a more demanding curriculum, this account suggests a tremendous gulf between the rhetoric of reform, on the one hand, and local practice and rhetoric, on the other. Recent instructional reforms appear to be progressing slowly everywhere.[38] My account suggests that this problem may be accentuated when it comes to the education of students who have traditionally been marginalized by the school system. In the schools studied, most educators flatly rejected the reforms as inappropriate. Understanding learning from a behaviorist perspective and seeing disadvantaged students chiefly in terms of their deficiency in basic language and behavioral skills, local educators shelved proposals for more intellectually challenging content and pedagogy. Believing that teaching the basics was a prerequisite to any instruction in more intellectually demanding content, teachers fixated on getting disadvantaged students up-to-speed on basic skills and never managed to get to more intellectually challenging content.

A web of beliefs that are interdependent and mutually self-supporting undergird these local educators' responses to state policies that pressed more intellectually rigorous instruction for all Americans. Thus to alter their beliefs about poor students, these local educators would also have to alter their beliefs and knowledge about learning, teaching, and classroom management. Beliefs that are "part of interlocking networks of beliefs" are not easily changed.[39] Moreover, teachers' beliefs about, and understanding of, teaching and learning are formed in childhood and adolescence through their lengthy "apprenticeship of observation" to teaching during their own schooling, and rarely adequately challenged in teachers' professional preparation.[40] Beliefs that are formed in childhood are especially resilient to change.[41]

It is unlikely that with time the rift between reformers' aspirations for all students and these local educators' convictions will narrow, absent some major interventions that would allow these educators to reconsider their knowledge and beliefs about learning, teaching, and students. Reformers offer local educators limited help in reconsidering their knowledge and beliefs about learning, teaching, and students, thereby failing to elaborate what their proposals might look like or involve in practice. Images of reformed practice in policy are frequently underdetermined and do not speak to the situations of practitioners who teach disadvantaged students. How might a teacher in a rural school get her first graders, who have not mastered basic English, to talk about books? How might one teach the procedure for adding decimals within the context of a discussion about place value? Simply telling teachers that all students can and should do intellectually demanding academic work is unlikely to be adequate in forging such tremendous instructional change. An urban school principal put it most poignantly noting, "I think it takes more than just saying everybody can learn and it takes more than just putting it out there and just saying do it. I mean there's some stepping stones in between." Reformers everywhere have offered few stepping stones that might help local educators bridge the gap between their existing practice and the ideal of a challenging pedagogy for all students. State policymakers in South Carolina and elsewhere have not developed a practice of policymaking that is capable of challenging local educators' web of beliefs and knowledge.

Based on my analysis, I identified a number of issues that might inform the design of policy and support the implementation process. To begin with, local implementation of state instructional policies that press intellectually rigorous content for all is dependent in part on altering not only local educators' beliefs about poor students but also their beliefs and knowledge about learning, teaching, and classroom management. Reform initiatives that mobilize opportunities for teachers to learn about teaching, learning, students, and content, as well as the relations among these, are more likely to be successful than those which focus exclusively on challenging prevalent beliefs about poor students and students of color.[42]

My analysis of Ms. Banks and Ms. Sosa suggests that interactions of various sorts are central in teachers' efforts to reconstruct their practice. First, there was the interaction between teachers' knowledge of instruction (subject matter, teaching, and learning) and their beliefs about disadvantaged students. Developing new understandings of mathematics and literacy instruction, these two teachers began to teach more challenging academic content and try out new instructional approaches. Observing their students' academic success with this more demanding content, these teachers generated evidence that their disadvantaged students were capable of handling more demanding intellectual content. They created the conditions that challenged their own convictions about disadvantaged students. Both teachers became convinced that their disadvantaged students could learn central disciplinary ideas and concepts as a result of the evidence, in the form of students' work and thinking, they generated in their classrooms. As teachers tried out more challenging pedagogy and engaged students in talking about mathematical and literacy ideas, they developed a better appreciation for students' resources for learning. These teachers began to see their students' resources, not just their deficiencies, and to see how these resources enabled them to learn mathematics and literacy. Further, these teachers also generated for themselves convincing evidence that their disadvantaged students were not only interested in learning, but also motivated to learn. The extent to which students' potentials are recognized, and therefore used by teachers, depends in part on teachers' conceptions of students that in turn appear to depend on teachers' understandings and conceptions of teaching, learning, and subject matter. Some might see this as a case of belief following action, but the evidence from these teachers suggests that the change process is not linear involving constant interaction between knowledge, beliefs, and practice.[43]

These two teachers' changing understandings of disadvantaged students interacted with their motivation to reconstruct their practice. Student success is a primary source of rewards for teachers[44] and these accounts suggest that it may be a key lever for change. For both teachers, their students' successes with more challenging content and interest in learning were primary sources of support for their efforts to reform. Students' success and interest was a key incentive for continued change because teachers noticed significant improvements in students' learning and interest. Seeing students' interest in, and success with, mathematics and literacy improve, these teachers were motivated to continue to reconstruct their teaching. In these interactions, we see that teachers' will to reform their teaching was fueled by their new understandings and skills that in turn fueled their efforts to further develop their knowledge.

My account suggests that the decisions teachers make about what content to teach and how to teach it influence whether and how reformers' aspirations for all Americans get played out locally. But teacher agency is constrained to some extent by what they know; that is, the alternatives and possibilities they can imagine for the education of poor students and students of color. With new knowledge about subject matter and instruction, teachers can reconstruct their practice in ways that enable them to see that their disadvantaged students can master more challenging content while also learning essential basic skills. The social and organizational conditions of teachers' work are important here. Some schools do create organizational supports in the form of classroom coaches or opportunities for teachers to meet and talk with one another about their practice. And research suggests that these supports do appear to enable teachers to revise their practice. In most schools, a scarcity of opportunities for teachers to learn about their practice—especially learning opportunities that are grounded in particular subject areas—and the absence of time and opportunity for most teachers to talk with colleagues about the ins and outs of teaching, influence teachers' enactment of policy.

NOTES

1. A version of this chapter appeared as an Institute for Policy Research (Northwestern University) Working Paper in the spring of 1998. The research reported herein was supported by the Education Policy and Practice Study, which is funded in part by Michigan State University, and by grants from the Pew Charitable Trusts (Grant No. 91-04343-000); Carnegie Corporation of New York (Grant No. B 5638); the National Science Foundation (Grant No. ESI-9153834); the Consortium for Policy Research in Education (CPRE) and the National Center for Research on Teacher Learning (NCRTL), both of which are funded by grants from the United States Department of Education, Office of Educational Research and Improvement (Grants No. OERI-G-008690011 and OERI-R-117G10011-94). A preliminary draft of this chapter, co-authored with Nancy Jennings, was presented at the annual meeting of the American Educational Research Association in April 1995. I am indebted to Nancy Jennings for her work on the preliminary draft and with data collection and analysis. I am also indebted to Charles Abelmann, David Cohen, William Corrin, Richard Elmore, Lauren Murphy, and Jim Rosenbaum for their helpful feedback on earlier drafts of this chapter. John Diamond and Jeremy Price provided helpful suggestions for reorganizing the next-to-last draft. I would also like to acknowledge the School of Education and Social Policy and the Institute for Policy Research at Northwestern University for supporting work on this chapter. The views expressed herein are mine and are not necessarily shared by the grantors.

2. South Carolina Mathematics Framework (Columbia, SC: South Carolina Department of Education, 1993), p. 10.

3. Principal, Butler Elementary School (South Carolina). Please note that all names and locations used in this chapter are pseudonyms.

4. Milbrey McLaughlin, "Learning from experience: Lessons from policy implementation," *Educational Evaluation and Policy Analysis* 9 (1987): pp. 171-178; *Educational Evaluation and Policy Analysis*, 12 (1990); John Schwille, Andrew Porter, Robert Floden, Donald Freeman, Linda Knappen, Therese Kuhs, and William Schmidt, "Teachers as policybrokers in the content of elementary school mathematics," in Larry Shulman and Gary Sykes, eds., *Handbook of Teaching and Policy* (New York: Longman, 1983).

5. South Carolina Mathematics Framework, p. 28.

6. Ibid., p. 29.

7. David Cohen, James Spillane, Nancy Jennings, and Scott Grant, *Reading Policy* (Ann Arbor, MI: University of Michigan, 1998); Deborah Ball and Suzanne Wilson, "Helping teachers meet the standards: New challenges for teacher educators," *The Elementary School Journal* 97 (1997): pp. 121-138.

8. Gloria Ladson-Billings, *The Dream Keepers: Successful Teachers of African American Children* (San Francisco: Jossey-Bass, 1994).

9. Ladson-Billings, *The Dream Keepers*; Lisa Delpit, "The silenced dialogue: Power and pedagogy in educating other people's children," *Harvard Educational Review* 58 (1988): pp. 280-298; Michelle Fine, *Chartering Urban School Reform* (New York: Teachers College Press, 1994); Michael Knapp, *Teaching for Meaning in High-Poverty Classrooms* (New York: Teachers College Press, 1995).

10. John Kingdon, *Agendas, Alternatives, and Public Policies* (Boston: Little Brown, 1984).

11. David Cohen, "Origins," in Arthur Powell, Eleanor Farrar, and David Cohen, eds., *The Shopping Mall High School* (Boston: Houghton Mifflin, 1985); David Labaree, "Curriculum, credentials, and the middle class: A Case study of a nineteenth century high school," *Sociology of Education* 59 (1986): pp. 42-57; David Labaree, *The Making of an American High School: The Credentials Market and the Central High School of Philadelphia, 1838-1939* (New Haven, CT: Yale University Press, 1988).

12. Michael Lipsky, *Street Level Bureaucracy: Dilemmas of the Individual in Public Services* (New York: Russell Sage Foundation, 1980).

13. Larry Cuban, *How Teachers Taught: Constancy and Change in American Classrooms, 1890-1990* (New York: Teachers College Press, 1993); Richard Weatherly and Michael Lipsky, "Street level bureaucrats and institutional innovation: Implementing special education reform," *Harvard Educational Review* 47 (1977): pp. 171-197.

14. Pierre Bourdieu, "Cultural reproduction and social reproduction," in Jerome Karabel and Albert Halsey, eds., *Power and Ideology in Education* (London: Oxford University Press, 1977), pp. 487-511.

15. Annette Lareau, "Social class differences in family-school relationships: The importance of cultural capital," *Sociology of Education* 60 (1987): pp. 73-85.

16. Cohen, Spillane, Jennings, and Grant, *Reading Policy; Educational Evaluation and Policy Analysis*, 1990; James Spillane and Nancy Jennings, "Aligned instructional policy and ambitious pedagogy: Exploring instructional reform from the classroom perspective," *Teachers College Record* 98 (1997): pp. 449-481.

17. Jean Anyon, "Social class and school knowledge," *Curriculum Inquiry* 11 (1981): pp. 3-42; Robert Connell, D. Ashendon, S. Kessler, and G. Dowsett, *Making the Difference: Schools, Families, and Social Division* (Sydney: Allen and Unwin, 1982); Paul Willis, *Learning to Labor* (New York: Columbia University Press, 1977).

18. Anyon, "Social class and school knowledge."

19. Thomas Good and Jere Brophy, *Looking in Classrooms* (New York: Harper and Row, 1987).

20. Shirley Brice Heath, *Ways with Words: Language, Life, and Work in Communities and Classrooms* (Cambridge, MA: Cambridge University Press, 1983).

21. Rebecca Barr, Nonglak Wiratchai, and Robert Dreeben, *How Schools Work* (Chicago: University of Chicago Press, 1983); Catherine Clark and Penelope Peterson, "Research on teacher thinking," in Merlin Wittrock, ed., *Handbook of Research on Teaching* (New York: Macmillan, 1986); Adam Gamoran, "Instructional and Institutional Effects of Ability Grouping," *Sociology of Education* 59 (1986): pp. 185-198; Deborah Meier, *The Power of their Ideas: Lessons for America from a Small School in Harlem* (Boston: Beacon Press, 1995).

22. Anthony Giddens, *Central Problems in Social Theory: Action, Structure, and Contradiction in Social Analysis* (Berkeley: University of California Press, 1979).

23. Matthew Miles and A. Michael Huberman, *Qualitative Data Analysis: A Source Book of New Methods* (Beverly Hills: Sage Publishers, 1984).

24. Only four of the thirty-two interviewees expressed views that differed from this perspective. I take their perspectives up in the next section.

25. Harold Stevenson and James Stigler, *The Learning Gap* (New York: Summit Books, 1992).

26. Burrhus Skinner, *Science and Human Behavior* (New York: Macmillan, 1953).

27. Robert Mills Gagné, *The Conditions of Learning* (New York: Holt, Rinehart, and Winston, 1970).

28. See, for example, Robert Glaser, "Education and thinking: The role of knowledge," *American Psychologist* 39 (1984): pp. 91-104; Gaea Leinhardt, "Development of an expert explanation: An analysis of a sequence of subtraction lessons," in Lauren Resnick, ed., *Knowing, Learning, and Instruction* (Hillsdale, NJ: Erlbaum, 1989); Lauren Resnick, "Learning in school and out," *Educational Researcher* 16 (1988): pp. 13-20.

29. Karen Fuson, Steve Smith, and Ana Maria Lo Cicero, "Supporting Latino first graders' ten-structured thinking in urban classrooms," *Journal for Research in Mathematics Education* (in press); Karen Fuson, *Latino children's construction of arithmetic understanding in urban classrooms that support thinking* (paper presented at the Annual Meeting of

the American Educational Research Association, New York, April 1996); Knapp, *Teaching for Meaning in High-Poverty Classrooms*; Daniel Mayer, "Measuring instructional practice: Can policymakers trust survey data?" *Educational Evaluation and Policy Analysis* 21 (1999): pp. 29-46.

30. Knapp, *Teaching for Meaning in High-Poverty Classrooms*.

31. Mayer, "Measuring instructional practice."

32. Ibid.

33. Gary Natriello, Edward McDill, and Aaron Pallas, *Schooling Disadvantaged Children: Racing Against Catastrophe* (New York: Teachers College Press, 1990).

34. Michelle Fine, "Making controversy," *Journal of Urban and Cultural Studies* 1 (1990): pp. 55-68; Virginia Richardson, Ursula Casanova, Peggy Placier, and Kar Guilfoyle, *School Children At Risk* (New York: Falmer Press, 1989).

35. Lareau, "Social Class Differences in Family-School Relationships"; Heath, *Ways with Words*.

36. Lisa Delpit, *Other People's Children: Cultural Conflict in the Classroom* (New York: New Press, 1995).

37. Delpit, *Other People's Children*; Ladson-Billings, *The Dream Keepers*.

38. *Educational Evaluation and Policy Analysis*, 1990; James Spillane and John Zeuli, "Reform and teaching: Exploring patterns of practice in the context of national and state mathematics reforms," *Educational Evaluation and Policy Analysis* 21 (1999): pp. 1-28.

39. Mary Kennedy, "The connection between research and practice," *Educational Researcher* 26 (1997): pp. 4-12.

40. Daniel Lortie, *School Teacher: A Sociological Study* (Chicago: University of Chicago Press, 1975), p. 61.

41. Kennedy, "The connection between research and practice."

42. G. William McDiarmid and Jeremy Price, *Prospective teachers' views of diverse learners: A study of the participants in the ABCD Project* (East Lansing, MI: National Center for Research on Teacher Learning, 1990).

43. Virginia Richardson, "Significant and worthwhile change in teaching practice," *Educational Researcher* 19 (1990): pp. 10-18.

44. Lortie, *School Teacher*.

Section Five
WHAT CAN BE SAID
ABOUT REFORM PROGRESS

CHAPTER XII

The Impact of Standards and Accountability
on Teaching and Learning in Kentucky[1]

PATRICIA J. KANNAPEL, LOLA AAGAARD, PAMELIA COE,
AND CYNTHIA A. REEVES

The Kentucky Education Reform Act

In June 1989, responding to a school finance lawsuit, the Kentucky Supreme Court declared the state's entire system of public schooling unconstitutional. The state legislature subsequently enacted the Kentucky Education Reform Act of 1990 (KERA), which mandated massive reforms of school curriculum, governance, and finance. The curriculum reforms of KERA reflect the national movement toward standards-based reform tied to an accountability program. This chapter addresses the effects of KERA on teaching and learning.

KERA sets forth goals that *all* students must meet, allows schools to determine how to reach those standards, and holds them accountable through a performance based testing instrument. The reform legislation requires schools to expect high levels of achievement for all students and identifies six student learning goals:

Patricia J. Kannapel and Pamelia Coe are education consultants; Lola Aagaard is an instructor in the Department of Leadership and Secondary Education at Morehead State University; and Cynthia A. Reeves is a Senior Project Associate in the Resource Center on Educational Equity at the Council of Chief State School Officers. Kannapel and Coe were co-directors of the Appalachia Educational Laboratory's study of the Kentucky Education Reform Act at the time this chapter was written. Aagaard and Reeves were researchers on the project.

1. Use basic communication and mathematics skills for purposes and situations they will encounter throughout their lives;

2. Apply core concepts and principles from mathematics, the sciences, the arts, the humanities, social studies, and practical living to situations they will encounter throughout their lives;

3. Become self-sufficient individuals;

4. Become responsible members of a family, work group, or community, including demonstrating effectiveness in community service;

5. Think and solve problems in school situations and in a variety of situations they will encounter in life, and;

6. Connect and integrate experiences and new knowledge from all subject matter fields with what they have previously learned, and build on past learning experiences to acquire new information through various media sources.

The 1994 legislature, in response to concerns that the state was teaching and testing values, prohibited the testing of students on learning goals three and four. The goals remained in effect, but only goals one, two, five, and six were further defined into fifty-seven academic expectations specifying what students should know and be able to do by the end of their schooling. Curriculum guidance was provided through *Transformations*,[2] a curriculum framework outlining a process for local curriculum development. In 1996, the Kentucky Department of Education released the *Core Content for Assessment*, identifying the content to be assessed under KERA goals one and two (the goals that focus on basic subject matter knowledge). A third curriculum document released in 1998, *Program of Studies for Kentucky Schools*,[3] outlined the *minimum* content required at each grade level.

A partially performance based assessment system (called the Kentucky Instructional Results Information System, or KIRIS) was developed and implemented from 1991 through 1998 to drive instruction, measure progress toward the goals, and hold schools accountable. At its most performance based, KIRIS included open-response questions, on-demand writing prompts, writing and mathematics portfolios, and performance events (requiring students to solve problems in groups, then respond to written questions individually). KIRIS was administered to students in grades four and five, seven and eight, and eleven and twelve; students were assigned performance ratings of novice, apprentice, proficient (the goal for all students), and distinguished in each tested subject. The goal was for all schools to reach an average score of *proficient* by 2014.

Scores for each biennium were averaged and combined with data on nonacademic factors (such as attendance and drop-out rates) to produce an accountability index for each school. Schools were expected to show specified levels of improvement on the index from one biennium to the next in order to earn cash rewards and avoid sanctions that included assistance from a Distinguished Educator.[4] During the 1996-98 biennium, in schools where scores declined by five points or more, Distinguished Educators were to evaluate certified staff every six months and recommend retention, dismissal, or transfers.

Numerous problems with the KIRIS test—including scoring reliability and validity, and complaints about the cumbersome nature of portfolios—resulted in removal of mathematics portfolios and performance events from the testing program. In 1998, the legislature replaced KIRIS with the Commonwealth Accountability Testing System (CATS), under development at the time this chapter was written. CATS continues to test students on the *Core Content* and includes a nationally normed test as part of the accountability system, gives more weight to nonacademic factors, and streamlines the writing portfolio. An interim accountability formula (in place while a permanent formula is devised) replaces mandatory assistance from Distinguished Educators to *all* schools "in decline" with nonmandatory assistance from Highly Skilled Educators to low-performing schools with declining scores.

School based decision making (SBDM) councils composed of the principal and elected teacher and parent representatives set policy to determine how to help students attain KERA goals. Council responsibilities include hiring a principal when a vacancy occurs and setting policy in key areas such as curriculum, instructional practices, professional development, school budget, and student assessment.

Kentucky deviates from the standards-based approach in mandating replacement of kindergarten through third grade with a nongraded primary program. This primary program was intended to create classrooms more responsive to individual differences in student learning styles and abilities by allowing students to progress at their own rates.[5] It was believed that students who had not acquired certain skills and capabilities by the end of the primary program, with three or four years of success behind them, would be better able to handle retention.[6]

Description of the Research

Throughout the 1990s, the Appalachia Educational Laboratory (AEL) studied the implementation of KERA in four rural school districts recommended by Kentucky educators and policymakers as "typical" districts (neither at the forefront of reform nor likely to subvert it). Two districts were located in Appalachian eastern Kentucky, one was in the Bluegrass region of central Kentucky, and the fourth was in the agricultural flatlands of western Kentucky. The identities of the districts remained confidential throughout the research. From 1990 through 1995, the research focused on reform implementation in all twenty schools in the four districts. From 1996 through 2000, the focus shifted from reform implementation to its effects on teaching and learning in six elementary schools in the four districts. Classroom experiences of the class of 2006 were targeted because this group entered school in 1993-94, the first year of primary program implementation.

The study was qualitative, including over the past decade more than 1,200 interviews with state policymakers, school administrators, teachers, school board members, parents, students, and community members. We spent more than 500 hours in classrooms and also observed professional development activities, school district meetings and parent events, and Kentucky Board of Education meetings. We regularly reviewed key documents such as local newspapers, school improvement plans, assessment results, lesson plans, and school board and school council minutes.

This chapter focuses primarily on the classroom effects of KERA in the six study schools, supplemented by findings of broader studies of KERA. Two research questions are addressed: (1) How has KERA influenced curriculum, instruction, and classroom assessment? and (2) How has KERA affected student learning?

Influence of KERA on Curriculum, Instruction, and Classroom Assessment

OVERVIEW

Embedded in the KERA learning goals and related statutes is the expectation that Kentucky teachers will change their approach to schooling to help all students achieve high standards; integrate subject matter across fields; engage students in problem solving, research, and real life activities; integrate authentic assessment tasks into the instructional program; and, in the primary grades, help individual students progress toward KERA goals rather than move age-groups of students through a specified curriculum. These practices run counter to the traditional classroom structure which has been highly resistant to change.[7]

The expected changes have proven difficult for Kentucky teachers, but some changes have occurred.

The two most widespread curricular effects of KERA were assessment driven: an increased emphasis on writing, and alignment of curriculum to the state test.

Writing emphasis. Numerous studies, including our own, have documented the increased emphasis on writing in Kentucky classrooms since 1990—a response to the strong written component of KIRIS.[8] Many teachers in the study districts reported that the emphasis on writing had positive effects. An eighth grade teacher commented:

For years we have been so concerned with [teaching] English in parts. You did a unit and then you went to another one and you never brought it all together. Somehow the kids never understood, "Why am I doing this?" So to me, actually seeing that they can communicate and use these skills is great.

Similarly, more than seventy percent of writing teachers responding to a 1996-97 statewide survey agreed that the KIRIS writing portfolio had a positive effect on writing instruction, while eighty percent said portfolios helped students write more and better, and seventy-eight percent believed portfolio instruction had made them more innovative teachers.[9]

In spite of their enthusiasm, teachers at the accountable grade levels reported that the focus on writing detracted from skills instruction and coverage of other content.[10] In response, the 1998 legislature reduced the number of required pieces in the elementary and middle school writing portfolio.

Curriculum alignment. Policymakers intended for local districts to use Kentucky's curriculum framework, *Transformations*, to develop their own curricula within the context of KERA goals and expectations.[11] Our study and others, however, found that the framework's lack of specific alignment to KIRIS, combined with its sheer size (over 500 pages), resulted in minimal use of the document.[12] In contrast, the *Core Content for Assessment*, which specifies the actual content to be assessed, was widely used to align curricula.[13] The alignment process was viewed as beneficial by many educators because it helped them collaboratively focus their efforts. A middle school principal commented in 1996:

Another thing I think we are on track with is curriculum alignment. We have done lots of professional development on this—looking at expectations and our curriculum and lessons plans, and seeing where we are covering these. Everything is not perfect but we are all moving in the same direction and have a pretty good sense of what those outcomes are that we may not be addressing.

While the *Core Content* was meant to be only *part* of a comprehensive curriculum,[14] many educators in the AEL study schools reported that tested subjects took precedence over others. A fourth grade teacher commented in 1998: "Trying to get to all the subjects is really difficult, so you tend to go with the ones you are really tested with and let the others slide. We do science, reading, and writing more than the others." A fifth grade teacher in another school reported in 1998 that she had stopped using an integrated language arts program because it did not cover the *Core Content*:

I used to use *Success in Reading and Writing* and really felt successful. We did thirty minutes of reading, thirty minutes of writing, thirty minutes of research, and thirty minutes of word study every day . . . When they developed the *Core Content*, I felt I might be leaving parts of content out, so felt I must get back to the textbook.

Similarly, statewide teacher surveys found widespread agreement that teachers at the testing grades de-emphasized nontested areas in favor of tested ones.[15]

While the emphasis on teaching to the test sometimes narrowed the curriculum, it led some of the study schools to expand curriculum into areas previously given scant attention. When art and humanities questions on KIRIS began to count in the accountability formula, some elementary schools began offering occasional arts programs or bringing in artists-in-residence. In addition, arts and humanities often appeared in teacher lesson plan books during the fifth grade year when this subject is tested.

INSTRUCTIONAL PRACTICES

Standards-based reform requires more challenging instruction in which all students engage in active problem solving, knowledge construction through analysis and synthesis of real life problems, hands-on experiences, and integration of subject matter.[16] This mode of teaching is sometimes referred to as "teaching for understanding."[17] The need to teach for understanding is implicit in KERA goals five and six, and in aspects of the KIRIS test and the mandated "critical attributes" of the primary program.

Studies have documented that for teachers to switch from the traditional, fact-based approach to teaching for understanding, they must have regular, ongoing support and modeling in the classroom.[18] Teachers in the AEL study schools and across the state received a great deal of professional development in the two years immediately following KERA, especially at the primary level, but these experiences rarely extended beyond a period of days nor included classroom follow-up. In addition, professional development across the state typically focused on general instructional techniques rather than on curriculum content linked to KERA goals and expectations.[19]

Even so, teachers in the study schools attempted many new instructional approaches aimed at introducing more variety, subject matter integration, thematic instruction, hands-on experiences, and group activities. The changes were especially evident at the primary level, where virtually all teachers experimented with hands-on and calendar activities to teach mathematics, thematic or interdisciplinary instruction, literature-based instruction, writing activities, and flexible seating arrangements. Some primary teachers also employed learning centers and cooperative learning activities. In general, teachers assigned less textbook work, seat work, and rote memorization than in the past.[20] Similar instructional changes in primary classrooms were reported statewide.[21]

Primary teachers found the new strategies labor intensive and time consuming, however, and worried that students were not acquiring "basic skills." Fourth and fifth grade teachers began to report that incoming students were unprepared for the state test. These pressures, combined with lack of follow-up support after initial professional development, led many primary teachers to return to more traditional "skill drill" practices.[22] Some new practices persisted in AEL study classrooms, however, including flexible seating arrangements, partner or group work, process writing, authentic literature as part of the reading program, and hands-on activities.[23]

Some changes consistent with standards-based reform also occurred above the primary level, including subject matter integration.[24] In the AEL study schools, "writing across the curriculum" was common as was correlation of children's literature with science and social studies topics. Integration of mathematics and science occurred occasionally. Teachers at one study school integrated science, social studies, mathematics, and language arts through a weather unit. Students wrote letters to various states inquiring about their weather patterns. They used the Internet to access weather data for their states of choice, then entered the data in a computer spreadsheet and graphed results. They tracked weather in their own area through local newspaper weather summaries.

Many fourth and fifth grade teachers in the AEL study schools daily or weekly used authentic literature for reading instruction and engaged students in hands-on science activities. Statewide research documented other instructional changes. More than half of fifth grade mathematics teachers surveyed reported increases in writing about mathematics, using calculators or computers to solve a problem, working on extended activities over several days, using manipulatives to solve problems, and solving nonroutine problems.[25]

The instructional changes Kentucky teachers made are in the direction of standards-based reform, but in the AEL study schools, classroom instruction continued to be teacher-directed and focused predominantly on factual knowledge, especially in the teaching of English, spelling, and mathematics. Occasional problem solving or thinking activities were observed in reading, social studies, and science—although science experiments often focused on following procedures rather than solving problems. Overall, there was scant evidence of student-directed instruction except in the occasional research project. Even here, topics were often assigned or limited by the teacher. Students had some degree of freedom in choosing writing topics. Statewide research also found that fact-based approaches predominated: the most common mathematics teaching activities reported on statewide surveys were practicing computation skills and working problems from a textbook, while the most common writing activity was practicing the mechanics of written English.[26]

When we questioned third, fourth, and fifth grade teachers about their continued reliance on teacher-directed, fact-based approaches, they offered a variety of explanations. They did not believe they could get through the *Core Content* while covering subject matter in any depth or engaging students in extended, problem-based activities. More integration of subject matter could help, but some found this to be a catch-22: integrating subject matter would require planning, practicing, and refining new methods, but covering the *Core Content* left them with insufficient time to do so. Teachers perceived that they must convey a vast body of factual knowledge, and they feared they might lose control of student learning and behavior if they allowed more student direction. Moreover, some teachers said they simply did not know how to "teach for understanding," and did not have the time or opportunity to learn.

Another factor contributing to teachers' focus on basic skills and knowledge is that the state test, *Core Content*, and *Program of Studies* emphasize KERA goals one and two, which focus on basic factual knowledge. After performance events were removed from KIRIS, remaining test items were mostly associated with goals one and two, and few with goals five and six.[27] Thus the assessment and accountability program itself provided little motivation for teachers to teach for understanding.

CLASSROOM ASSESSMENT PRACTICES

Kentucky's initial assessment design included two major strands: accountability assessment and continuous assessment. Most of the state's assessment resources, however, went into development and implementation of the accountability test, leaving few resources to develop models for assessing the progress of individual students toward KERA goals.[28] The closest the state came to developing a continuous assessment tool was the Kentucky Early Learning Profile (KELP) for use in the primary grades. The KELP, however, was not directly linked to KERA goals and expectations, was not made mandatory, and was viewed by many teachers as burdensome and time consuming. Consequently, the KELP was not widely used around the state.[29]

The lack of emphasis on continuous assessment at the state level likely contributed to a corresponding lack of attention at the local level. Primary teachers attempted authentic assessment strategies as one of the "critical attributes" of the primary program, but the techniques they used were cumbersome and were rarely linked to KERA goals and expectations.[30]

Above the primary level, most changes in classroom assessment were in response to the accountability test. Teachers across the state and in the AEL study schools had students practice responding to open-response questions and on-demand writing prompts.[31] Many of the AEL study schools, as well as those visited by Kelley and Protsik,[32] required teachers to post in their classrooms a list of steps to answering open-response questions. Teachers in the study schools added open-response questions or on-demand writing prompts to multiple-choice unit tests throughout the school year, while more intensive test practice occurred in the weeks immediately preceding testing.

The intense focus on test preparation and implementing the primary program's critical attributes obscured the need to develop instruments for assessing individual student progress toward KERA goals and expectations. Only one of the AEL study schools, Orange County

Elementary School (OCES), developed a formal system for regularly assessing individual student progress within and across grade levels. This system was only loosely tied to KERA goals and expectations, but it was a start. At OCES, continuous assessment of students went hand-in-hand with a schoolwide ethic of high expectations for all students. Teachers recognized that helping all students achieve required identifying areas where individual students needed assistance. In other schools, efforts at raising whole school test scores tended to focus on covering the *Core Content* or engaging in general instructional activities that teachers hoped would make a difference for students. Perhaps this was part of the reason OCES was the only study school to meet its KIRIS goal every biennium.

Evidence of Increased Student Learning

The true measure of KERA's success is improved learning for *all* students. Looking first at test scores, elementary schools in the AEL study and across the state improved average student performance on KIRIS in all academic areas. The greatest gains occurred in reading (from 32 to 58 on the academic index),[33] mathematics (from 22 to 44), and science (from 18 to 37).[34] High school students also improved their test scores considerably. Middle school students had the lowest scores and improved the least, although all academic areas improved except writing where scores remained flat.[35] The validity and reliability of KIRIS, however, were never firmly established. A panel of national testing experts noted that large increases on KIRIS did not correspond to equivalent gains on nationally normed tests.[36] KIRIS is the only test, however, that is linked to Kentucky's academic goals and expectations, so greater gains on KIRIS are to be expected.[37] Improvements are almost certainly attributable, as well, to the considerable amount of test preparation in Kentucky schools.

Other achievement measures show less dramatic achievement gains. The National Assessment of Educational Progress (NAEP), whose open-response format is similar to KIRIS and CATS, was administered to a sample of Kentucky schools during the reform period. Kentucky fourth graders improved their NAEP reading scores from 213 to 218 between 1992 and 1998 to exceed the national average (215) for the first time. Eighth graders exceeded the national average in reading (261) by one point in 1998 (the first year that eighth grade NAEP reading scores were published by state). Fourth graders improved faster in mathematics than their counterparts in most other states, to come within two points of the national average (222), compared to a four-point gap in 1992.[38]

Kentucky's improved NAEP scores have been questioned due to the decrease in the numbers of Kentucky students with disabilities who took the test between 1994 and 1998. Two statistical analyses were conducted to examine this issue. One analysis concluded that had the proportion of students with disabilities remained constant, Kentucky's gain would no longer be statistically significant.[39] Another analysis concluded that excluding students with disabilities had only "modest" effects on the 1998 scores.[40]

Test results are also available from the nationally normed Comprehensive Test of Basic Skills (CTBS). Using this test to judge progress is problematic, however, because the CTBS/4 was administered the year before KERA's passage, but was not administered statewide again until 1997. By then, the test (now called the CTBS/5) had been newly normed, preventing the valid comparison of pre- and post-KERA results. In addition, a review of CTBS/5 test materials indicated that it does not measure Kentucky's academic expectations very well.[41] Nevertheless, CTBS national percentile scores for Kentucky's third grade students increased from 50 to 55 between 1997 and 2000, while sixth grade scores increased from 50 to 52, and ninth grade scores increased from 48 to 49.[42]

Results from all three tests suggest that achievement for Kentucky students has improved, at least at the elementary level. The dramatic rise in KIRIS scores, as contrasted to other measures, is very likely related to test preparation activities, teachers' focus on tested content, and greater alignment of KIRIS to Kentucky's learning goals and academic expectations. Only by keeping the same test in place for a period of years, and by supplementing test score data with other indicators of success, will it be possible to determine whether schools are genuinely increasing students' knowledge and skills or whether rising test scores are an artifact of test preparation.

Not only are test scores rising, but parents in the AEL study districts and across the state believe student learning has improved—a noteworthy finding given the transitional state of Kentucky schools over the past decade. In the AEL study schools, more than three-fourths of twenty-nine parents of randomly selected students reported in 1998-99 that their children were learning more—and at a faster rate—than they would have expected. One parent contrasted her daughter's elementary experience with a son who did not receive his elementary education under KERA.

They did not have all of this when [the brother] was in elementary school. The things she learns and writes, it is a lot more than what he ever did. A couple of weeks ago, they wrote a brochure like going on vacation . . . And they have been studying China and doing portfolios . . . I don't remember him getting into depth like they do now.

These findings mirror statewide data. A 1999 statewide survey found that a majority of public school parents believed that student learning over the past five years had improved in the areas of computer skills, writing, thinking and problem solving, reading, knowledge of basic subject matter, and mathematics computation. Further, a majority of parents believed schools were doing a good job preparing students for college, work, self-sufficiency, basic skills, and citizenship.[43]

HELPING *ALL* STUDENTS ACHIEVE

While student achievement has increased overall, Kentucky has not yet produced equitable achievement results on KIRIS and NAEP for minority students and those from low-income households.[44] Educator beliefs about student capabilities likely play a role here. In the AEL study, the exception proves the rule. The school in our study with the highest percentage of poor students (OCES with seventy percent of students eligible for free or reduced lunch) achieved the highest KIRIS scores among the study schools in recent years, demonstrated the fastest rate of improvement on KIRIS, and attained CTBS scores that were well above the state average and nearly as high as those of the two study schools with the fewest at-risk students. OCES was characterized by a schoolwide ethic that all of their students could succeed—a commitment inspired by both a district philosophy of high achievement and inclusion for all students, and by a principal whose own low-income background instilled in her a mission to encourage and assist all children to succeed.

Educators at the other study schools neither spoke as positively about their students nor displayed the same level of commitment to helping all achieve. Over the ten years of research, two schools experienced significant increases in the proportion of low-income students enrolled. Teachers were sometimes skeptical about these students' abilities and were unaccustomed to adapting their teaching to meet different student needs and learning styles. A teacher at one of these schools, when asked for her reaction to the KERA expectation that all students will achieve at high levels, responded:

It will never happen, not [at our school], that all will achieve at the proficient level. From the time I came here until now, the town and the housing have deteriorated to low-income housing. We have a few set families that have good students, but so many have moved in here for the low-income housing that are not education-oriented, they are not job-oriented, they are welfare-oriented. Their children come to school with the idea that they will stay until they can drop out. They get no help at home, you get nothing back from home . . . Not all will achieve at the proficient level. I feel it is impossible . . . I'm butting my head against the wall.

Educators at a third school with more than fifty percent of students qualifying for free or reduced lunch and the only substantial minority population in their school district were often heard to attribute the school's erratic test performance to the kind of students the school served. In explaining the school's low KIRIS scores in 1994, the following remark was fairly typical: "We're doing a great job. You have to look at what we're working with."

Except at OCES, most teachers expressed reservations throughout the last decade about the concept that *all* students can achieve at high levels, although many were willing to agree that *most* students can rise to higher expectations. But teachers were skeptical that all students are capable of reaching the "proficient" level on the state test—which is the state's method of judging whether schools have succeeded with all students. One teacher commented, "I have kids who are novice students, and that's all they are ever going to be." Similarly, a 1996-97 statewide RAND survey found that sixty-three percent of fifth grade teachers and seventy percent of eighth grade teachers agreed that some students will never perform above the novice level no matter what teachers do.[45]

There is evidence, however, that teachers' perceptions of student abilities have changed. Since 1994, the Kentucky Institute for Education Research has monitored educators' agreement with the KERA principle that all children can learn and most at high levels. The percentage of teachers who agreed with the statement rose from thirty-five percent in 1994 to sixty-eight percent in 1999.[46] The change may reflect teachers pushing students to higher levels of achievement because of accountability pressures, then raising their expectations when students do better than anticipated—a phenomenon reported by Holland[47] in her case study of a single Kentucky district. An elementary school principal in an AEL study school described how student performance led teachers to raise their expectations of students:

I think we are becoming more aware of all the students than we have [been] in the past . . . partially because [of] rewards and sanctions hanging out there over the top of us . . . When I came here, the seventh and eighth grades were absolutely horrible. All we could think about was, "Boy, in two years they'll be gone . . . " Well, those were the kids that we got these [high] scores with on the eighth grade assessment. I pointed out to [the teachers], "You exceeded your threshold in the eighth grade by a little over a point and you did it with those types of students." To me, that was probably a much bigger motivator than rewards or sanctions was. They realize that they have had a degree of success, where I don't think they really thought before that they could.

A special education teacher commented:

KERA has really changed the complexion of special education. It used to be you had your little IEP [individual education plan] and you started where the student was and took them along. Now I have to do portfolios with students. It is a lot of work for me, but I have seen how these students can really write, much more than in the past. I have had to raise my expectations of students, and I have learned that they can do a great deal more than I thought.

Discussion

The results of Kentucky's standards-based reform have been mixed as might be expected when a change of this magnitude is attempted. Since 1990, Kentucky policymakers have held firmly to the vision of helping all students reach challenging goals and have kept substantial funding intact to help this happen, leading to positive changes. Entire schools are now focused on the same goals and curricular content and are coordinating their efforts across grade levels and subjects. Classroom instruction has become more interesting and interactive. Students have greater access to instructional materials and to art and humanities instruction. Student achievement has improved on most measures and remained stable on others, and parents have been satisfied with the level of student learning under KERA. Even greater success might be achieved if attention is given to two key issues: (1) the need to develop positive incentives for change together with accountability systems, and (2) the need to provide the professional development and time teachers need to make the desired changes.

ACCOUNTABILITY STRUCTURE

Kentucky's assessment and accountability program gave schools greater curricular focus and motivated teachers to push students to higher performance levels, but educators in all but one study school were more preoccupied with test scores than with helping each student achieve high standards. Changes in classroom assessment, for the most part, reflected preparation for the state assessment. Absent in most places was any system for tracking the progress of individual students toward KERA goals and expectations. Similarly, Stecher and Barron[48] found that the accountability system caused Kentucky teachers to focus on "the most proximal aspects of the system (tests) rather than the more distant goals it is supposed to promote (curriculum and performance standards)." In addition, external rewards and sanctions provided insufficient motivation for teachers to create classrooms where basic content and higher order skills were taught simultaneously through authentic activities that develop all students' conceptual understanding of subject matter. These observations suggest the need to supplement or expand accountability systems in at least three areas.

First, looking at multiple indicators of success might help teachers get beyond test scores. Wheelock[49] suggests that to improve teaching and learning, accountability systems should focus not only on test scores but on classroom practices that are likely to lead to success for students. A related idea is a school quality review process in which schools account for student learning, professional practice, equity, opportunity to learn, and community building.[50] Kentucky is currently developing a scholastic audit that examines some of these factors, but as it is currently conceived, the audit will be required only in schools with declining test scores. Making such a tool available to all schools might help teachers focus on professional practice as it relates to student learning, rather than solely on improving test scores.

Another way to supplement the accountability system is to link external and internal incentives for change. Internal reward systems could include salary increases for staff development related to changes in practice, as well as released time for teachers to engage in the intensive work required to implement standards-based reform.[51]

A third avenue is to blend high-stakes testing programs with high-quality classroom assessment so that important decisions about student learning are based on specific information about how individual students are performing.[52] This was the original intent in Kentucky, but classroom assessment was nearly lost in a single-minded focus on school accountability.

PROFESSIONAL DEVELOPMENT AND SUPPORT

If standards-based reform is to succeed, a professional development structure must be created that can provide the kind of training and support teachers need to teach higher order skills to diverse learners, to regularly evaluate individual student learning and adapt instruction accordingly, and to make policy decisions designed to improve learning for all students. The Kentucky Department of Education has begun to develop new models of professional development through "teacher academies" that focus on deepening teachers' subject matter knowledge. Continued work in this direction is needed, and could probably best be accomplished through collaboration among state departments of education, professional associations, and higher education institutions.

Related to professional development is the need to restructure teacher time. Virtually every study of KERA implementation, as well as the literature on standards-based reform, emphasizes the need to provide teachers with time and compensation to implement a reform that requires them to engage in intensive and ongoing professional development and to make major changes in classroom practice.[53] Some thoughtful and creative study of the issue of restructuring teacher time is needed at the national, state, and local levels.

Conclusion

Standards-based reform as implemented in Kentucky has resulted in school curricula that are more focused and aligned with state standards, and classrooms that are better equipped as well as more interesting, active, and enjoyable. Evidence from various assessment measures indicates that the reform has paid off in terms of student achievement, especially at the elementary level. But the goal of high achievement for all students has yet to be attained.

It must be remembered, however, that reform has only begun in Kentucky. While proponents of standards-based reform envision a unified system in which all the pieces cohere and classrooms are centers of active student learning, we might do well to think of standards-based reform as it played out in Kentucky as yet another example of "tinkering toward Utopia."[54] It has brought about positive changes, but there is more tinkering to be done at the state, district, and school levels before reaching the envisioned Utopia. Some might argue that the work to be done requires much more than "tinkering," but until public education is sufficiently funded to provide teachers with the professional education, support, and time they need to implement the labor-intensive changes required by standards-based reform, educational policymakers and researchers will have to settle for positive changes in smaller increments.

NOTES

1. Throughout the 1990s, the Appalachia Educational Laboratory (AEL) studied the implementation of the Kentucky Education Reform Act in four rural Kentucky school districts. This chapter is based on work sponsored wholly or in part by the Office of Educational Research and Improvement, United States Department of Education, under contract number RJ96006001. Its contents do not necessarily reflect the views of OERI, the Department, or any other agency of the United States government.

2. Kentucky Department of Education, *Transformations: Kentucky's Curriculum Framework* (Frankfort, KY: Author, 1993).

3. Kentucky Department of Education, *Program of Studies for Kentucky Schools, Grades Primary-12* (Frankfort, KY: Author, 1998).

4. Distinguished Educators were administrators and teachers, selected through an application process, who were released from their school districts for two to four years and received a salary supplement to assist schools which failed to meet their state testing goals. Distinguished Educators received intensive training from the Kentucky Department of Education before and during their service to schools.

5. Jack Foster, *Redesigning Public Education: The Kentucky Experience* (Lexington, KY: Diversified Services, Inc., 1999).

6. Kentucky Department of Education, *Kentucky's Primary School: The Wonder Years, Program Description I* (Frankfort, KY: Author, 1991).

7. Larry Cuban, *How Teachers Taught: Constancy and Change in American Classrooms, 1890-1990* (New York: Teachers College Press, 1993); Richard Elmore, "Getting to scale with good educational practice," *Harvard Educational Review* 66 (1996): pp. 1-26; William Firestone, David Mayrowetz, and Janet Fairman, "Performance based assessment and instructional change: The effects of testing in Maine and Maryland," *Educational Evaluation and Policy Analysis* 20 (1998): pp. 95-113; David Tyack and Larry Cuban, *Tinkering Toward Utopia: A Century of Public School Reform* (Cambridge, MA: Harvard University Press, 1995); David Tyack and William Tobin, "The 'grammar' of schooling: Why has it been so hard to change?" *American Educational Research Journal* 31 (1995): pp. 453-479.

8. Appalachia Educational Laboratory, "Instruction and assessment in accountable and nonaccountable grades," *Notes from the Field 4* (Charleston, WV: Author, 1994); Appalachia Educational Laboratory, "Five years of education reform in rural Kentucky," *Notes from the Field 5* (Charleston, WV: Author, 1996); Connie Bridge, Margaret Compton-Hall, and Susan Chambers Cantrell, *Classroom Writing Practices Revisited: The Effects of Statewide Reform on Classroom Writing Practices* (Lexington, KY: Institute on Education Reform, University of Kentucky, 1996); Mark J. Fenster, *An assessment of "middle" stakes educational accountability: The case of Kentucky* (Paper presented at the annual meeting of the American Educational Research Association, New York, NY, April 1996); Patricia Kannapel, Pamelia Coe, Lola Aagaard, Beverly Moore, and Cynthia Reeves, "Teacher responses to rewards and sanctions: Effects of and reactions to Kentucky's high stakes accountability program," in Betty Lou Whitford and Ken Jones, eds., *Accountability, Assessment, and Teacher Commitment: Lessons from Kentucky's Reform Effort* (Albany: SUNY Press, 2000), pp. 127-146; Carolyn Kelley and Jean Protsik, "Risk and reward: Perspectives on the implementation of Kentucky's school based performance award program," *Educational Administration Quarterly* 33 (1997): pp. 474-505; Daniel Koretz, Sheila Barron, Karen Mitchell, and Brian Stecher, *Perceived Effects of the Kentucky Instructional Results Information System (KIRIS)* (Santa Monica, CA: RAND, 1996); Brad Matthews, *The Implementation of Performance Assessment in Kentucky Classrooms* (Frankfort, KY: Kentucky Institute for Education Research, 1995); Brian Stecher and Sheila Barron, *Quadrennial Milepost Accountability Testing in Kentucky* (Los Angeles: National Center for Research on Evaluation, Standards, and Student Testing, UCLA, 1999).

9. Brian Stecher, Sheila Barron, Tessa Kaganoff, and Joy Goodwin, *The Effects of Standards-Based Assessment on Classroom Practices: Results of the 1996-97 RAND Survey of Kentucky Teachers of Mathematics and Writing* (Los Angeles: National Center for Research on Evaluation, Standards, and Student Testing, UCLA, 1998).

10. Kannapel, Coe, Aagaard, Moore, and Reeves, "Teacher responses to rewards and sanctions"; Koretz, Barron, Mitchell, and Stecher, *Perceived Effects of the Kentucky Instructional Results Information System (KIRIS)*.

11. Kentucky Department of Education, *Transformations: Kentucky's Curriculum Framework*.

12. Appalachia Educational Laboratory, "Instruction and assessment in accountable and nonaccountable grades"; Appalachia Educational Laboratory, *The Needs of Kentucky's Teachers for Designing Curricula Based on Kentucky's Academic Expectations* (Charleston, WV: Author, 1995); Thomas Corcoran and Barbara Matson, *Evaluation of NSF's Statewide Systemic Initiatives (SSI) Program: A Case Study of Kentucky's SSI (PRISM), 1992-1997* (Menlo Park, CA: SRI International, 1998); Koretz, Barron, Mitchell, and Stecher, *Perceived Effects of the Kentucky Instructional Results Information System (KIRIS)*.

13. G. Williamson McDiarmid, Jane David, Patricia Kannapel, Pamelia Coe, and Thomas Corcoran, *Professional Development: Meeting the Challenge* (Lexington, KY: Partnership for Kentucky Schools and The Prichard Committee for Academic Excellence, 1997); Office of Education Accountability, *Annual Report* (Frankfort, KY: Author, 1997); Office of Education Accountability, *Annual Report* (Frankfort, KY: Author, 1998); Arthur Thacker, R. Gene Hoffman, and Lisa Koger, *Course Contents and KIRIS: Approaches to Instructional and Curriculum Design in Middle School Science and Social Studies* (Radcliff, KY: Human Resources Research Organization, 1998).

14. Kentucky Department of Education, *Core Content for Assessment, Version 1.0* (Frankfort, KY: Author, 1996); Brad Matthews, "Curriculum reform," in Jane Lindle, Joseph Petrosko, and Roger Pankrantz, eds., *1996 Review of Research on the Kentucky Education Reform Act* (Frankfort, KY: Kentucky Institute for Education Research, 1997), pp. 51-77.

15. Koretz, Barron, Mitchell, and Stecher, *Perceived Effects of the Kentucky Instructional Results Information System (KIRIS)*; Stecher and Barron, *Quadrennial Milepost Accountability Testing in Kentucky*; Stecher, Barron, Kaganoff, and Goodwin, *The Effects of Standards-Based Assessment on Classroom Practices*.

16. David Cohen, "What is the system in systemic reform?" *Educational Researcher* 24 (1995): pp. 11-17, 31; Richard Elmore, "Introduction: On changing the structure of public schools," in Richard Elmore, ed. *Restructuring Schools: The Next Generation of Educational Reform* (San Francisco: Jossey-Bass Publishers, 1990), pp. 1-28; Hendrik Gideonse, "Organizing schools to encourage teacher inquiry," in Richard Elmore and Susan Fuhrman, eds., *Restructuring Schools: The Next Generation of Educational Reform* (San Francisco: Jossey-Bass Publishers, 1990), pp. 97-124; Jennifer O'Day, Margaret Goertz, and Robert Floden, "Building capacity for education reform," *CPRE Policy Briefs* (Philadelphia, PA: Consortium for Policy Research in Education, 1995); Marshall Smith and Jennifer O'Day, "Systemic school reform," in Susan Fuhrman and Betty Malen, eds., *The Politics of Curriculum and Testing: The 1990 Yearbook of the Politics of Education Association* (London: Falmer Press, 1991), pp. 233-267.

17. Milbrey McLaughlin and Joan Talbert, "Introduction: New visions of teaching," in David Cohen, Milbrey McLaughlin, and Joan Talbert, eds., *Teaching for Understanding: Challenges for Policy and Practice* (San Francisco: Jossey-Bass Publishers, 1993), pp. 1-10.

18. Deborah Ball and Sylvia Rundquist, "Collaboration as a context for joining teacher learning with learning about teaching," in David Cohen, Milbrey McLaughlin, and Joan Talbert, eds., *Teaching for Understanding: Challenges for Policy and Practice* (San Francisco: Jossey-Bass Publishers, 1993), pp. 13-42; Ruth Heaton and Magdalene Lampert, "Learning to hear voices: Inventing a new pedagogy of teacher education," in

David Cohen, Milbrey McLaughlin, and Joan Talbert, eds., *Teaching for Understanding: Challenges for Policy and Practice* (San Francisco: Jossey-Bass Publishers, 1993), pp. 43-83; Sarah McCarthey and Penelope Peterson, "Creating classroom practice within the context of a restructured professional development school," in David Cohen, Milbrey McLaughlin, and Joan Talbert, eds., *Teaching for Understanding: Challenges for Policy and Practice* (San Francisco: Jossey-Bass Publishers, 1993), pp. 130-163.

19. McDiarmid, David, Kannapel, Coe, and Corcoran, *Professional Development*.

20. Appalachia Educational Laboratory, "Kentucky's primary program," *Notes from the Field 3* (Charleston, WV: Author, 1993); Appalachia Educational Laboratory, "Evolution of the primary program in six Kentucky Schools," *Notes from the Field 6* (Charleston, WV: Author, 1998).

21. Connie Bridge, *The Implementation of Kentucky's Primary Program 1995: A Progress Report.* (Lexington, KY: Institute on Education Reform, University of Kentucky, 1995); James Raths and John Fanning, *Primary School Reform in Kentucky Revisited* (Lexington, KY: The Prichard Committee, 1993).

22. Appalachia Educational Laboratory, "Evolution of the primary program in six Kentucky schools"; Raths and Fanning, *Primary School Reform in Kentucky Revisited*.

23. Appalachia Educational Laboratory, "Evolution of the primary program in six Kentucky schools."

24. Stecher, Barron, Kaganoff, and Goodwin, *The Effects of Standards-Based Assessment on Classroom Practices*.

25. Ibid.

26. Stecher and Barron, *Quadrennial Milepost Accountability Testing in Kentucky*; Stecher, Barron, Kaganoff, and Goodwin, *The Effects of Standards-Based Assessment on Classroom Practices*.

27. Kentucky Department of Education, *KIRIS Accountability Cycle 2 Technical Manual* (Frankfort, KY: Author, 1997); Joseph Petrosko, "Assessment and accountability," in *Review of Research on the Kentucky Education Reform Act* (Lexington, KY: Institute on Education Reform, forthcoming); Anthony Nitko, *A Guide to Tests in Kentucky: A Description and Comparison of the Comprehensive Test of Basic Skills, the California Achievement Tests, the TerraNova (CTBS5), and the Kentucky Instructional Results Information System Assessment* (Frankfort, KY: Kentucky Institute for Education Research, 1997).

28. Foster, *Redesigning Public Education: The Kentucky Experience*; Edward Kifer, "Development of the Kentucky Instructional Results Information System (KIRIS)," in Thomas Guskey, ed., *High Stakes Performance Assessment: Perspectives on Kentucky's Educational Reform* (Thousand Oaks, CA: Corwin Press, 1994), pp. 7-18.

29. Office of Education Accountability, *Annual report* (Frankfort, KY: Author, 1999).

30. Office of Education Accountability, "Evolution of the primary program in six Kentucky schools"; Ellen McIntyre and Diane Kyle, "Primary program," in Jane Lindle, Joseph Petrosko, and Roger Pankrantz, eds., *1996 Review of Research on the Kentucky Education Reform Act* (Frankfort, KY: Kentucky Institute for Education Research, 1997), pp. 119-142.

31. Appalachia Educational Laboratory, "Evolution of the primary program in six Kentucky Schools"; Kelley and Protsik, "Risk and reward: Perspectives on the implementation of Kentucky's school based performance award program"; Koretz, Barron, Mitchell, and Stecher, *Perceived Effects of the Kentucky Instructional Results Information System (KIRIS)*; McIntyre and Kyle, "Primary program."

32. Kelley and Protsik, "Risk and reward: Perspectives on the implementation of Kentucky's school based performance award program."

33. The state KIRIS goal was for all schools to obtain an average score of 100 (the "proficient" level) on a 140-point scale.

34. Susan Weston, "KIRIS data on improvement in student performance," memorandum to Robert Sexton, Prichard Committee for Academic Excellence, June 15, 1999.

35. Ibid.

36. Ronald Hambleton, Richard Jaeger, Daniel Koretz, Robert Linn, Jason Millman, and Susan Phillips, *Review of the Measurement Quality of the Kentucky Instructional Results Information System 1991-1994* (Frankfort, KY: Office of Education Accountability, 1995).

37. Nitko, *A Guide to Tests in Kentucky: A Description and Comparison of the Comprehensive Test of Basic Skills, the California Achievement Tests, the TerraNova (CTBS5), and the Kentucky Instructional Results Information System Assessment.*

38. Susan Weston, "NAEP data on Kentucky performance," memorandum to Robert Sexton, Prichard Committee for Academic Excellence, March 19, 1999.

39. John Mazzeo, John Donoghue, and Catherine Hombo, "A summary of initial analyses of 1998 state NAEP exclusion rates," memorandum to Pascal D. Forgione, Commissioner of Education Statistics, NCES, March 12, 1999.

40. David Hoff, "Kentucky's 1998 NAEP gains declared statistically significant," *Education Week* 19 (1999), p. 6.

41. Nitko, *A Guide to Tests in Kentucky: A Description and Comparison of the Comprehensive Test of Basic Skills, the California Achievement Tests, the TerraNova (CTBS5), and the Kentucky Instructional Results Information System Assessment.*

42. Kentucky Department of Education, "Briefing packet, state and regional release, 2000 CTBS/5 results for exiting primary, grades 6 and 9" (Frankfort, KY: Author, 2000).

43. Kentucky Institute for Education Reform, *1999 Statewide Education Reform Survey of Teachers, Principals, Parents, and General Public* (Lexington, KY: Author, 1999).

44. Joseph Petrosko, "Assessment and accountability"; Phillip Roeder, *Educational Reform and Equitable Excellence* (Lexington, KY: RDS Publishing Co., 1999); Weston, "KIRIS data on improvement in student performance"; Weston, "NAEP data on Kentucky performance."

45. Stecher, Barron, Kaganoff, and Goodwin, *The Effects of Standards-Based Assessment on Classroom Practices: Results of the 1996-97 RAND Survey of Kentucky Teachers of Mathematics and Writing.*

46. Kentucky Institute for Education Research, *Statewide Education Reform Survey* (Frankfort, KY: Author, 1995); Kentucky Institute for Education Research, *A Review of the 1996 Statewide Education Reform Survey Data* (Frankfort, KY: Author, 1996); Kentucky Institute for Education Research, *1996 Statewide Education Reform Survey of Teachers, Principals, Parents, and General Public* (Frankfort, KY: Author, 1997); Kentucky Institute for Education Research, *1999 Statewide Education Reform Survey of Teachers, Principals, Parents, and General Public.*

47. Holly Holland, *Making Change: Three Educators Join the Battle for Better Schools* (Portsmouth, NH: Heinemann, 1998).

48. Stecher and Barron, *Quadrennial Milepost Accountability Testing in Kentucky.*

49. Anne Wheelock, "A new look at school accountability," in Betty Lou Whitford and Ken Jones, eds., *Accountability, Assessment, and Teacher Commitment: Lessons from Kentucky's Reform Efforts* (Albany: State University of New York Press, 2000), pp. 179-198.

50. David Ruff, Debra Smith, and Lynne Miller, "The view from Maine: Developing learner-centered accountability in a local control state," in Betty Lou Whitford and Ken Jones, eds., *Accountability, Assessment, and Teacher Commitment: Lessons from Kentucky's Reform Efforts* (Albany: State University of New York Press, 2000), pp. 163-178; Betty Lou Whitford and Ken Jones, "Kentucky lesson: How high stakes accountability undermines a performance based curriculum vision," in Betty Lou Whitford and Ken Jones, eds., *Accountability, Assessment, and Teacher Commitment: Lessons from Kentucky's Reform Efforts* (Albany: State University of New York Press, 2000), pp. 9-24.

51. Elmore, "Getting to scale with good educational practice."

52. Richard Stiggins, "Assessment, student confidence, and school success," *Phi Delta Kappan* 81 (1999), pp. 191-198.

53. Appalachia Educational Laboratory, "Special feature: KERA through the eyes of teachers," *Notes from the Field 2* (Charleston, WV: Author, 1992); Appalachia Educational Laboratory, "Kentucky's primary program"; Appalachia Educational Laboratory, "Five years of education reform in rural Kentucky"; Jane David, *School Based Decision Making: Linking Decisions to Learning* (Lexington, KY: The Prichard Committee, 1994); Tom Donahoe, "Finding the way: Structure, time, and culture in school improvement," *Phi Delta Kappan* 75 (1993), pp. 298-305; Elmore, "Getting to scale with good educational practice"; Gideonse, "Organizing schools to encourage teacher inquiry"; McDiarmid, David, Kannapel, Coe, and Corcoran, *Professional Development: Meeting the Challenge*; Ellen McIntyre, Ric Hovda, and Diane Kyle, "Lessons on creating nongraded primary programs or implementing other systemic changes," in Ric Hovda, Diane Kyle, and Ellen McIntyre, eds., *Creating Nongraded K-3 Classrooms: Teachers' Stories and Lessons Learned* (Thousand Oaks, CA: Corwin Press, 1996), pp. 181-188; Judith Newman, "We can't get there from here: Critical issues in school reform," *Phi Delta Kappan* 80 (1998), pp. 288-296; O'Day, Goertz, and Floden, "Building capacity for education reform"; Raths and Fanning, *Primary School Reform in Kentucky Revisited*; Gary Sykes, "Fostering teacher professionalism in schools," in Richard Elmore, ed., *Restructuring Schools: The Next Generation of Educational Reform* (San Francisco: Jossey-Bass Publishers, 1990), pp. 56-96; Suzanne Wilson, Carol Miller, and Carol Yerkes, "Deeply rooted change: A tale of learning to teach adventurously," in David Cohen, Milbrey McLaughlin, and Joan Talbert, eds., *Teaching for Understanding: Challenges for Policy and Practice* (San Francisco: Jossey-Bass Publishers, 1993), pp. 84-129.

54. Tyack and Cuban, *Tinkering Toward Utopia: A century of public school reform.*

CHAPTER XIII

Conclusion

SUSAN H. FUHRMAN

Evidence about the effects of standards-based reforms on student achievement is just beginning to accumulate. Grissmer and Flanagan[1] have suggested that alignment of standards, curriculum, and assessment, along with accountability, are largely responsible for strong gains in some states. Grissmer[2] finds that state and local data show some progress as noted earlier in this volume.

This yearbook has focused on antecedent questions that are being addressed by many current studies and that are easier to answer at this stage in the reform process. Some have to do with the central theory of the reform: Are policies being aligned around standards? Do they embody incentives that motivate schools, teachers, and students to reach the standards? The others have to do with actual changes in practice. Is content and pedagogy changing in the directions sought by reformers?

The chapters in this book have mixed answers to these questions. They report progress, but they also report numerous gaps in reform design and challenges in implementation. But the most common answer to these questions is that there is no one answer for each context. Instead, we see an enormous amount of variation on both the policy development and change measures. In some states and districts there's greater alignment than in others; in some places the incentives have more power; in some classrooms there's more change and innovation than in others.

Variation is the typical response to policy change, especially in our very decentralized education system. Much has been written about how implementers' views of reforms and the incentives for compliance (often called "will") as well as their underlying knowledge, access to resources, and belief systems (often called "capacity") affect their responses.[3]

Susan H. Fuhrman is Dean, and the George and Diane Weiss Professor of Education at the Graduate School of Education, University of Pennsylvania. She also is chair of the management committee of the Consortium for Policy Research in Education.

We know, for example, that district response to state policy can range from resistance, to pro forma compliance, to some sort of mutual accommodation ("mutual adaptation" in McLaughlin's words), to proactive use of external reforms to achieve internal strategic goals.[4]

It may be that in the case of standards-based reforms, variation is even more pronounced than usual and should be expected. Unlike simple reforms that are easily understood, standards-based reforms are enormously complex. The classic example of a mandate that includes within it all the information needed for compliance is the "sixty-five mile per hour speed limit." Drivers know what that means and what they must do to comply.[5] Policies about teaching all students to high standards are at the other end of the complexity continuum. Reasonable people have different understandings of many aspects of these policies, including how to define the terms "all students," "high," and "standards."

Further, standards-based reforms require dramatic changes in policy configuration, in operations at various levels of government, and in instructional practice. They require very unfamiliar behaviors. No level of government has practice in assuring that policies cohere, which is an underlying tenet of standards-based reform. In fact, political incentives drive policymakers toward new, distinct efforts that call attention to the sponsor instead of toward policies that build on previous efforts.[6] Old policies are seldom eliminated, so even a set of new policies that are "coherent" within themselves are likely to clash with existing policies that remain on the books. In terms of operations, as most of the chapters in this volume make clear, states are entering into new accountability relationships with schools, and both they and districts are being called upon to help schools—through professional development, assistance in data interpretation, and other efforts—build the capacity necessary to meet the new requirements. Both the accountability roles—actually attaching consequences to student performance—and the capacity-building roles entail new kinds of behaviors for states and districts.[7] As far as changes in classroom practice are concerned, the new reforms envision more challenging and sophisticated content, methods that engage students more actively in problem solving, and learning and pedagogics that embrace varied learners in rigorous learning experiences. These are daunting challenges for teachers.[8]

Expecting variation, however, is quite different from understanding it in a way that helps policymakers and educators address it. The chapters in this volume go a long way toward unpacking the sources and nature of the variation associated with both alignment or coherence and changes in practice. They also indicate that while some sources of the variation might be addressed, some are more deep-seated and less amenable to change.

Variation as a Consequence of Policy Design

A considerable amount of the varied responses at both the policy level—putting policies together, aligning curriculum to standards, aligning assessments to standards and curriculum, and developing accountability—and the classroom level reflect differences in standards-based policy design. States and districts have made decisions in shaping these policies that in turn shape their implementation. We see variation across jurisdictions because of this, but we also see in these chapters that some of the design features within a jurisdiction can also result in less, rather than more, commonality in response.

AVAILABILITY OF CURRICULUM LINKED TO STANDARDS

As Clune points out, a particularly weak link in standards-based reform policies in the nine states he examined is the absence of model curricula, new materials, and model teaching units. That means that teachers frequently have to rely on content standards as the sole guidance about *what* to teach. If standards are vague, as they often have to be to generate sufficient political support, or large in number, because additive approaches were used to get buy-in from various constituencies, it is very difficult for teachers to interpret what teaching to them meant. In the absence of actual curriculum—or at least much further definition of standards and more guidance about priorities among standards—teachers are likely to vary considerably in which standards they emphasize and which material they use to teach each standard. So one clear source of variation is policies that were too vague, or that had gaps in them, like the provision of specific curriculum.

In the absence of curriculum provided by states and districts, most teachers appear to be relying on assessments to set the specifications for curriculum. If standards are vague or voluminous, teachers focus their attentions on what is covered on the assessment. Kannapel, Aagaard, Coe, and Reeves tell us that Kentucky teachers, who, unlike those in many other states, actually had a curriculum framework, *Transformations*, tied to its academic expectations, did not find it specific enough. Its lack of direct alignment to the assessment system and its mammoth size (over 500 pages) severely limited its utility. In 1996, the state agency released the *Core Content for Assessment*, which laid out specific content to be assessed, divided by subject area and by testing levels. This document was, according to the authors, immediately seized upon to define and align curriculum. Likewise, Wilson and Floden found teachers in each of their sites focusing more on assessed content. Maryland teachers, for example, were focusing on content covered in the Maryland State Performance Assessment Program, and teachers in Michigan mentioned the Michigan Educational Assessment Program as a major influence.

A number of scholars have worried that focusing on tested content can severely narrow the curriculum.[9] Teachers discard favorite units and drill students in assessed content. Sometimes that drill exceeds "instruction" and falls over into overt "test preparation." In those cases it appears that the content is being learned only in context of a specific test, without any broader application.

ABSENCE OF ALIGNED ASSESSMENTS

The authors in this book, however, are less likely than some others to frame the main relationship between assessment and instruction as a problem of narrowing the curriculum around tested content. Although some do point to narrowing effects,[10] a larger problem for our authors is the lack of alignment between curriculum and assessments. It's one thing if part of the curriculum is assessed and part isn't. One might lament the fact that teachers will naturally gravitate to what is measured and skimp on the unmeasured material. But it's an even more serious problem if the test and the standards and curriculum have so little in common that the assessments used are not a fair measure of whether the standards (either a part or all) are being taught and learned. In the latter case, the alignment underlying the theory of standards-based reform has not been accomplished and the theory, as Clune clearly points out, and as Supovitz echoes with respect to the effects of aligning professional development to student learning goals, cannot be assessed. We don't know if teachers are teaching students to standards if the assessments focus on something other than the standards. We don't know if teacher professional development aligned to the standards changes teacher effectiveness if the assessments are not aligned to standards.

Goertz tells us that, although we can expect a time lag between state creation of standards and the development and implementation of an assessment to measure performance on these standards, a number of states in her fifty-state survey describe using norm-referenced tests designed to measure the knowledge and skills of students across the country, rather than the knowledge and skills embodied in specific state standards. Porter and Smithson analyzed alignment issues in six states. Their conclusion that "Instruction in a state was, in general, no more aligned to that state's test than it was aligned to the tests of other states" is telling. They do not report whether the assessments are aligned to standards, and admit that non-alignment of instructional content may not be a problem if the test is a basic skills variety of the kind Goertz is talking about.

If alignment problems keep us from assessing the progress of reform, they also underscore why so many researchers find variation in response. Some teachers are responding to standards that are vague and hard to match to curriculum, some to assessments that truly reflect standards, some to assessments that only cover a small part of standards, and some to assessments that don't match standards much at all.

THE ACCOUNTABILITY STRUCTURE

Another aspect of design that directly affects variation in response is the "bite" of the accountability system. The extent to which new standards-based accountability systems are affecting motivation to improve performance depends in large measure on several design features. It matters whether there are stakes or consequences for good or poor performance. It matters where stakes are placed—on schools, students, or individual adults. It matters what the actual stakes are and whether they are credible—whether the state will really close a failing school or really provide a sizeable bonus.[11] It matters how high the goals are set—goals that are too high may not be seen as attainable and worth striving for.

In most of the states and districts studied by Goertz, teachers themselves faced few formal consequences for failure to reach goals. Generally, districts used performance data to support rather than punish, and where consequences existed, they were generally higher for students and principals than for individual teachers. For example, in Minnesota, one of many states with a high school graduation test, the students bore the only stakes in the system. In such circumstances, teachers were less directly affected, and focused on improving performance. But as Kannapel, Aagaard, Coe, and Reeves make clear, in Kentucky it was schools, not students, which felt the consequences. They credit Kentucky's accountability system with giving schools greater curricular focus and motivating teachers to push students to higher performance levels, although they worry about preoccupation with test scores rather than with helping each student achieve to high standards.

Placement of stakes interacts with other features of accountability design. If schools are the unit of accountability, it is not necessary to test every student in every grade. Rather, students can be sampled to get a picture of the school's progress. However, as Goertz points out, if students' promotion or graduation hinge on testing, individual testing is required. Individual testing is often also favored by parents who want regular reports on their own child's progress. When only samples are tested, it may be the teachers in the tested grades that feel the impact the most and other teachers in the schools may not sense much fall-out from the accountability system. Further, the distance between current performance and goals matters. When very low-performing schools face very high improvement goals, they can give up. As DeBray, Parson, and Woodworth conclude, states frequently do not set structures for low-performing schools to create short-term goals for continuous improvement, so they can have some benchmarks against which to mark progress over time.

Fairman and Firestone's contrast of Maine and Maryland highlights the effects of differences in accountability design. Because of the threat of school "reconstitution" for low and declining performance, Maryland districts responded directly to state tests, whereas in Maine, where scores were published but no other consequences were provided, ". . . districts had generally low will to respond to the state standards and, in particular, state assessment." For example, one superintendent the authors visited did not even open the state test results until asked to as part of the interview.

In summary, as our chapters make clear, much of the varied response to standards-based reform depends on policy design; on the specificity of standards and their elaboration into curriculum; on the alignment of assessment, curriculum, and standards; and on the features of the accountability system. Yet it is also clear that much variation also stems from how these designs were interpreted by people at different levels of the system, with differing skills and beliefs. Therefore a second theme of the book is that the implementation of standards-based reform depends a great deal on differences in capacity.

Variation as a Consequence of Differences in Capacity

Capacity issues are important at all levels of the system. Standards-based reform requires state level policymakers and educators who can manage valid, representative standard-setting processes, assess and choose assessments to measure attainment of standards, and design accountability systems and other policies that support standards. Optimally, the state must also have the capacity to support standards-based reform at other levels of governance (i.e., to support capacity-building activities). Districts also have design and support functions, creating policy systems and providing personnel and materials that help schools improve instruction. Importantly, districts also mediate between state policy and schools; their capacity to interpret and tailor state policies to their own settings is vital. And, of course, capacity at the school and classroom levels is most essential; principals and teachers must believe in their own ability and that of their students to reach high standards, and they must have the knowledge and skills, as well as sufficient material resources, to achieve such goals.

The authors in this volume show clearly how these abilities vary from state to state, district to district, school to school, and classroom to classroom.

CAPACITY AT THE STATE LEVEL

Goertz points out that all states try to make some provision for assistance to schools, including supporting and funding school improvement planning processes and technical assistance. However, many states report having insufficient resources to achieve their goals. Goertz uses the example of California, which in 1999-2000, designated 3,144 schools as underperforming, but was only able to include 430 in the first year of its Immediate Intervention/Underperforming Schools Program. Studying the same eight states as Goertz, Massell concludes that while states used the same basic strategies to support school use of assessment data to improve instruction—supporting school improvement processes, or offering professional development on data interpretation, for example— they vary in how they design and use these mechanisms. Some state agencies have less of their own capacity to support such processes; others are just new to the business of accountability and need time to grow expertise. Clune further supports this theme: time is important. From his study of nine states participating in the Statewide Systemic Initiatives Program, he finds that "successful states built on pre-existing reforms of the 1980s, with continuity rather than discontinuity between the earlier period and the new period of standards-based reform." Similarly, Hannaway and Kimball find that district and school reports of reform progress were more positive in "early reform" states with more experience in the process.

An important aspect of state capacity to support reform is political stability. A stable political environment assures that policies are in place long enough to allow implementation to take place. Further, instability reinforces what educators already sense about much reform: "This too shall pass," so why bother changing what we do?

Kannapel, Aagaard, Coe, and Reeves give a clear sense of the importance of a stable political environment in Kentucky. Changes did come to the standards-based reform design over the period studied, but they were more evolutionary than revolutionary, leading to incremental adjustment rather than large upsets in the implementation process. In their words, "Since 1990, Kentucky policymakers have held firmly to the vision of helping all students reach challenging goals and have kept substantial funding intact to help this happen, leading to positive changes." In contrast, in California, in Wilson and Floden's words, "state mandates were in flux." Teachers were getting "confusing and conflicting messages."

CAPACITY AT THE DISTRICT LEVEL

As in the case of states, districts differ in resources and expertise; they also vary in their experience in spearheading and supporting reform. Some districts offer coherent and sophisticated professional development, require and/or help schools plan to improve instruction and achievement, support the use of achievement data in planning, and supplement state accountability by providing additional incentives and support. Others resist reform; many fall somewhere in between active, effective support and resistance.

One factor explaining these differences is district size. Both Hannaway and Kimball, and Fairman and Firestone cite size as the key district characteristic that affects ability to support reform. Hannaway and Kimball believe this is because larger districts are better connected to helpful sources of information and assistance. As an example, the largest districts in their study were about twice as likely to report that subject matter associations were very helpful in reform efforts. Also, of course, larger districts have specialized staff available to help schools. Fairman and Firestone think this latter point is the most important. In the larger districts they studied, the Maryland districts, size correlated with curriculum directors, subject matter specialists, and testing directors. The Maryland districts had about twelve of these people who could support school efforts, compared to one in the Maine districts. Even though the Maryland districts also had many more students, they still maintained double the number of specialized central office staff per student.

Size is certainly not the only factor affecting district capacity. Fairman and Firestone also talk about political flexibility, the ability to buffer school improvement efforts from vigorous constituencies. In the larger Maryland districts, which serve several towns, boards were less responsive to sectional or special interests. In the authors' opinion, this left them interestingly freer to attend to the state and, therefore, more responsive to the reform agenda. The authors apparently see a zero-sum game between local versus state orientation.

To Fairman and Firestone, district responsiveness to the state highlights the importance of another aspect of capacity that affects variation: belief in the authority of the reform agenda. In both Maryland districts, the administrators felt strongly compelled to comply to the state's agenda, even when they personally did not support the instructional goals. They saw a link between rising test scores and funding support from the county, and they also frequently met with state personnel who pushed the reform.

Belief also encompasses the sense that the goals are achievable. Administrators must think that the district can make progress for them to put wholehearted support behind it. As Massell says, "If educators think the outcomes are irrelevant to their students, and/or the goals unattainable, they seem less likely to invest energy and resources in creative strategies to improve on these measures." The expectation that goals can be achieved, sometimes called expectancy,[12] can be affected by policy design. If goals are too high, then many can see them as unachievable. But expectancy is also influenced by belief in student abilities, and in the abilities of educators to offer appropriate opportunities to learn. If educators think students are incapable of learning challenging material and/or that they themselves lack the knowledge and skills to teach the material, their expectancy is low, even if they think that reaching the goals is important and that positive and/or negative consequences will be forthcoming.

According to Massell, beliefs about the ability to achieve the goals were important influences in determining district efforts to support data use, particularly data from the accountability/assessment system, by local schools. Some districts that she calls "intensive users" see data as indispensable tools in the reform effort. They see the potential for more instructionally-oriented professional dialogues, better and more targeted professional development, and improved decision making through better planning and evaluation processes. On the other hand are districts that do little with data, perhaps moving curriculum units around and putting in some add-on remedial programs, but not truly addressing instructional implications.

District variation in support for reform clearly affects school variation. But it is not true that every school in supportive districts is making equal progress. Neither is the reverse true. Specific factors at the school and classroom level also come into play.

CAPACITY AT THE SCHOOL AND CLASSROOM LEVEL

The authors in this volume give us many pictures of teachers and schools responding to reform. Some of the vignettes are very exciting and promising, suggesting that standards are catalyzing more challenging and ambitious instruction. We have an elementary school principal and teacher in California who are active reformers as evidenced by rich examples of student work and many innovative pedagogics.[13] In Rivera High School in New York, teachers accepted the "Regents-for-all" policy enthusiastically, feeling personally responsible for student progress, using data to improve instruction, adding instructional time, and increasing professional development.[14] A fifth grade teacher of "disadvantaged students" in South Carolina was focusing increasingly on understanding mathematical concepts rather than on skills and procedures. For example, she involved students in designing their own number systems.[15] In the Glen Lake School in Vermont, teachers were shocked at low test results and used state-mandated Action Planning to set ambitious data-driven goals, to broaden the literature curriculum, and, to emphasize open-ended mathematics questions, to change the algebra sequence.[16]

Some of the vignettes are much more disturbing. Worksheets and board work on basic skills characterized Mrs. Brady's South Carolina classroom. Students worked on exercises largely alone. She said she planned to do higher level work, but basic skills took up too much time and she felt that the state reforms were not realistic given the basic skill deficits.[17] In Robinson High School in New York, teachers complied with external requirements, for example, by eliminating a lower track so that all students could take regular Regents exams, but they did little else to prepare. There was no professional development aimed at making necessary instructional changes. Similarly, in Garrison High School in Vermont, no real attempts were made to change curriculum. In fact, English teachers who were interviewed said there was no real English curriculum, and while they "were aware of the school's low scores . . . they weren't particularly disposed to fundamentally changing their practice."[18]

Many of the schools and teachers visited by authors in this volume fell somewhere in between the positive and negative accounts just described, balancing the old and the new. Mrs. Chandler, in a Maryland elementary school, combined a new textbook based on the standards with much of her traditional practice. In Marlowe School in Kentucky, teachers did more writing instruction, as they were encouraged to by the state assessment, but they also had daily oral language exercises on grammar and spelling.[19] Fairman and Firestone report that Maryland teachers they studied added larger, multi-step problems in mathematics of the kind included on the state assessment and used more hands-on and group work. But ". . . teachers rarely used these activities as a vehicle to move beyond computational procedures and a step-by-step approach." In the Kentucky schools studied by Kannapel, Aagaard, Coe, and Reeves, teachers used newer practices, such as the incorporation of authentic literature for reading instruction and hands-on science activities. But these were added into classrooms that still continued to be teacher-directed and focused primarily on basic skills and factual knowledge. The authors remind us that the Kentucky assessment also emphasizes basic factual knowledge, with few items covering higher level goals. But the pattern of adding in some new practices seen as standards-based while maintaining much of traditional practice, what Wilson and Floden call "balance," is a strong one that crosses study states.

It is worth noting that the variation just described occurs within and across states. In states with high stakes for schools but not for students (e.g., Kentucky), high stakes for students but not for schools (e.g., New York), states phasing in high stakes for both schools and students (e.g., Maryland), and states with low stakes for everyone (e.g., Vermont), there are exciting examples of change, depressing examples of poor practice, and many examples of mixed or moderate change, with a "balance" of old and improved practice. Variation at the school and teacher level is clearly not erased by the presence of strong incentives, even though some policymakers have argued that accountability is enough. Just because there are stakes, schools do not automatically develop capacity, certainly not the abilities necessary to sustain deep improvement in practice.

What aspects of capacity explain variation in pursuit of reform objectives and improvement in practice? Some of the factors are those we have long known to distinguish more from less effective schools. Wilson and Floden, and DeBray, Parson, and Woodworth write about the importance of principal leadership in supporting excellent teachers. For example, Rivera High School's principal and department chairs held teachers accountable for student performance.[20] Teacher knowledge and skills are also important; Fairman and Firestone, and Kannapel, Aagaard, Coe, and Reeves discuss the need for much more and better professional development than what they observed. Supovitz cites several studies that show a strong relationship between intensive, standards-based professional development and teaching practice, but that kind of professional development is rare.[21]

Another interesting aspect of capacity highlighted in this volume is the sense of unity of purpose around improved student performance. In the higher performing schools studied by DeBray, Parson, and Woodworth, there were internal accountability systems, collective responsibility, and shared expectations about student progress that could be marshaled in response to the external accountability system. In contrast, in the lower performing schools, collective norms did not exist, teachers operated in isolation, and while they complied with the new state policies, the compliance was superficial and not meaningful.

In the absence of collective goals about improved student performance, teachers very often fall back on their own individual expectations about their students.[22] One of the strongest themes emerging from this volume is the devastating effect of low expectations. Teachers who don't believe their students can achieve new standards don't try very hard to improve instruction and student performance.

BELIEF SYSTEMS AND TEACHING PRACTICE

A teacher in a Kentucky school with a growing proportion of low-income children told Kannapel, Aagaard, Coe, and Reeves, "Their children come to school with the idea that they will stay until they can drop out. They get no help at home, you get nothing back from home . . . Not all will achieve at the proficient level. I feel it is impossible . . . I'm butting my head against the wall." This statement could have been made by many of the teachers described in these chapters. Across study states, teachers believed that low-income, "disadvantaged" children could not achieve the new state standards. Witness Mrs. Carlton, a fifth grade teacher in South Carolina, who believed her students needed discipline above all else. The thematic units she understood the state to be promoting were not appropriate to the very structured classroom environment she believed necessary.[23] Or observe an English teacher at Robinson High School in New York speaking about her students as too behind to pass Regents exams, ". . . we're dealing with kids who are mostly drowning."[24] A principal in a low performing school studied by Massell viewed the state test as "substantively inappropriate" for her urban students, tied to "performance standards that the very lowest achievers are unlikely to meet."

In the above examples, the low expectations play out in maintained emphasis on basic skills despite new state and/or district standards emphasizing problem solving and conceptual understanding, and tightly ordered classrooms focused on worksheets and drills despite the visions of new more student-centered pedagogics in standards documents. When such teachers encounter the new accountability systems, they may simply give up, as did the New York English teacher just quoted. But most try to do something to increase student performance: at least adding tested information into the curriculum, and sometimes doing extensive test preparation.

The authors in this volume see the culture of low expectations as not just a characteristic of the poorest teacher responses they observe but also as an important reason for the more mixed picture of teaching practice they report as predominant. Even teachers who are enthusiastic about reform goals, or those who may be better prepared than others in terms of their own knowledge and skills, or those with supportive principals and other factors in their favor can doubt that poor and underprepared students can reach standards. They may try to protect them by assuring that they still keep healthy doses of basic skills in their practice and that they mix in some more challenging work without reaching too high. As Wilson and Floden tell us, teachers report that instruction is influenced by standards-based reform, especially by the assessment system, but they also take account of students' particular needs. Specifically, "they held on to what they knew students needed to master mathematics and English Language Arts—the 'basics.'" So one of the reasons for the balance between the old and the new, the mixture of the familiar and the traditional, is that teachers are worried about students achieving more challenging material with more innovative pedagogics. They are, to borrow the title of Wilson and Floden's chapter, "hedging their bets."

If the bad news is that low expectations can kill standards-based reform, then the good news authors in this volume report is that reform itself, along with some other helpful practices, can begin to change those expectations. These findings suggest some reason to hope for progress, even if it takes a very long time.

Changing Beliefs and the Future of Standards-based Reform

One important finding of this book is that standards-based reform itself can begin to overcome the low expectations that are so damaging to reform goals. Kannapel, Aagaard, Coe, and Reeves cite specific evidence that teachers' perceptions of student abilities have changed over the years that Kentucky has been engaged in standards-based reform. In 1994, only thirty-five percent of teachers agreed with the Kentucky reform principle that all children can learn and most at high levels. By 1999, sixty-eight percent agreed. How did this change occur? In the context of a stable reform environment, teachers made incremental changes in their practice, and student performance, even in the most disadvantaged settings, improved. The assessment system provided clear focus on key goals, the accountability system enhanced motivation, curriculum changed to align to the standards, more professional development occurred than before, and students learned more. As Clune would put it, the theory of standards-based reform worked in this case, and its success convinced teachers that students really could learn more challenging material. The evidence became clear. Even if, as reform critics argue, the curriculum has been narrowed around the testing and more authentic instructional improvement is neither encouraged by the current accountability structure nor supported by sufficient, sophisticated professional development, changing teachers' perceptions of student abilities to such a great extent would be a remarkable achievement in itself, one that could have lasting ramifications.

Massell agrees that experience with reform can change teachers' impressions about the capacity of students to achieve. She feels that the prevalence of data appears to be altering some educators' attitudes about the ability of different groups. She cites a Maryland principal who says that seeing student achievement results in the way the accountability system presents them eliminates the excuses teachers make about lack of parent involvement and other problems of low-achieving students. The principal says the new system has "emphasized, re-emphasized, that it is teachers as people who make the difference."

It appears that the impact of standards reforms on teachers' beliefs can be boosted by the same kind of intensive, curriculum-based professional development shown by Supovitz to be effective in improving teacher knowledge and skills. The two South Carolina teachers described by Spillane as effectively improving their practice did so by deepening their understanding of mathematics and literacy instruction. Then, trying out more challenging academic content and new instructional approaches, they saw some students they previously thought incapable succeed. As Spillane puts it, "They created the conditions that challenged their own convictions about disadvantaged students . . . With new knowledge about subject matter and instruction, teachers can reconstruct their practice in ways that enable them to see that their disadvantaged students can master more challenging content while also learning essential basic skills."

Of course, organizational supports such as coaches and opportunities for teachers to meet and talk about practice are important. But the news that excellent professional development geared to standards cannot only improve knowledge and skills and change practice, but also change teachers' beliefs in profound ways, is very encouraging. It offers some existence proofs that the theory of standards-based reform, the idea that high standards for all—linked to other policies like professional development—can improve instruction and achievement. It may be that such professional development, linked to opportunities for collaboration at the school site, can create the kind of collective responsibility for student learning discussed by DeBray, Parson, and Woodworth.

The bottom line is that these findings offer hope for continued educational improvement if enough political stability can be created to sustain the standards agenda and if policymakers come to realize that accountability is not enough—it must be accompanied by capacity-building, including high quality, intensive professional development. And, according to Massell, Hannaway and Kimball, Fairman and Firestone, and others, some state and local policymakers are getting the message about the importance of added capacity.

The hope for such benefits from standards-based reform does not remove the need to remain watchful about potential dangers, such as narrowing the curriculum and excessive test preparation. But it does suggest that we might be optimistic about incremental progress. Perhaps the "balance" of old and new observed by Wilson and Floden and others reflects a snapshot in time. Perhaps in another five years, assuming stability and continued investment in capacity, observations would yield even more positive results. The chapters in this volume hold out that possibility, and they give guidance about some of the conditions that will be necessary for such progress to occur.

NOTES

1. David Grissmer and Ann Flanagan, *Exploring Rapid Achievement Gains in North Carolina and Texas* (Washington, DC: National Education Goals Panel, 1998).

2. David Grissmer, Ann Flanagan, Jennifer Kawata, and Stephanie Williamson, *Improving Student Achievement: What State NAEP Test Scores Tell Us* (Santa Monica, CA: RAND, 2000).

3. For a summary, see Milbrey McLaughlin, "Learning from experience: Lessons from policy implementation," *Educational Evaluation and Policy Analysis* 9 (1987): pp. 171-178; *Educational Evaluation and Policy Analysis* 12 (1990).

4. Susan Fuhrman, William Clune, and Richard Elmore, "Research on education reform: Lessons on the implementation of policy," *Teachers College Record* 90 (1988): pp. 237-257.

5. Lorraine McDonnell and Richard Elmore, "Getting the job done: Alternative policy instruments," *Educational Evaluation and Policy Analysis* 9 (1987): pp. 133-152.

6. Susan Fuhrman, ed., *Designing Coherent Education Policy: Improving the System* (San Francisco: Jossey-Bass, 1993).

7. Susan Fuhrman, "The new accountability," *CPRE Policy Briefs* (Philadelphia: Consortium for Policy Research in Education, 1999); Diane Massell, "The district role in building capacity: Four strategies," *CPRE Policy Briefs* (Philadelphia: Consortium for Policy Research in Education, 2000).

8. David Cohen and James Spillane, "Policy and practice: The relations between governance and instruction," in Gerald Grant, ed., *Review of Research in Education* 18 (Washington, DC: American Educational Research Association, 1992), pp. 4-49.

9. Linda McNeil, *Contradictions of Control: School Structure and School Knowledge* (New York: Routledge, 1988); Stephen Klein, Linda Hamilton, Daniel McCaffrey, Brian Stecher, Abby Robyn, and Delia Burroughs, *Teaching Practices and Student Achievement: Report of the First-Year Findings from the "Mosaic" Study of Systemic Initiatives in Mathematics and Science* (Santa Monica, CA: RAND, 2000).

10. See Kannapel, Aagaard, Coe, and Reeves' chapter in this volume.

11. Carolyn Kelley, Herbert Heneman III, and Anthony Milanowski, *School-Based Performance Award Programs, Teacher Motivation, and School Performance: Findings from a Study of Three Programs* (Philadelphia: Consortium for Policy Research in Education, 2000).

12. Ibid.

13. See Wilson and Floden's chapter in this volume.

14. See DeBray, Parson, and Woodworth's chapter in this volume.

15. See Spillane's chapter in this volume.

16. See DeBray, Parson, and Woodworth's chapter.

17. See Spillane's chapter.

18. See DeBray, Parson, and Woodworth's chapter.

19. See Wilson and Floden's chapter.

20. See DeBray, Parson, and Woodworth's chapter.

21. Michael Garet, Beatrice Birman, Andrew Porter, Laura Desimone, Rebecca Herman, and Kwang Suk Yoon, *Executive Summary, Designing Effective Professional Development: Lessons from the Eisenhower Program* (Washington, DC: United States Department of Education, 1999).

22. Charles Abelmann and Richard Elmore, with Johanna Even, Susan Kenyon, and Joanne Marshall, *When Accountability Knocks, Will Anyone Answer?* (Philadelphia: Consortium of Policy Research in Education, 1999).

23. See Spillane's chapter.

24. See DeBray, Parson, and Woodworth's chapter.

Name Index

N.B. The Notes at the end of each chapter have not been indexed.

Aagaard, Lola, 11, 265, 267, 270, 273–275
Abelmann, Charles, 172, 177, 184

Ball, Deborah Loewenberg, 126
Barron, Sheila, 256
Baxter, Gail, 88–89
Blank, Rolf, 65
Borman, Kathryn, 65
Bourdieu, Pierre, 221
Bransford, John, 91
Brennan, Robert, 88
Burger, Donald, 89
Burger, Susan, 89
Burns, Marilyn, 140, 197

Clinton, William, 5
Clune, William, 8, 15, 265–266, 269, 276
Coe, Pamelia, 11, 265, 267, 270, 273–275
Cohen, David, 84–86, 126
Cuban, Larry, 143
Cyert, Richard, 102

David, Jane, 153, 156
DeBray, Elizabeth, 10, 268, 273–274, 277
Delpit, Lisa, 231
Detterman, Douglas, 90

Elmore, Richard, 99, 148, 172, 177, 184

Fairman, Janet, 9, 268, 270–271, 273, 277
Firestone, William, 9, 134, 268, 270–271, 273, 277
Flanagan, Ann, 8, 263
Floden, Robert, 10, 266, 270, 273, 275, 277
Friedkin, Noah, 101
Fullan, Michael, 83

Goertz, Margaret, 8–9, 266–269
Goldman, Susan, 88–89
Grasmick, Nancy, 149
Grissmer, David, 8, 263
Guthrie, James, 99

Hannaway, Jane, 9, 102, 269–270, 277
Hiebert, James, 126, 128
Hill, Heather, 84, 86
Hunter, Madeline, 199

Kahle, Jane, 84
Kannapel, Patricia, 11, 265, 267, 270, 273–275
Kawata, Jennifer, 8
Kelley, Carolyn, 250
Kennedy, Mary, 62, 83, 86, 94
Kersaint, Gladis, 65
Kim, Jason, 65
Kimball, Kristi, 9, 269–270, 277
Knapp, Michael, 7

LeFever, Karen, 84
Lieberman, Ann, 83–84
Little, Judith Warren, 83
Louis, Karen Seashore, 134

March, James, 102
Marder, Camille, 24
Marek, Edmund, 83
Marsh, David, 84
Massell, Diane, 10, 187, 189, 269, 271, 274, 276–277
Mayer, Daniel, 84
McLaughlin, Milbrey, 134, 264
Methven, Suzanne, 83

Nocochea, Juan, 101
Noyce, Pendred, 65

O'Day, Jennifer, 13–14, 20
Osthoff, Eric, 15

Parson, Gail, 10, 268, 273–274, 277
Perkins, David, 90
Pine, Jerry, 88–89
Porter, Andrew, 9, 17, 62, 65, 93, 194–195, 267
Protsik, Jean, 250

Reeves, Cynthia, 11, 265, 267, 270, 273–275
Richardson, Lloyd, 65
Rosenblum, Sheila, 134
Rothman, Robert, 148
Routman, Regie, 234
Rowan, Brian, 63–64

Sanders, William, 92
Schwartz, Daniel, 91

Shanker, Albert, 2
Shavelson, Richard, 88–89
Smith, Marshall, 13–14, 20
Smithson, John, 9, 65, 93, 267
Solomon, Gavriel, 90
Spillane, James, 10, 128, 134, 276
Stecher, Brian, 256
Sternberg, Robert, 90
Stigler, James, 126–127
Supovitz, Jonathan, 9, 84, 88, 93, 266, 276

Talbert, Joan, 102
Thompson, Charles, 128

Thorndike, Edward, 90
Turner, Herbert, 84, 93

Wheelock, Anne, 256
White, Paula, 15
Williamson, Stephanie, 8
Wilson, Suzanne, 10, 266, 270, 273, 275, 277
Woodworth, Katrina, 10, 268, 273–274, 277
Woodworth, Robert, 90

Zucker, Andrew, 24

Subject Index

N.B. The Notes at the end of each chapter have not been indexed.

A+ Plan for Education, 46

Accountability, 208–211; design elements, 45–48; district role in, 48–51; external and internal, weak alignment of, 184–185; performance based, 39–41; structure, 255–256, 267–268; state, and testing, 150–151; student and adult, 55

Accountability policies, state, 42–48

Accountability systems, effects of performance based, 51–54; locally-defined, 44–45, 50–51; public reporting, 44; state-defined, 45, 48–49; types of, 44–45

Act 60, 171, 181, 183, 191

Advanced Placement, 3

Alignment, 13–14, 62–63; curriculum, 246–247; lack of, 55–56; poor, 89–91

American Association for the Advancement of Science, 60

American Federation of Teachers, 2

America's Choice, 94

Appalachia Educational Laboratory, 244, 247–254

Assessment, absence of, 28, 266–267; state, 66–67

Belief systems, teaching practice, and, 274–275

British Assessment of Performance Unit, 88

Business Roundtable, The, 5

California Achievement Test, 88–89

California Learning Assessment System, 42–43, 86

California Mathematics Framework, 84, 86

Capacity, 57–58; district level, 270–272; school and classroom level, 272–274; state level, 269–270; teacher will, and, 141–142

Causality, 61–62, 92–93

Causation, 20–22

Challenge Initiative, 50

Challenges, attitudinal, 160–162

Classroom assessment practices, 250–251

Colorado State Assessment Program, 156–157, 165

Committee for Fiscal Equity, 40

Common Core of Data, 100, 103, 111

Commonwealth Accountability Testing System, 244, 251

Communication, 211–213

Comprehensive School Reform Design, 148

Comprehensive Tests of Basic Skills, 88–89, 252–253

Consortium for Policy Research in Education, 41, 50, 54–55, 57, 85–86, 92, 94, 195

Core Content for Assessment, 243–244, 246–247, 249–251, 265

Council of Chief State School Officers, 5, 73

Curricular effects, 246–247

Curriculum, guides, 66; linked to standards, 265–266

Data, absence of, 28; complexity of, 166; effects of, 167; incentives for, 155–156; use, 162–165, 189–190

Degrees of Reading Power, 89

District mediation, 134

Early Childhood Development and Academic Assistance Act of 1993 (Act 135), 218–219, 222

Education Commission of the States, 5

Education Trust, The, 94

Eisenhower Program, 74

Elementary and Secondary Education Act, 60, 103

Equity, 56–57

Excellence Movement, 2–4

First International Mathematics and Science Study, 2

Frameworks, 66

From the Capitol to the Classroom, 1

Goals 2000, 5, 103, 107, 110, 201–202. *See* Table 2, 110

Immediate Intervention/Underperforming Schools Program, 58, 269

Improving America's Schools Act, 40

Incentives, 29
Individuals with Disabilities Education Act, 40
Information networks, 117
Instruction, ambitious, 223, 231
Instructional practices, 247–250
Internet technology, 152
Invitations, 234

Kentucky Board of Education, 245
Kentucky Department of Education, 243, 257
Kentucky Early Learning Profile, 250
Kentucky Education Reform Act of 1990, 242–245, 247–248, 250–257
Kentucky Institute for Education Research, 254
Kentucky Instructional Results Information System, 243–244, 246–247, 250–254
Kentucky Long-Term Accountability Model, 47
Kentucky Supreme Court, 242

Learning, evidence of increased, 251–253; teaching, and, 205–208

Maine Educational Assessment, 127, 130–131, 139, 142
Maryland Assessment Consortium, 131, 135, 139
Maryland School Performance Assessment Program, 7, 127, 129–131, 135–139, 164, 166, 198–200, 266
Maryland State Department of Education, 133
Math: A Way of Thinking, 233
Mathematics A, 6, 71
Merck Institute for Science Education, 85–86, 92, 94
Mexican American Legal Defense and Education Fund, 40
Michigan Educational Assessment Program, 89, 201–202, 210, 266

Nation at Risk, A, 1–2
National Academy of Education, 5
National Academy of Sciences, 5
National Alliance for Business, 5
National Assessment of Educational Progress, 7–8, 18, 68–69, 71, 78, 251–253
National Center for Education and the Economy, 94
National Center for Education Statistics, 74

National Council of Teachers of Mathematics, 5–6, 14, 60, 66, 73, 83, 125, 130, 136, 138–140, 142, 199, 219, 229
National Evaluation of the Eisenhower Professional Development Program, 64
National Governors' Association, 5, 39
National Institute for Science Education, 13, 22–23, 27
National Research Council, 73
National Science Education Standards, 83
National Science Foundation, 5, 7–8, 13, 15, 20–21, 23–24, 26, 28–29, 65, 84, 93–94
New Standards Reference Exam, 171, 179–182, 184, 186

Ohio Statewide Systemic Initiative, 84
Organisation for Economic Co-operation and Development, 73

Pew Charitable Trusts, The, 5
Policy enactment and access to knowledge, 220
Professional development, 152–154; comprehensiveness of, 165–166; effective, 82–84; logic of, 81–82; support, and, 256–257; teaching practice, and, 84–85
Professional Development and Appraisal System, 44
Programs of Studies for Kentucky Schools, 243, 250
Promoting data, local role in, 153; state role in, 149–153; variations in, 156
Prospects, 63

RAND, 86, 254
Reading Leaders, 152
Reconstitution, 129–130
Reform Up Close, 73–76
Regents Competency Tests, 171, 176–177
Regents One, 71
Responsibility, individual, 185–186
Restructuring Movement, 3–4

SAT-9, 197, 209–210
School improvement planning, 152, 154–155
School Performance Indices, 47
School Recognition Program, 44
Schools, high-performing, 188–189; low-performing, 189–191
Schoolwide response, lack of, 177–178
Second International Mathematics and Science Study, 2
Socio-economic status, 63–64
SRI International, 15, 18–21

Standards, assessment, and, 125–127; content, 66
Standards-based curriculum, 15–18
Standards-based policy, 15–17
Standards-based reform, development of, 1–5; disparate meanings of, 195–196; future of, and changing beliefs, 275–277; impact of, 213–215; student learning, and, 5–6; theory of, 15–18, 30
Stanford-9, 7, 86, 90
State and local efforts, effects of, 160–165
State Collaborative on Assessment and Student Standards, 73
State policy, 128–134; capacity building, and, 131; context, 218–220; district configuration, and, 132–134; district will, and, 129–130
State Systemic Initiatives Program, 7, 13, 15, 18, 19, 20, 23–25, 28–29, 269
Stretch Regents, 71
Student achievement, 15–18; gain in, 87; teaching practice, and, 86–87
Success in Reading and Writing, 247
Surveys of the enacted curriculum, 65, 68
Systemic reform, 13–14

Texas Assessment of Academic Skills, 7, 160
Texas Essential Knowledge and Skills, 49, 52
Third International Mathematics and Science Study, 64, 76, 83, 126–128, 131
Time, lack of sufficient, 91
Title I, 5, 40–41, 47, 55, 58, 60, 107, 136, 149, 151, 153, 157, 159
Transformations, 243, 246, 265

United States Department of Education, 2, 103
University of Chicago School Mathematics Program, 167
Upgrading Mathematics Project, 78
Urban Institute, The, 100
Urban Systemic Initiatives, 14, 30, 65–66

Variation, 268–269

Weather Channel, 21
Westat, 100
Whole school restructuring, 29–30

RECENT PUBLICATIONS OF THE SOCIETY

1. The Yearbooks

100:1 (2001) *Education Across a Century: The Centennial Volume.* Lyn Corno, editor. Cloth.

100:2 (2001) *From Capitol to the Cloakroom: Standards-based Reform in the States.* Susan H. Fuhrman, editor. Cloth.

99:1 (2000) *Constructivism in Education.* D. C. Phillips, editor. Cloth.

99:2 (2000) *American Education: Yesterday, Today, and Tomorrow.* Thomas L. Good, editor. Cloth.

98:1 (1999) *The Education of Teachers,* Gary A. Griffin, editor. Cloth.

98:2 (1999) *Issues in Curriculum,* Margaret J. Early and Kenneth J. Rehage, editors. Cloth.

97:1 (1998) *The Adolescent Years: Social Influences and Educational Challenges.* Kathryn Borman and Barbara Schneider, editors. Cloth.

97:2 (1998) *The Reading-Writing Connection.* Nancy Nelson and Robert C. Calfee, editors. Cloth.

96:1 (1997) *Service Learning.* Joan Schine, editor. Cloth.

96:2 (1997) *The Construction of Children's Character.* Alex Molnar, editor. Cloth.

95:1 (1996) *Performance-based Student Assessment: Challenges and Possibilities.* Joan B. Baron and Dennie P. Wolf, editors. Cloth.

95:2 (1996) *Technology and the Future of Schooling.* Stephen T. Kerr, editor. Cloth.

94:1 (1995) *Creating New Educational Communities.* Jeannie Oakes and Karen Hunter Quartz, editors. Cloth.

94:2 (1995) *Changing Populations/Changing Schools.* Erwin Flaxman and A. Harry Passow, editors. Cloth.

93:1 (1994) *Teacher Research and Educational Reform.* Sandra Hollingsworth and Hugh Sockett, editors. Cloth.

93:2 (1994) *Bloom's Taxonomy: A Forty-year Retrospective.* Lorin W. Anderson and Lauren A. Sosniak, editors. Cloth.

92:1 (1993) *Gender and Education.* Sari Knopp Biklen and Diane Pollard, editors. Cloth.

92:2 (1993) *Bilingual Education: Politics, Practice, and Research.* M. Beatriz Arias and Ursula Casanova, editors. Cloth.

91:1 (1992) *The Changing Contexts of Teaching.* Ann Lieberman, editor. Cloth.

91:2 (1992) *The Arts, Education, and Aesthetic Knowing.* Bennett Reimer and Ralph A. Smith, editors. Cloth.

89:1 (1990) *From Socrates to Software: The Teacher as Text and the Text as Teacher.* Philip W. Jackson and Sophie Haroutunian-Gordon, editors. Cloth.

89:2 (1990) *Educational Leadership and Changing Contexts of Families, Communities, and Schools.* Brad Mitchell and Luvern L. Cunningham, editors. Paper.

Order the above titles from the University of Chicago Press, 11030 S. Langley Ave., Chicago, IL 60628. For a list of earlier Yearbooks still available, write to the Secretary, NSSE, University of Illinois at Chicago, College of Education, MC 147, 1040 W. Harrison, Chicago, IL 60607.

2. The Series on Contemporary Educational Issues

This series has been discontinued.

The following volumes in the series may be ordered from the McCutchan Publishing Corporation, P.O. Box 774, Berkeley, CA 94702-0774. Phone: 510-841-8616; Fax: 510-841-7787.

Academic Work and Educational Excellence: Raising Student Productivity (1986). Edited by Tommy M. Tomlinson and Herbert J. Walberg.
Adapting Instruction to Student Differences (1985). Edited by Margaret C. Wang and Herbert J. Walberg.
Choice in Education (1990). Edited by William Lowe Boyd and Herbert J. Walberg.
Colleges of Education: Perspectives on Their Future (1985). Edited by Charles W. Case and William A. Matthes.
Contributing to Educational Change: Perspectives on Research and Practice (1988). Edited by Philip W. Jackson.
Effective Teaching: Current Research (1991). Edited by Hersholt C. Waxman and Herbert J. Walberg.
Moral Development and Character Education (1989). Edited by Larry P. Nucci.
Motivating Students to Learn: Overcoming Barriers to High Achievement (1993). Edited by Tommy M. Tomlinson.
Radical Proposals for Educational Change (1994). Edited by Chester E. Finn, Jr. and Herbert J. Walberg.
Reaching Marginal Students: A Prime Concern for School Renewal (1987). Edited by Robert L. Sinclair and Ward Ghory.
Restructuring the Schools: Problems and Prospects (1992). Edited by John J. Lane and Edgar G. Epps.
Rethinking Policy for At-risk Students (1994). Edited by Kenneth K. Wong and Margaret C. Wang.
School Boards: Changing Local Control (1992). Edited by Patricia F. First and Herbert J. Walberg.

The two final volumes in this series were:

Improving Science Education (1995). Edited by Barry J. Fraser and Herbert J. Walberg.
Ferment in Education: A Look Abroad (1995). Edited by John J. Lane.

These two volumes may be ordered from the Book Order Department, University of Chicago Press, 11030 S. Langley Ave., Chicago, IL 60628. Phone: 312-669-2215; Fax: 312-660-2235.

CABRINI COLLEGE LIBRARY
610 KING OF PRUSSIA RD.
RADNOR, PA 19087-3699

DEMCO